山东省社科规划重点项目研究成果(项目批准号:20BYYJ02)

法律法规常用句式汉英翻译研究

——以《中华人民共和国民法典》为例

胡志军 张静 著

山东大学出版社
SHANDONG UNIVERSITY PRESS
·济南·

图书在版编目(CIP)数据

法律法规常用句式汉英翻译研究 ：以《中华人民共和国民法典》为例 / 胡志军，张静著. -- 济南 ：山东大学出版社，2025. 4. -- ISBN 978-7-5607-8828-9

Ⅰ. D90-055

中国国家版本馆 CIP 数据核字第 20258M42E8 号

责任编辑 肖淑辉

封面设计 蓝海文化

法律法规常用句式汉英翻译研究

FALÜ FAGUI CHANGYONG JUSHI HANYING FANYI YANJIU

——以《中华人民共和国民法典》为例

出版发行 山东大学出版社

社　　址 山东省济南市山大南路 20 号

邮政编码 250100

发行热线 (0531)88363008

经　　销 新华书店

印　　刷 济南乾丰云印刷科技有限公司

规　　格 720 毫米×1000 毫米 1/16

20.75 印张 308 千字

版　　次 2025 年 4 月第 1 版

印　　次 2025 年 4 月第 1 次印刷

定　　价 78.00 元

前 言

面临实现中华民族伟大复兴的战略全局和世界百年未有之大变局，法律翻译作为跨法系对话的桥梁，战略价值日益凸显。我国已成为世界第二大经济体，积极倡导构建人类命运共同体，并在“一带一路”倡议框架下与130多个国家签署了合作协议，法律翻译已突破传统语言转换的范畴，演变为维护国家法律主权、参与全球治理、促进国际规则对接的战略工具。

法律法规句式结构的核心特点可概括为五个方面，即规范性、一致性、逻辑性、技术性和简洁性。规范性和一致性主要体现在句式结构表述严谨规范、重复率高，一致性强，用同样的句式结构表达同样的句式意义，避免曲解和误解，便于在法律实践中统一标准。逻辑性主要体现在大量使用判断句、条件复句、因果复句、转折复句、并列复句等句式结构，便于在法律实践中实现严密的逻辑推理。技术性主要体现在大量使用法律术语，准确表达法律意义。简洁性主要体现在省略冗余成分，突出核心要义。

《中华人民共和国民法典》（简称《民法典》）是法律文本的典型代表。《民法典》是中华人民共和国第一部以“法典”命名的法律，于2020年5月28日由第十三届全国人民代表大会第三次会议通过，自2021年1月1日起施行。《民法典》共1260条，包括总则编、物权编、合同编、人格权编、婚姻家庭编、继承编、侵权责任编，形成了系统完备的民事法律体系，被称为“社会生活的百科全书”。

通过对《民法典》句子结构的分析，可以看出法律语言通过高度结构化的表达，将复杂的社会关系转化为明确、可操作的行为规则，既保障了法律的权威性，也便于司法实践中的准确适用。《民法典》的英译有多个版本。其中两个译本具有一定的代表性：一是全国人大常委会法制工作委员会组织中外专家翻译并收入到国家法规总库的官方译本；二是北大法宝组织翻译团队翻译的译本。这两个译本质量高，各有特色，也存在一些有待商榷的问题，值得认真借鉴和深入研究。

法律法规句式结构的翻译至关重要。我们在《民法典》的文本中提炼了30个具有代表性的常用句式结构。本书针对所提炼的句式结构，首先，探讨每个句式结构的特点和在《民法典》中的使用情况；其次，选取《民法典》中的典型例句和与之对应的上述两个译本中的译文，并通过表格对比列出；最后，对两个译文进行比较分析，并对各个句式结构的英文翻译提出可供参考的建议。

在分析过程中，我们参考了多种文献资料，如相关的著作、论文、教材、词典等。另外，为了准确甄别、选用法律英语中的词语和结构，我们利用了四个法律数据库的资源，即香港法例库（https://www.elegislation.gov.hk/）、英国立法库（https://www.legislation.gov.uk/browse）、美国法典库（http://uscode.house.gov/）和美国联邦法规库（https://www.ecfr.gov/）。这些英文法律数据库内容极为丰富，语言规范地道，为本书研究提供了重要参考。

本书是山东省社会科学规划研究重点项目（20BYYJ02）的部分成果。感谢山东省社会科学规划办公室作为年度重点项目立项资助。本项研究曾作为课程研究项目，在山东大学外国语学院2022级和2023级英语翻译专业硕士研究生的“法律翻译”课程中，分组开展研讨活动。在研讨活动中，各组研究生在句式结构提炼、资料收集整理和译文对比分析等方面，做了一些颇具价值的工作。部分研究成果成为本书的前期研究资料，在此向各位同学表示感谢。特别感谢2023级研究生崔馨文基于梳理的资料，按照本书的内容和格式要求，撰写了部分句式翻译研究的初稿。感谢2024级研究生刁惠兰和袁雨媞细心校对部分书稿。在课程研讨和著作成书过程中，同学们积极参与，也颇有收获。因此，本项研究起到了“科研育人”的效果。

法律翻译博大精深，作者水平颇为有限，书中内容难免浅陋粗疏。不对之处、不当之处、不足之处，敬请批评指正。

作　者

2025年2月

目　录

1 “是”字结构的翻译

1.1 结构特点及其在《民法典》中的运用

1.1.1 结构特点

本节讨论的是狭义上的“是”字结构，即以动词“是”作谓语或谓语中心的判断句，呈现为“A 是 B”结构。刘月华等(2019)认为“是”是动词，基本意思表示“肯定”，起判断作用，几乎一切实词和一切短语都可以充当“是”的主语和宾语，比如名词及名词短语、代词、数词、动词及动词短语、形容词及形容词短语、主谓短语等。根据主语和宾语的关系，“是”字结构可以分成八种类型：表示等同和归类、表示说明、表示解释、表示“存在”、强调宾语、表示肯定、“是”字前后词语相同、表示“无例外”。

1.1.2 在《民法典》中的运用

“是”字结构在《民法典》中一共出现了 82 次，绝大多数情况下，主语和宾语都是名词或名词短语，如第 133 条规定：“**民事法律行为是**民事主体通过意思表示设立、变更、终止民事法律关系的**行为**。”个别情况以代词作主语，如第 849 条规定：“完成技术成果的个人享有在有关技术成果文件上写明**自己是**技术成果完成者的权利和取得荣誉证书、奖励的权利。”还有 14 处宾语是动词短语，如第 1079 条中，“婚姻登记机关查明**双方**确实**是自愿**

离婚，并已经对子女抚养、财产以及债务处理等事项协商一致”，“双方”是名词，而“自愿离婚”是动词短语。

《民法典》中的“是”字结构可分为四种类型：

(1)表示等同

本类型在《民法典》中数量最多，通常是给某个法律术语、概念或情形下定义，一般是相关章节的第一个条款，旨在确立一个清晰且具有确定性的含义，为后续的法律适用提供统一的标准，如第 57 条规定：“法人是具有民事权利能力和民事行为能力，依法独立享有民事权利和承担民事义务的组织。”这种情况下，“A 是 B”可以改写成“B 是 A”，意思成立而且没有变化。

(2)表示归类

“是”字前后的主语和宾语都是名词或名词短语，但是，“A 是 B”不能改写成“B 是 A”，B 的涵盖比 A 宽泛，如第 1160 条中，“……死者生前是集体所有制组织成员的，归所在集体所有制组织所有”。

(3)强调宾语

这种情况下，“是”的宾语通常为形容词或动词词组，如第 311 条规定了受让人取得不动产或者动产的所有权的情形，其一是“受让人受让该不动产或者动产时是善意”，“善意”此处是形容词，意指受让人“不知道或者不应当知道转让人为无权处分人”的心理状态。还有更多的这种类型出现在“的”字结构中，如第 1239 条规定：“……能够证明损害是因受害人故意或者不可抗力造成的，不承担责任。”用于强调宾语时，省略掉“是”字，句意不会发生变化。

(4)表示说明

这种类型很少，只找到一处，第 34 条规定：“监护人的职责是代理被监护人实施民事法律行为，保护被监护人的人身权利、财产权利以及其他合法权益等。”“是”后的宾语是对主语“监护人的职责”的说明。

1.2 译文对比

表 1.1 《民法典》中"是"字结构的翻译对比

序号	出处(条)	原文	北大法宝译文(法宝版译文)	国家法规总库译文(总库版译文)
1	114	…… 物权是权利人依法对特定的物享有直接支配和排他的权利,包括所有权、用益物权和担保物权。	… A real right is the right holder's exclusive right to directly dominate a specific thing in accordance with the law, including ownership, usufruct, and security interest.	… Real rights are the rights to directly and exclusively control a specific thing by the right holder in accordance with law, which consists of the ownership, right to usufruct, and security interests in the property.
2	180	因不可抗力不能履行民事义务的,不承担民事责任。法律另有规定的,依照其规定。 不可抗力是不能预见、不能避免且不能克服的客观情况。	Where the non-performance of civil obligations is caused by a force majeure, no civil liability shall arise therefrom, except as otherwise provided for by any law. A force majeure means any objective circumstance that is unforeseeable, inevitable, and insurmountable.	A person who is unable to perform his civil-law obligations due to *force majeure* bears no civil liability, unless otherwise provided by law. "*Force majeure*" means objective conditions which are unforeseeable, unavoidable, and insurmountable.
3	464	合同是民事主体之间设立、变更、终止民事法律关系的协议。 ……	A contract refers to an agreement between the parties to civil legal relations for the establishment, modification, and termination of civil legal relations. …	A contract is an agreement on the establishment, modification, or termination of a civil juristic relationship between persons of the civil law. …

续表

序号	出处（条）	原文	北大法宝译文（法宝版译文）	国家法规总库译文（总库版译文）
4	469	当事人订立合同，可以采用书面形式、口头形式或者其他形式。 书面形式是合同书、信件、电报、电传、传真等可以有形地表现所载内容的形式。	The parties may enter into a contract in written, oral, or any other form. "Written form" means a written contract, letter, telegram, telex, facsimile, or any other form that can tangibly express the contents thereof.	The parties may conclude a contract in writing, orally, or in other forms. A writing refers to any form that renders the content contained therein capable of being represented in a tangible form, such as a written agreement, letter, telegram, telex, facsimile, or the like.
5	23	无民事行为能力人、限制民事行为能力人的监护人是其法定代理人。	The guardian of a person without capacity for civil conduct or with limited capacity for civil conduct shall be the statutory agent of the person.	The guardian of a person who has no or limited capacity for performing civil juristic acts is the legal representative of the person.
6	203	期间的最后一日是法定休假日的，以法定休假日结束的次日为期间的最后一日。	Where the last day of a time period falls on a legal holiday, the day after the legal holiday shall be the last day of the time period.	Where the last day of a time period falls on a legal holiday, the day after the holiday is deemed as the last day of the period.

续表

序号	出处（条）	原文	北大法宝译文（法宝版译文）	国家法规总库译文（总库版译文）
7	488	……有关合同标的、数量、质量、价款或者报酬、履行期限、履行地点和方式、违约责任和解决争议方法等的变更，是对要约内容的实质性变更。	... The modification relating to the subject matter, quality, quantity, price or remuneration, time or place or method of performance, liabilities for breach of contract, method of dispute resolution, etc. shall constitute the substantial modification of an offer.	... An alteration concerning the object of the contract, the quantity, quality, price or remuneration, period of performance, place and manner of performance, default liability, the means of dispute resolution, or the like is a material alteration to the content of an offer.
8	549	有下列情形之一的，债务人可以向受让人主张抵销： …… （二）债务人的债权与转让的债权是基于同一合同产生。	Under any of the following circumstances, a debtor may claim set-off against the assignee: ... (2) The obligation owed to the debtor and the claim assigned arise from the same contract.	A debtor may claim a set-off against the assignee under either of the following circumstances: ... (2) the debtor's claim and the assigned claim are generated on the basis of the same contract.
9	1175	损害是因第三人造成的，第三人应当承担侵权责任。	Where any harm is caused by a third party, the third party shall assume the tort liability.	Where a damage is caused by a third person, the third person shall bear tort liability.

续表

序号	出处（条）	原文	北大法宝译文（法宝版译文）	国家法规总库译文（总库版译文）
10	34	监护人的职责是代理被监护人实施民事法律行为，保护被监护人的人身权利、财产权利以及其他合法权益等。	The duties of a guardian include but are not limited to representing the ward in performing juridical acts and protecting the personal rights, property rights, and other lawful rights and interests of the ward.	The duties of a guardian are to represent the ward to perform civil juristic acts and to protect the personal, proprietary, and other lawful rights and interests of the ward.

1.3 译文分析

经过统计可以看出，两个版本的处理较为统一，多数译为系动词 be 的相应形式，少量译文使用 mean、refer to、省译等表达方式。因此，针对《民法典》中“是”字结构的四种类型，我们对比分析两个版本的对应译文，力图在具体语境中探讨更为可取的翻译方法。

1.3.1 表示等同的“是”的翻译

这一类型通常用于给某一法律语词下定义，绝大多数情况下，两个版本都倾向于使用系动词 be，比如例句 1 和例句 3 的总库版译文；但有时也译为 mean，如例句 2 和例句 4 的法宝版译文；还有时译为 refer to，如例句 3 的法宝版译文和例句 4 的总库版译文。

根据《韦氏词典》的释义，系动词 be 和 mean 都可用于下定义、做解释，基本可以通用，但 refer to 意思稍有不同，词典解释为 to have a direct connection or relationship to (something)，它着眼于某物与其他事物的关系。比如“What does the word refer to?”和“What does the word mean?”

意思不同，refer to不是问该词的含义，而是问该词在描述或指代什么。

在数据库中检索两词，发现refer to在香港法例库（HKeL）中出现了175次，通常指"提交""参考""引用""指（代）的是"，而定义条款中全部使用了mean一词。

在美国联邦法规库（eCFR）中，以21 CFR Chp.1为例，§600.3是专门的定义条款部分，在全部44条定义中，除去表示"包括""适用于"的5条，使用mean的占30条，使用系动词be的有7条，使用refer to的有2条。进一步考察mean和be的具体用法，mean既可以用于"语词定义"，亦可以用于"内涵定义"（汪全胜、张鹏，2013：15）。"语词定义"是指规定或说明词语意义的定义，如"(b) *Secretary* means the Secretary of Health and Human Services and any other officer or employee of the Department of Health and Human Services to whom the authority involved has been delegated."。"内涵定义"即真实定义，是指反映事物本质属性的定义，如"(k) *Proper name*, as applied to a product, means the name designated in the license for use upon each package of the product."。使用系动词be的条文，如"(2) *A therapeutic serum* is a product obtained from blood by removing the clot or clot components and the blood cells."。"a therapeutic serum"是医学术语，词义不为人熟知。又如"(6) *A protein* is any alpha amino acid polymer with a specific, defined sequence that is greater than 40 amino acids in size. When two or more amino acid chains in an amino acid polymer are associated with each other in a manner that occurs in nature, the size of the amino acid polymer for purposes of this paragraph (h)(6) will be based on the total number of amino acids in those chains, and will not be limited to the number of amino acids in a contiguous sequence."先给出protein的常规性定义，接着注明在本款(h)(6)下该定义发生的改变。可见，mean用于规定某词或某概念在法律上或法条语境中的含义，而be一般用于明确一个常规词或概念的常规性含义。

我国《民法典》定义条款中表示等同类型的"是"字结构，涉及的概念或术语(如法人、物权、不可抗力等)都不是常规词,而是在法律语境中的用词,因此可以与国际惯例接轨,使用 mean 来替代系动词 be。

例句 2 中,法宝版把“不可抗力”译为“a force majeure”,经过查询,数据库中 force majeure 的用法,均无冠词 a,如果指某次不可抗力事件,美国联邦法规库(eCFR)译为“a force majeure event”。另外,总库版把 force majeure 斜体并且标注引号,这种形式在电子版香港法例库(HKeL)中从未出现,在美国联邦法规库(eCFR)和美国法典库(GovInfo)中也极为少见,基本都是把该词斜体,HKel 还会使用斜体加粗体。由此,建议我们的英译也遵循此例,把“是”译为 mean,把“是”前面的术语或概念斜体。但是,鉴于《民法典》中的此类条款不像中国香港或英美国家一样集中列为一部分,而是分散于整部法典,为避免突兀,可不用粗体。

例句 4 中,法宝版把“书面形式”译为 written form,字面上看似一致,实则不妥。in written form 和 in writing 都是指“以/用书面形式”,written form 不同于 a written form 或 a writing,后两者意思相同,均指以书面形式呈现的一个实例,如信件、文件等;而前者指“书面形式”这种概念,是一种形式类型名称。法宝版译文用形式类型名称作主语,宾语是属于此类型的各个实例,再用 mean 作谓语动词,实在是逻辑不通。因此,不妨将译文改为“A *written form* means a written contract, letter, telegram, telex, facsimile, or any other form that can tangibly express the contents thereof.”。

1.3.2 表示归类的“是”的翻译

对于这一类型,两个版本多数译为系动词 be 的相应形式,可以表达“属于”“担当”“构成”等意思。但例句 5 中,法宝版译文使用了 shall,是否恰当呢?根据《布莱克法律词典》第十版的释义,法律文本中 shall 的用法只有“has a duty to; more broadly, is required to”这一表示“命令”或“义务”的意义才是标准的用法。法定代理人所享有的代理权是由法律规定的,法定代理权的终止分为两种情况:一是被代理人取得完全民事行为能力或恢复完全民事行为能力；二是监护人的监护资格被撤销。可见，此处的“监护人”担当“法定代理人”，是法律赋予的权利，更是义务，加上 shall 着实必要。

例句 6 中，两个版本都译成 fall on，因为条文讲的是“最后一日是法定休假日”，用 fall on 表达“适逢某一日期”，是为地道的翻译。

例句 7 中，法宝版把“是”译为 constitute，属实没有必要，be 本身就有“构建”的含义。而且“是”字本身比较泛义，源语法条并未明确表现出此类变更构成(constitute)实质性变更，还是具有“实质性变更”的性质，总库版译为同样泛义的系动词 be 可谓恰当。另外，法宝版对 shall 的添加也属失范。在原生英语法律语料库中，与 shall 搭配的主语为有灵主语(各种义务承担者)和无灵主语(各种义务)(李晋、董晓波，2021)，此句中“有关合同……等的变更”，不属于与 shall 搭配的主语的范畴，并且与“对要约内容的实质性变更”之间没有“义务”或“要求”关系。

1.3.3 强调宾语的“是”的翻译

这一类型中，“是”字后面的宾语都为动词短语，“是”字用于强调宾语，突出宾语内容的重要性，如果省略掉“是”字，句意不会发生变化。译文中，两个版本都省译了“是”字，如例句 8 和例句 9，直接用动词短语中的动词作谓语，简洁又明确，是可取的译法。

1.3.4 表示说明的“是”的翻译

这种类型只有例句 10 一处，法宝版译文“include but are not limited to”中，用 include 翻译“是”字没有问题，因为“是”的宾语是对主语“职责”的列举说明。但 but are not limited to 却是误译，该条文中的“等”指的是被监护人的合法权益尚未尽数列举，不是监护人的职责列举未尽。法宝版加上 but are not limited to，实为扩大了监护人的职责范围，与法条不符。总库版译为“be to”结构，取其表示责任之意，可视为系动词 be 的变形，是可取译法。

小　结

《民法典》中的"是"字结构均呈现为"A 是 B"结构，根据主语和宾语的关系，可分为四种类型。①表示等同的，通常用于给某个法律术语或概念下定义，建议与国际惯例接轨，把"是"译为 mean，"是"前面的术语或概念斜体呈现。②表示归类的，取系动词 be 作"属于""担当""构成"等的意思，译为系动词 be 与其主语相应的适当形式，但需注意情态动词 shall 的规范使用。③强调宾语的，可省译"是"字。④表示说明的，就例句 10 而言，可译为 be to 结构，也可用 include 表示列举。

2 “对”字结构的翻译

2.1 结构特点及其在《民法典》中的运用

2.1.1 结构特点

“对”字作为现代汉语高频介词，通常用来标记或引出动作的对象，或引入与动作有关的人或事物。在法律条文中，“对”字可以引出某个特定的主题、情形、条件或人群，表明法律条文所讨论的焦点或适用对象，确保法律条文的精确性和清晰性。“对”字有时可以替换为“对于”，用以明确法律规定的适用对象或适用范围。但更多情况下，“对”字的动作性、指向性更强，意思相当于“向”“跟”，用于提示行为动作所针对的对象，不可替换为“对于”。

2.1.2 在《民法典》中的运用

在《民法典》中“对”字结构一共出现了154次，其中“对于”加宾语的结构出现了10次。有的“对”字结构表示动作的对象，受句中主要动词的支配，如第35条规定：“**对被监护人有能力独立处理的事务**，监护人不得干涉。”句中“干涉”是主要动词，其宾语即为“对”引出的对象“被监护人有能力独立处理的事务”。而在第533条中，“……继续履行合同对于当事人一方明显不公平的，受不利影响的当事人可以与对方重新协商……”此处的

“当事人一方”表示同动作“不公平”有关的人或事物，不受“不公平”的支配。

“对”字结构可分为两种情况：

(1)出现在句首

出现在句首的“对”字结构可以分为“对/对于……的”“对/对于……”和“对……的……”三种。

“对/对于……的”通常引出法律行为适用的情形或条件，如第534条规定：“对当事人利用合同实施危害国家利益、社会公共利益行为的，市场监督管理和其他有关行政主管部门依照法律、行政法规的规定负责监督处理。”

“对/对于……”通常引出法律行为针对的对象，表示所描述对象具有特殊性，提请关注，如第942条规定：“对物业服务区域内违反有关治安、环保、消防等法律法规的行为，物业服务人应当及时采取合理措施制止、向有关行政主管部门报告并协助处理。”

“对……的……”结构通常在句中作主语，“对”不可替换成“对于”，“的”字后面是动作性名词，前面是该动作名词针对的对象，如第1001条规定：“对自然人因婚姻家庭关系等产生的身份权利的保护，适用本法第一编、第五编和其他法律的相关规定。”本句的主语是“对自然人因婚姻家庭关系等产生的身份权利的保护”，其中“保护”是动作性名词，“保护”的对象是“自然人因婚姻家庭关系等产生的身份权利”，由“对”字引出。

(2)出现在句中

“对”字出现在句中的情况居多，基本结构为“对＋对象＋动作”，“对”不可替换成“对于”。该结构中“对象”是“动作”所指向的目标或相关联的对象。如第622条中的“该期限仅视为买受人对标的物的外观瑕疵提出异议的期限”，“标的物的外观瑕疵”是动作“提出异议”的相关对象，“对”字意思为“关于”“有关”；第696条中“债权人未经保证人书面同意转让债权的，保证人对受让人不再承担保证责任”，“承担保证责任”所指向的目标对象是“受让人”，“对”字意思为“向”“朝”。

2.2 译文对比

表 2.1 《民法典》中“对”字结构的翻译对比

序号	出处（条）	原文	北大法宝译文（法宝版译文）	国家法规总库译文（总库版译文）
1	291	不动产权利人对相邻权利人因通行等必须利用其土地的，应当提供必要的便利。	The right holder of an immovable shall provide necessary convenience if the right holder of a neighboring immovable has to use the land thereof for passage or any other purpose.	A person entitled to the real rights in immovable property shall provide necessary convenience for the persons entitled to an adjacent right who have to utilize his land for passage, and the like.
2	738	依照法律、行政法规的规定，对于租赁物的经营使用应当取得行政许可的，出租人未取得行政许可不影响融资租赁合同的效力。	**Where** any law or administrative regulation requires a lessee to obtain administrative license for the operation and use of the leased property, the failure of the lessor to obtain administrative license does not affect the validity of the financial leasing contract.	**Where** the operation or use of a leased object requires an administrative license in accordance with the provision of laws or administrative regulations, the failure of the lessor to obtain such administrative license does not affect the validity of the contract for financing lease.
3	262	对于集体所有的**土地和森林、山岭、草原、荒地、滩涂等**，依照下列规定行使所有权： ……	The ownership of collectively-owned land, forest, mountain, grassland, waste land or intertidal zone, among others, shall be exercised in accordance with the following provisions: …	**With respect to** the collectively-owned land, forests, mountain ridges, grasslands, unreclaimed land, mudflats, and the like, the ownership thereof shall be exercised in accordance with the following provisions: …

续表

序号	出处（条）	原文	北大法宝译文（法宝版译文）	国家法规总库译文（总库版译文）
4	286	……对于物业服务企业或者其他管理人执行政府依法实施的应急处置措施和其他管理措施，业主应当依法予以配合。	... The owners shall, in accordance with the law, cooperate with the property management service enterprise or any other manager in the execution of emergency response measures and other management measures legally taken by the government.	... With respect to the emergency measures and other management measures implemented by the government in accordance with law that are carried out by the property management service enterprise or other managers, the unit owners shall, in accordance with law, be cooperative.
5	942	…… 对物业服务区域内违反有关治安、环保、消防等法律法规的行为，物业服务人应当及时采取合理措施制止、向有关行政主管部门报告并协助处理。	... For any violation of the relevant laws and regulations on public security, environmental protection, and fire protection, among others, in the property management service area, the property management service provider shall, in a timely manner, take reasonable measures to stop the violation, make a report to the relevant authority, and assist in handling.	... For any violation of the relevant laws or regulations on public security, environmental protection, fire protection, and the like in the property management service area, the property management service provider shall, in a timely manner, take reasonable measures to stop the violation, make a report to the competent department, and render assistance to the department in handling the violation.

续表

序号	出处（条）	原文	北大法宝译文（法宝版译文）	国家法规总库译文（总库版译文）
6	61	…… 法人章程或者法人权力机构**对**法定代表人代表权**的**限制，不得对抗善意相对人。	... Any restriction **on** the legal representative's right of representation imposed by the bylaws or the supreme organ of the legal person shall not be set up against bona fide opposite parties.	... Any restrictions **on** the legal representative's power to represent the legal person which is stipulated in the articles of association or imposed by the governing body of the legal person may not be asserted against a bona fide counterparty.
7	38	被监护人的父母或者子女被人民法院撤销监护人资格后，除**对被监护人**实施故意犯罪的外，确有悔改表现的，经其申请，人民法院可以在尊重被监护人真实意愿的前提下，视情况恢复其监护人资格……	Where the ward's parent or child shows true repentance after being disqualified from guardianship by the people's court, except one having committed an intentional crime **on** the ward, the people's court may, by respecting the ward's true will and according to the circumstances, reinstate his or her guardianship upon his or her application ...	Where a ward's parent or child, who has been disqualified as a guardian by the people's court for reasons other than having committed an intentional crime **against** the ward, and who has truly repented and mended his ways, applies to the people's court for reinstatement, the people's court may, upon considering the actual situation and upon the satisfaction of the prerequisite that the true will of the ward is respected, reinstate the guardian ...

续表

序号	出处(条)	原文	北大法宝译文(法宝版译文)	国家法规总库译文(总库版译文)
8	1039	国家机关、承担行政职能的法定机构及其工作人员**对于**履行职责过程中知悉的自然人的**隐私和个人信息**,应当予以保密,不得泄露或者向他人非法提供。	The state organs, statutory institutions assuming administrative functions, and their staff members shall keep confidential the privacy and personal information of natural persons known in the course of fulfilling duties, and shall not disclose it or illegally provide it for others.	State organs and the chartered institutions assuming administrative functions as well as their staff shall keep confidential the privacy and the personal information of natural persons known to them during the performance of their responsibilities, and may not disclose or illegally provide it to others.
9	1074	有负担能力的祖父母、外祖父母,**对于**父母已经死亡或者父母无力抚养的未成年**孙子女、外孙子女**,有抚养的义务。 ……	Paternal or maternal grandparents who can afford it shall have the duty to support their paternal or maternal grandchildren who are minors and whose parents are dead or have no means to support them. …	Paternal or maternal grandparents, if financially capable, have the duty to raise their minor grandchildren whose parents are deceased or are incapable of such raising. …
10	92	…… 依法设立的宗教活动场所,具备法人条件的,可以申请法人登记,取得捐助法人资格。**法律、行政法规对**宗教活动场所**有规定的**,依照其规定。	… A venue for holding religious activities formed in accordance with the law and satisfying the conditions for a legal person may apply for legal person registration and obtain the status of a donation-based legal person, subject to any provisions of laws and administrative regulations relating to the venues for holding religious activities.	… A site legally established to hold religious activities may be registered as a legal person and attains the status of a donation-funded legal person if it meets the requirements for being a legal person. **Where there are laws or administrative regulations providing for** the religious sites, such provisions shall be followed.

续表

序号	出处（条）	原文	北大法宝译文（法宝版译文）	国家法规总库译文（总库版译文）
11	198	**法律对**仲裁时效**有规定的**，依照其规定；没有规定的，适用诉讼时效的规定。	**Where any law prescribes** arbitration, such a law shall apply; otherwise, the provisions on extinctive prescription for actions shall apply.	**Any provisions of law regulating** the limitation period for arbitration shall be followed; in the absence of such provisions, the provisions on limitation period for litigation provided herein shall be applied *mutatis mutandis*.
12	289	**法律、法规对**处理相邻关系**有规定的**，依照其规定；法律、法规没有规定的，可以按照当地习惯。	**Where** the handling of neighboring relations **is provided for by any law or regulation**, the provisions thereof shall prevail; or if the law or regulation is silent, such relations may be handled according to local customs.	**Where there are laws and regulations providing for** adjacent relationships, those provisions shall be applied. Where there are no such provisions, local customs may be followed.

2.3 译文分析

以下对比分析两个版本中"对"字结构的相应译文，探讨各种情况下较为可取的翻译方法。

2.3.1 "对/对于……的"结构的翻译

在法宝版译文中，本结构通常译为条件句，使用的连接词有 if(如例句 1)和 where(如例句 2)。在总库版译文中，有的译为 where 引导的条件句(如例句 2)，有的则改变了原文语句结构，进行意译，如例句 1 拆分了"对"

字结构，把“相邻权利人”译为不动产权利人“提供必要的便利”的对象，把“对”字结构描述的情形译为“相邻权利人”的定语。

根据Coode的分析法，一条完整的法律条文通常要包括至少三个要素成分：法律主体、法律行为，以及如果该条文要付诸实施或具有可操作性，所必需的适当情况或特定条件（李克兴，2013）。“对/对于……的”结构在法律条文中的作用正是引出法律行为适用的情形或条件，与“的”字结构作状语的情形一般无异。根据动态对等原则，在翻译法律文本时，要注意保持原文及译文之间的法律效力上的对等，必须注重语言及文体的特点。也就是说，作为法律条文的要素成分之一，“对/对于……的”结构也要译成英文版条文中的情形或条件。因此，例句1中，总库版的意译处理不可取。

例句2中，两个版本都译为where引导的条件句。where作条件句的引导词，比if更正式。此外，where通常置于句首，引导充分法律条件句。因此，where-条件句可以充分表明例句2法条所适用的情形，很合适。

例句1中，法宝版译文使用if-条件句，置于主句之后，也是可接受的译法。但是考虑到法律翻译的一致性原则，我们要坚持用同一措辞表示同一概念。如果将例句1的法条稍稍调整语序，可变为“对相邻权利人因通行等必须利用其土地的，不动产权利人应当提供必要的便利”，意思与原条文无异，因此，不妨也译为where-条件句。

2.3.2 “对/对于……”结构的翻译

例句3、例句4、例句5同属于这种结构。法宝版的译文多数倾向于省译，如例句3和例句4，将“对/对于……”结构拆分，融入主句结构。总库版译文倾向于使用“with respect to”介宾短语，像原文一样置于句首。

“对/对于……”出现在句首，通常引出法律行为针对的对象，表示所述对象的特殊性，使人们注意到其需要特别处理的法律特征，突出所述对象，如例句3对“所有权”的范围予以强调，即包括“集体所有的土地和森林、山岭、草原、荒地、滩涂等”，译文中也应实现这种突出效果，而法宝版的省译处理，缺少这种效果，不可取。

总库版译文将“with respect to”介宾短语置于句首，不但实现了上文所说的突出效果，而且在语义上与原文非常相符。根据《韦氏词典》，with respect to 指 about or concerning something or someone; in relation to，常用于引入关于某个主题或事项的说明或解释，强调对该主题或事项的关注或关系，通常译为“关于、就……而言、涉及到”。例句 3 和例句 4 中的“对于”都可以用“涉及到”进行替换。

例句 5 中，两个版本都译为“for”引导的介宾短语，并且置于句首，虽然也不错，但是，for 作为介词用法甚多，在某些情况下虽然可以表示对某个对象、目的或目标的指向或关系，但强调的是指向性。例句 5 中的“对”可以替换成“涉及到”，也可以替换成“针对”，译为 for 无可厚非，但是考虑到同一性原则，with respect to 的适用范围更广，建议统一用 with respect to 翻译“对/对于……”结构。

2.3.3 “对……的……”结构的翻译

对“对……的……”在句中作主语的结构，两个译本的处理一致，都将“的”字后面的动作性名词译为相应的名词，在译文中仍作主语，把“对”译成与该名词搭配的恰当介词，后跟“的”字前面的内容，即该动作名词针对的对象，如例句 6。这种译法实现了原文与译文在形式和内容上的双重对等，是为可取，此处不再赘述。

2.3.4 “对＋对象＋动作”结构的翻译

这种结构在《民法典》中数量最多，“对象”指“动作”指向的对象，两个译本基本都采用直译方法，根据适用的动词短语，“对”有时译为介词，如例句 7，有时省译，如例句 8 和例句 9。

例句 7 中，尽管两个版本选用的动词短语一样，但介词不同，法宝版译成“on”，总库版译成“against”。on 在此处用于指示方向，表明“实施故意犯罪”指向的对象，而 against 不但指出故意犯罪的目标对象，还表明故意犯罪对目标对象造成的侵犯和不利。因此，总库版略胜一筹。

例句 8 和例句 9 使用了省译，因为译本中的英语动词是及物动词，“对”字引出的动作对象受其支配，顺理成章地译为动作短语的宾语，句式简洁，清晰又紧凑。

此外，《民法典》中 8 次出现了“法律对……有规定的”句式，也可归入这一结构。多数情况下，法宝版译为 Where any laws provide for...（3 次），总库版译为 Where there are laws providing for...（5 次），可见，对“对……有规定”的翻译，两个版本均倾向使用 provide for，其他表达还有 govern（1 次）、regulate（1 次）和 prescribe（1 次）。

考察词义，四者都可译为“规定”，但侧重点不同：govern 主要强调管理、管辖，regulate 强调规范、调节，而 prescribe 和 provide for 都有以条文形式制定具体要求的意思，可见后两者更符合“法律对……有规定的”语义。根据数据库检索结果，provide for 与法律、法规连用的词频更高（见表 2.2），鉴于此，选择 provide for 翻译“有规定的”更合适。

表 2.2 “法律对……有规定的”的英文表达方式及检索频次

表达方式	国内	国外		
	香港法例库	英国立法库	美国联邦法规库	美国法典库
law(s) prescribe	1	19	4	2853
regulation(s) prescribe	71	>200	35	10260
law(s) provide for	2	119	43	15104
regulation(s) provide for	114	>200	23	7668

例句 10 中，法宝版译文使用 subject to，将前后两句连到了一起，把“法律、行政法规对宗教活动场所有规定的”译为“any provisions of laws and administrative regulations <u>relating to</u> the venues for holding religious activities”。relate to 指“与……有关”，用在此处不够严谨，“对……有规定的”指法条对某一事物的具体事宜提出具体要求，并非只是与该事物相关，因此，该译文不合适。

例句 11 中，总库版没有把“法律对……有规定的”译为条件句，而是与后句“依照其规定”合并成一个简单句。前文提到，“……的”结构用于提出法律条文中的情形或条件要素，为了使条文要素完整、措辞规范，译文最好保留该要素形式，译成 where 引导的条件句。

例句 12 中，法宝版译文使用了 provide for 的被动形式，可以看作是变通译法，但鉴于措辞的同一性原则，最好还是保持主动形式，与其他处译文一致。总库版译文是“Where there are laws and regulations providing for...”。首先，there be 句型稍显累赘，不如像法宝版一样直接用“法律、法规”作主语，更符合简明英语的趋势；其次，“法律、法规对……有规定的”指的是任一法律或法规有规定，法律和法规之间是“或者”关系，不是“并且”关系，因此，应当改为“Where any law or regulation provides for...”。

小　结

“对”字介宾结构在《民法典》中的出现频率较高，用以引出某个特定的情形、条件、人群或事物，确保法律条文的精确性和清晰性。一般分为四种情况：①“对/对于……的”出现在句首，惯常用以表明法律行为适用的情形或条件，可以译为 where-条件句。②“对/对于……”也在句首，通常引出法律行为适用的对象，译文可以使用 with respect to 介宾短语，同样置于句首，以突出所述对象。③“对……的……”常在句中作主语，翻译时可将“的”字后面的动作性名词译为相应的名词，在译文中仍作主语，把“对”译成与该名词搭配的恰当介词，后跟“的”字前面的内容，即该动作名词指向的对象。④出现在句中的“对”字结构，一般呈现为“对＋对象＋动作”结构，根据适用的英语动词短语，“对”可译为与之搭配的介词，若动作对象直接受动词支配，且动词为及物动词，可将动作对象译为动词的宾语，“对”字省译。固定句式“法律、法规对……有规定的”建议译为“Where any law or regulation provides for...”。

3 “为”字结构的翻译

3.1 结构特点及其在《民法典》中的运用

3.1.1 结构特点

“为”字有两个读音（wéi 和 wèi）。在《民法典》中，读二声的情况包括：①动词，表示判断，同“是”字；②动词，表示“做、干”，如权利人请求特定义务人为或者不为一定行为；③动词，表示“变成、成为”，如恢复为、登记为、约定为、批准为；④动词：视为；⑤名词：行为；⑥表示被动，如为国家所有、为他人知晓；⑦出现在“以……为……”结构中，表示“作为”，如以……为由、以……为条件、以……为内容，等等。读四声的情况，通常作介词，呈现为“为+O+V/VP”结构，“O”代表“为”的宾语，“V/VP”代表动词和动词性成分。鉴于“为”字用法太多，本节根据出现频率，仅讨论作动词表示判断的“为”“视为”，以及作介词的“为”。

3.1.2 在《民法典》中的运用

（1）表示判断的“为”

在《民法典》中，本结构一共出现了 79 次。“为”是文言泛义动词，很多时候可以译成现代汉语的“是”字，如第 17 条规定：“十八周岁以上的自然人为成年人。不满十八周岁的自然人为未成年人。”现代法律文本中使用了大量的汉语文言成分，“为”字作谓语表示判断即为其一，是体现法律文本“庄典性”的重要手段（张文，2020）。

（2）“视为”

本结构表示被动意义，在《民法典》中出现了44次。在法律上，“视为”这一语词表达的是法律拟制制度、推定制度和注意规定（张海燕，2012），意思是将某一行为或事实按照法律规定的效果进行处理。作为动词，“视为”在条文中通常作谓语，后接宾语，有时有明确的主语，如第18条规定：“**十六周岁以上的未成年人**，以自己的劳动收入为主要生活来源的，**视为**完全民事行为能力人。”也有时主语不明确，如第503条规定：“无权代理人以被代理人的名义订立合同，被代理人已经开始履行合同义务或者接受相对人履行的，**视为**对合同的追认。”“视为”的主语不是某个确定的人或事物，而是整个“的”字结构所表达的情形。

（3）作介词的“为”

“为”作介词读四声，在《民法典》中出现了46次，可分为两种情况。其一，“为”用于引进受益对象，意思是“替、给”，如第1141条规定：“遗嘱应当**为缺乏劳动能力又没有生活来源的继承人**保留必要的遗产份额。”保留遗产份额的受益对象是“缺乏劳动能力又没有生活来源的继承人”。

其二，“为”用于引进原因或目的，“为”后面的宾语可以是名词或名词性词组，也可以是动词或动词性词组，有时可以用“为了”代替。如第999条规定：“**为公共利益**实施新闻报道、舆论监督等行为的，可以合理使用民事主体的姓名、名称、肖像、个人信息等。”“公共利益”是名词词组，是实施所述行为的原因。又如第169条规定：“在紧急情况下代理人**为了维护被代理人的利益**需要转委托第三人代理的除外。”“维护被代理人的利益”是动词词组，是代理人转委托第三人代理的目的。

“为”引进目的时，有时会省略主语，把“为＋O＋V/VP”结构中的“为＋O”和V/VP之间用逗号隔开，起到强调作用。如第1008条规定：“**为研制新药、医疗器械或者发展新的预防和治疗方法，需要进行临床试验**的，应当依法经相关主管部门批准并经伦理委员会审查同意，向受试者或者受试者的监护人告知试验目的、用途和可能产生的风险等详细情况，并经其书面同意。”

3.2 译文对比

表 3.1 《民法典》中"为"字结构的翻译对比

序号	出处（条）	原文	北大法宝译文（法宝版译文）	国家法规总库译文（总库版译文）
1	1145	继承开始后，遗嘱执行人为遗产管理人……	After the opening of succession, the testamentary executor shall be the estate administrator...	Upon opening of a succession, the executor of the will is the administrator of the estate...
2	1153	夫妻共同所有的财产，除有约定的外，遗产分割时，应当先将共同所有的财产的一半分出为配偶所有，其余的为被继承人的遗产。 ……	When a decedent's estate is partitioned, half of the joint property acquired by the spouses shall, unless otherwise agreed upon, be first allotted to the surviving spouse as his or her own property; and the remainder shall constitute the decedent's estate. …	When partitioning an estate, where community property of husband and wife is involved, unless otherwise agreed upon, half of the community property shall be allocated first to the surviving spouse as separate property, while the remaining property shall be part of the decedent's estate. …
3	16	涉及遗产继承、接受赠与等胎儿利益保护的，胎儿视为具有民事权利能力。但是，胎儿娩出时为死体的，其民事权利能力自始不存在。	Where the protection of the interests of a fetus is involved in, among others, a succession or acceptance of a gift, the fetus shall be presumed to have capacity for civil rights. However, in case of a stillborn, the fetus's capacity for civil rights has never existed.	A fetus is deemed as having the capacity for enjoying civil-law rights in estate succession, acceptance of gift, and other situations where protection of a fetus' interests is involved. Provided, however, that a stillborn fetus does not have such capacity *ab initio*.

续表

序号	出处（条）	原文	北大法宝译文（法宝版译文）	国家法规总库译文（总库版译文）
4	18	…… 十六周岁以上的未成年人，以自己的劳动收入为主要生活来源的，**视为**完全民事行为能力人。	... A minor attaining the age of sixteen and primarily relying on his or her own labor income in living **is deemed** a person with full capacity for civil conduct.	... A minor aged sixteen or above whose main source of support is the income from his own labor **is deemed as** a person with full capacity for performing civil juristic acts.
5	159	附条件的民事法律行为，当事人为自己的利益不正当地阻止条件成就的，**视为**条件已经成就；不正当地促成条件成就的，**视为**条件不成就。	For a juridical act subject to a condition, if a party prevents the fulfillment of the condition by improper means for its own benefits, the condition **shall be deemed** fulfilled; or if a party hastens the fulfillment of a condition by improper means, the condition **shall not be deemed** fulfilled.	Where a condition is attached to a civil juristic act, if a party, for the sake of its own interests, improperly obstructs the fulfillment of the condition, the condition **is deemed as** having been fulfilled; if a party improperly facilitates the fulfillment of the condition, the condition **is deemed as** not having been fulfilled.
6	519	连带债务人之间的份额难以确定的，**视为**份额相同。 ……	Where the shares of joint and several debtors are difficult to determine, the shares **shall be treated as** being equal. ...	Where it is difficult to determine the share of obligation among the debtors subjected to joint and several liabilities, each debtor **is deemed to** owe an equal share. ...

续表

序号	出处(条)	原文	北大法宝译文(法宝版译文)	国家法规总库译文(总库版译文)
7	290	不动产权利人应当为相邻权利人用水、排水提供必要的便利。……	The right holder of an immovable shall provide necessary convenience for water use and drainage by the right holder of the neighboring immovable. …	A person entitled to the real rights in immovable property shall provide a person entitled to an adjacent right in the immovable property the necessary convenience for the use of water or drainage. …
8	1106	收养关系成立后,公安机关应当按照国家有关规定为被收养人办理户口登记。	After an adoptive relationship is established, the public security organ shall, in accordance with the relevant provisions issued by the state, handle the household registration for the adopted person.	Upon establishment of an adoptive relationship, the public security department shall facilitate household registration for the adoptee in accordance with the relevant regulations of the State.
9	117	为了公共利益的需要,依照法律规定的权限和程序征收、征用不动产或者动产的,应当给予公平、合理的补偿。	Fair and reasonable indemnification shall be made if any immovable or movable is expropriated or requisitioned for public interest according to the authority and procedures prescribed by laws.	Where, for the purpose of public interests, immovable or movable property is expropriated or requisitioned according to the scope of authority and the procedure provided by law, fair and reasonable compensation shall be paid.

续表

序号	出处（条）	原文	北大法宝译文（法宝版译文）	国家法规总库译文（总库版译文）
10	169	…… 转委托代理未经被代理人同意或者追认的，代理人应当对转委托的第三人的行为承担责任；但是，在紧急情况下代理人为了维护被代理人的利益需要转委托第三人代理的除外。	… Without the principal's consent to or ratification of the appointment, the agent shall be liable for the acts of the third party appointed by the agent, unless it is necessary for the agent to appoint the third party in case of emergency to safeguard the interests of the principal.	… If re-delegation of authority to a third person is not consented to or ratified by the principal, the agent shall be liable for the acts performed by the third person, unless the agent redelegates his authority to a third person in an emergency situation in order to protect the interests of the principal.
11	681	保证合同是为保障债权的实现，保证人和债权人约定，当债务人不履行到期债务或者发生当事人约定的情形时，保证人履行债务或者承担责任的合同。	" Contract of suretyship " means a contract by which a surety performs the obligation or assumes the responsibility under an agreement between the surety and the creditor in order to protect the realization of the obligation, in case the debtor fails to perform the obligation due, or the circumstances agreed upon by the parties occur.	A suretyship contract is a contract under which a surety and a creditor agree, for the purpose of ensuring the enforcement of an underlying claim, that the surety shall perform the obligation or bear the liability when the debtor fails to perform the obligation when it is due or a circumstance as agreed by the parties occurs.

续表

序号	出处（条）	原文	北大法宝译文（法宝版译文）	国家法规总库译文（总库版译文）
12	1	为了保护民事主体的合法权益，调整民事关系，维护社会和经济秩序，适应中国特色社会主义发展要求，弘扬社会主义核心价值观，根据宪法，制定本法。	This Code is enacted in accordance with the Constitution for the purposes of protecting the lawful rights and interests of the parties to civil legal relations, regulating civil relations, maintaining the social and economic order, meeting the developmental requirements of socialism with Chinese characteristics, and upholding core socialist values.	This Code is formulated in accordance with the Constitution of the People's Republic of China for the purposes of protecting the lawful rights and interests of the persons of the civil law, regulating civil-law relations, maintaining social and economic order, meeting the needs for developing socialism with Chinese characteristics, and carrying forward the core socialist values.

3.3 译文分析

针对《民法典》中“为”字结构的运用情况，我们对两个版本的对应译文进行了对比分析，探讨更为可取的翻译方法。

3.3.1 表示判断的“为”的翻译

表示判断的“为”与现代汉语中的“是”极为相似，通常属于“是”字结构中表示归类的情况，如例句1—4，意思是“属于”“担当”“构成”等，翻译方法也应当与“是”字结构表示归类的情况一致，此处不再赘述，但需注意以下两点：

第一，情态动词shall的规范使用。例句1中，遗嘱执行人担当遗产管理人，既是法律赋予的权利，更是法律赋予的义务，具有法律强制性，符合shall表示“命令”或“义务”的意义，因此法宝版译文比总库版更为可取。例句2中，两版译文都使用了shall，其实是混淆了规定与义务的概念。仔细分析源语，我们就会发现主语“其余的（财产）”并非有灵主体，也非实际的施事主体，它与“被继承人的遗产”之间不是命令（mandatory duty）的关系，不符合shall的规范使用。

第二，“为”字译为系动词be是常用译法，但也有例外，需根据语境和行文灵活处理。如例句3中，“胎儿娩出时为死体的”，法宝版译文“in case of a stillborn”实际是“in case it is a stillborn”的变通。根据《韦氏词典》，stillborn主要用作形容词，虽也有名词的标注，但没有任何作名词的例句，而且查询各大英美法规数据库，常用表达均为a stillborn child或a stillborn animal，故此，建议此处修改为“in case it is stillborn”。总库版译文直接译为a stillborn fetus，并与后句组合，译成一个简单句，也是可取的做法。值得一提的是，总库版译文用provided that句式翻译原文的但书部分，表示例外情况，而且用拉丁文*ab initio*表示“自始”，符合立法文本“专业性”的语言特征，是更为可取的译文。

3.3.2 “视为”的翻译

法宝版译文中，译为“be deemed”的计23处，如例句4和例句5；译为“be treated as”的计20处，如例句6。总库版译文中，译为“be deemed as”的计21处，如例句3—5；译为“be deemed to”的计23处，如例句6。

在数据库中检索词频可知，be deemed的出现频次最高，其次是be treated as，而be deemed as最少。（见表3.2）根据《牛津词典》中的用法说明和《韦氏词典》中的例句，be deemed后面可以搭配不定式，也可以直接搭配名词、形容词，但是没有与as的搭配，可见be deemed as的用法失于规范，as多余了。

表 3.2 "视为"的英文表达方式及检索频次

表达方式	国内	国外		
	香港法例库	英国立法库	美国联邦法规库	美国法典库
be deemed	3006	>200	7155	432205
be deemed as	5	148	47	6755
be treated as	853	>200	5952	238895

例句 3 中,法宝版还译成"be presumed to"。根据《布莱克法律词典》,presume 一词指 to accept something as true until it is shown not to be true;deem 指 to treat something as true as if ① it were really something else, or ② it has qualities that it does not have。在香港法例库(HKeL)中检索两词,发现 be presumed to 译为"推定";be deemed 译为"视为""当作",指"看成是、认为是"。可见, be presumed to 表示法定的预设,即法律上假定某事是真实的,除非有证据证明相反。这种表达方式强调在法律上的先验假设,通常需要对其进行证明推翻,在立法文件中可对应"推定"。而 be deemed 强调一种法定的虚拟性,即便实际情况可能并非如此,法律也将其认定为成立,正好与汉语语境中的"视为"含义相符。

同为"视为",法宝版在例句 4 中译为 is deemed,在例句 5 中又添加使用了情态动词 shall,有何区别呢? 除了《布莱克法律词典》,《加纳现代英语用语词典》(第 4 版,2016 年)也指出,目前 shall 在法律文件中主要用于设定强制性义务或者职责(duty)。也就是说,shall be deemed 具有"要求"或"义务"的含义,对应汉语中的"应当/必须视为",例句 5 源语法条并没有对应词或明显的强制性或强调性语气,可见是对 shall 的滥用和误用了。考察香港法例库(HKeL)中的中英版本,凡是 shall be deemed 都有对应词"须",而不加 shall 的,要么指已经明确的认定,要么不强调"强制性",表明只是一种法律规定。如《西九文化区管理局条例》Section 21 Subsection 13 中规定:"Where the Chief Executive in Council refuses to approve a development plan which <u>is deemed to be a draft plan by virtue of</u>

subsection (8), the Authority shall, as soon as reasonably practicable after such refusal, prepare another development plan for the purposes specified in subsection (1)(a), (b) and (c)..."这里的"视为"是基于subsection (8),是已明确的认定。又如《仲裁条例》Section 10 中规定:"Without affecting subsection (1), if a written communication (other than communications in court proceedings) is sent by any means by which information can be recorded and transmitted to the addressee, the communication is deemed to have been received on the day it is so sent."。此处的"视为"是法律规定,没有明显的强调语气。故此,法律文本汉英翻译实践中,"视为"前有"必须""须""应当"字样的,可使用 shall,其余没有明显强制、强调语气的,不要滥用 shall。

至于 be treated as,《牛津词典》释义为 to behave towards someone or deal with something in a particular way,对应汉语词组"按照……处理"。与 be deemed 相比,be treated as 正式程度较低,可以用于更多的日常场景,在法律文本中的使用频率较低。虽然二者在数据库中的意思相差无几,几乎可以通用,但是考虑到法律语词同一性原则,建议统一措辞,不妨译为认可度相对更高的"be deemed"。例句 6 中,由于"视为"的主语在源语法条中不明确,两版译文选用了不同主语,法宝版可以修改为"the shares are deemed equal"。

3.3.3 作介词的"为"的翻译

作"替、给"的意思时,如例句 7 和例句 8,两个版本都译为介词 for,毋庸赘述。但例句 7 中,"为相邻权利人用水、排水提供必要的便利",法宝版译为"provide necessary convenience for water use and drainage by the right holder of the neighboring immovable",即 provide something for something;总库版译为"provide a person entitled to an adjacent right in the immovable property the necessary convenience for the use of water or drainage",即 provide somebody something for something。而根据《牛津高

级英语词典》，provide 作"提供"意思时，用法有四：provide something；provide something for somebody；provide somebody with something；provide something to somebody。分析源语条文，"便利"的受益人应当是"相邻权利人"，因此，法宝版应当修改为"provide necessary convenience for the right holder of the neighboring immovable in water use and drainage"，总库版可以修改为"provide a person entitled to an adjacent right in the immovable property with the necessary convenience for the use of water or drainage"。

当"为"字表原因或目的时，两个版本共有四种译法：for、for the purpose(s) of、to、in order to。首先，关于 for the purpose(s) of，两个版本都有使用，如例句 9 和例句 11 的总库版，以及例句 12 的两版译文，但是，尽量用这个介词短语表达"就(有关)章、条、款、节而言"的意思，而用 for 表示目的，更符合简明英语的规范。作为美国简明英语运动中极具权威性和代表性的文件，《2010 年简明写作法案》(Public Law 111-274－*Plain Writing Act of 2010*)的第二条清晰阐释了其制定目的，即通过促进公众采用一种他们可以理解并使用的沟通方式，与政府实行清晰明了的沟通，从而提高联邦政府的工作效率，更好地履行对公众的责任①。法律文本翻译的选词如果意义不够单一，难免会增加读者的理解难度，妨碍法律沟通效率，因此，为了体现立法文本的规范性、严谨性，保证译文的清晰简明，在表意正确的情况下，最好还是选用意义单一的表达方式。

其次，当"为"字后面的宾语是动词短语时，可以使用"to do"或"in order to do"结构，如例句 10、例句 11 的法宝版译文。二者的区别在于，to 表达了一个更加直接和简洁的目的或行为导向，对行为的动机或意图没有强调意味；in order to 更加正式，强调为了实现某个结果而采取的行动。当"为＋O＋V/V"结构省略主语，并且"为＋O"和 V/VP 之间用逗号隔开时，

① 原文为："The purpose of this Act is to improve the effectiveness and accountability of Federal agencies to the public by promoting clear Government communication that the public can understand and use."。See https://www.govinfo.gov/content/pkg/PLAW-111publ274/pdf/PLAW-111publ274.pdf.

通常表达强调意义，如例句 9、例句 11 和例句 12。此时可以使用更为正式、严谨的 in order to，以示强调。

小 结

“为”字结构在《民法典》中的用法众多，本节选取出现频率较高的三种情况进行讨论，即作动词表示判断的“为”“视为”，以及作介词的“为”。①表示判断的“为”字结构通常属于“是”字结构中表示归类的情况，一般译为系动词 be，但是具体语境和行文有时也会产生例外译法。②“视为”在《民法典》中通常表达被动意义，指将某一行为或事实按照法律规定的效果进行处理，不妨使用正式用语 be deemed，后面可搭配名词、形容词或动词不定式。需要注意的是，翻译作动词的“为”时，务必规范使用情态动词 shall。③对于作介词的“为”，如果取“替、给”之意，可以译为介词 for；如果表示目的，根据行文和语境，建议译为 for something 或 to do something，如果有强调意义，不妨译为 in order to do something。如此，句式简洁明快，词义单一，又能突出重点，符合简明英语的时代趋势。

4 “因”字结构的翻译

4.1 结构特点及其在《民法典》中的运用

4.1.1 结构特点

“因”字结构在法律文本中通常用于表明某一情形、事物或行为出现或发生的缘由或条件，其基本结构为“因＋O＋V/VP”或“因＋O＋小句”。O代表宾语，可以是名词或名词短语、动词或动词短语，或者小句。如“因正当防卫造成损害的，不承担民事责任”，其中O是名词短语“正当防卫”，VP是“造成损害”，该“因”字结构出现在“的”字句中，厘清了出现此种情形（“造成损害的”）的原因。又如“因出卖人故意或者重大过失不告知买受人标的物瑕疵的，出卖人无权主张减轻或者免除责任”，此处的“因”是连词，连接两个小句，说明了法律行为（后句）出现的条件（前句）。

4.1.2 在《民法典》中的运用

鉴于法律文本“庄典性”的语体特征，大量使用汉语文言成分（张文，2020），《民法典》中表示因果关系的标记词均为“因”字，而非现代汉语的双音词“因为”。“因”字结构在《民法典》中一共出现了177次，可以分为作介词和作连词两种情况。

(1)作介词

本结构在《民法典》中甚为常见,O为名词或名词短语、动词或动词短语。尽管V/VP都可看作O的影响或结果,但细细分析,大致又可划分为五种情况:

① O是V/VP的凭借、依据。如第230条规定:“因继承取得物权的,自继承开始时发生效力。”该条规定的情形是:物权是**凭借/通过**继承获得的。又如第118条对债权的定义:“债权是因合同、侵权行为、无因管理、不当得利以及法律的其他规定,权利人请求特定义务人为或者不为一定行为的权利。”“权利人请求特定义务人为或者不为一定行为”的**依据**是“合同、侵权行为、无因管理、不当得利以及法律的其他规定”。

②O是V/VP的目的。如第1060条规定:“夫妻一方因家庭日常生活需要而实施的民事法律行为,对夫妻双方发生效力,但是夫妻一方与相对人另有约定的除外。”“实施民事法律行为”的目的是满足“家庭日常生活需要”。

③O是V/VP的时间、时机。如第62条规定:“法定代表人因执行职务造成他人损害的,由法人承担民事责任。”“执行职务”不是“造成他人损害”的目的,而是时间。

④O是V/VP的内容。如第1230条规定:“因物权的归属、内容发生争议的,利害关系人可以请求确认权利。”发生“争议”的原因是对“物权的归属、内容”有歧义,可见,“争议”的内容是“物权的归属、内容”。

⑤O是V/VP的直接原因(cause),在《民法典》中经常用于“因……造成……”“因……致使……”等结构。如第935条中的“因委托人死亡或者被宣告破产、解散,致使委托合同终止将损害委托人利益的”,该情形中,“委托合同终止”是由“委托人死亡或者被宣告破产、解散”直接造成的。

(2)作连词

“因”在本结构中连接两个小句,多数情况表示原因,少数情况表示条件。如第917条规定的“因仓储物本身的自然性质、包装不符合约定或者超过有效储存期造成仓储物变质、损坏”,“仓储物本身的自然性质、包装不符合约定或者超过有效储存期”是导致“仓储物变质、损坏”的原因。又如第122条规定:“因他人没有法律根据,取得不当利益,受损失的人有权请求其返还不当利益。”“他人没有法律根据”和“取得不当利益”是“受损失的人有权请求其返还不当利益”的条件。

4.2 译文对比

表 4.1 《民法典》中“因”字结构的翻译对比

序号	出处（条）	原文	北大法宝译文（法宝版译文）	国家法规总库译文（总库版译文）
1	112	自然人<u>因</u>婚姻家庭关系等<u>产生</u>的人身权利受法律保护。	The personal rights of a natural person <u>arising from</u> marriage or family relations, among others, shall be protected by law.	The personal rights of a natural person <u>arising from</u> a marital or familial relationship are protected by law.
2	322	<u>因</u>加工、附合、混合而<u>产生</u>的物的归属，有约定的，按照约定……	Where there is an agreement on the attribution of the property <u>arising from</u> processing, attachment, or mixing, such an agreement shall prevail...	A thing, that is created <u>as a result of</u> processing, or combining or mixing with another thing or things, shall be owned as agreed if there is such an agreement...
3	229	<u>因</u>人民法院、仲裁机构的法律文书或者人民政府的征收决定等，导致物权设立、变更、转让或者消灭的，自法律文书或者征收决定等生效时发生效力。	Where a real right is created, modified, transferred, or extinguished <u>in accordance with</u> the legal document of a people's court or an arbitration institution or an expropriation decision made by a people's government, among others, it shall have binding force from the time when the legal document or expropriation decision, among others, becomes valid.	Where a real right is created, altered, transferred, or extinguished <u>as a result of</u> a legal document issued by the people's court or an arbitration institution, or based on an expropriation decision made by the people's government, the creation, alteration, transfer, or extinguishment of the real right becomes effective at the time when the legal document or expropriation decision enters into effect.

续表

序号	出处（条）	原文	北大法宝译文（法宝版译文）	国家法规总库译文（总库版译文）
4	296	不动产权利人因用水、排水、通行、铺设管线等利用相邻不动产的，应当尽量避免对相邻的不动产权利人造成损害。	Where the right holder of an immovable uses the neighboring immovable for water use, drainage, passage, laying pipelines, or any other purpose, the right holder shall do the best to avoid causing any damage to the right holder of the neighboring immovable.	A person entitled to the real rights in immovable property who utilizes the adjacent immovable property for the purpose of using water, drainage, passage, laying pipelines, or the like, shall spare no effort to avoid causing damage to the person entitled to the real rights in the adjacent immovable property.
5	591	…… 当事人因防止损失扩大而支出的合理费用，由违约方负担。	... The reasonable expenses incurred by the other party to prevent the aggravation of losses shall be borne by the party in breach.	... The reasonable expenses incurred by a party in preventing the aggravation of the loss shall be borne by the breaching party.
6	34	…… 因发生突发事件等紧急情况，监护人暂时无法履行监护职责，被监护人的生活处于无人照料状态的，被监护人住所地的居民委员会、村民委员会或者民政部门应当为被监护人安排必要的临时生活照料措施。	... In case of emergency or under any other emergency circumstance, the guardian is temporarily unable to perform the duty of guardianship and the ward's life is unattended, the urban residents' committee, villagers' committee, or civil affairs department of the place of the ward's domicile shall arrange for necessary daily care for the ward.	... Where a guardian is temporarily unable to perform his duties owing to an emergency such as an unexpected incident, thus leaving the ward in an unattended situation, the residents' committee, the villagers' committee, or the civil affairs department in the place where the ward's domicile is located shall make arrangement as a temporary measure to provide necessary life care for the ward.

续表

序号	出处（条）	原文	北大法宝译文（法宝版译文）	国家法规总库译文（总库版译文）
7	1088	夫妻一方因抚育子女、照料老年人、协助另一方工作等负担较多义务的，离婚时有权向另一方请求补偿，另一方应当给予补偿……	Where one of the spouses performs more duties in bringing up children, taking care of the elderly or assisting the other spouse in his or her work, that spouse shall have the right to claim compensation from the other spouse in the case of divorce, and the other spouse shall make compensation...	Where one spouse is burdened with additional duties for raising children, looking after the elderly, or assisting the other spouse in his work, the said spouse has the right to request for compensation upon divorce against the other party, and the other party shall make due compensation...
8	234	因物权的归属、内容发生争议的，利害关系人可以请求确认权利。	Where any dispute arises over the attribution or content of a real right, the interested parties may file a claim for confirmation of the right.	Where a dispute arises over the attribution or contents of a real right, an interested person may request for confirmation of the right.
9	594	因国际货物买卖合同和技术进出口合同争议提起诉讼或者申请仲裁的时效期间为四年。	For a dispute arising from a contract for the international sale of goods or a technology import or export contract, the time limit for instituting an action or applying for arbitration is four years.	The limitation period for filing a lawsuit or arbitration on a dispute arising from a contract for international sale of goods and a contract for the import and export of technology is four years.

续表

序号	出处(条)	原文	北大法宝译文(法宝版译文)	国家法规总库译文(总库版译文)
10	593	当事人一方因第三人的原因造成违约的,应当依法向对方承担违约责任。当事人一方和第三人之间的纠纷,依照法律规定或者按照约定处理。	Where a party is in breach because of a third party, it shall be liable to the other party for breach in accordance with the law. Any dispute between the party and such third party shall be handled in accordance with the law or as agreed.	A party who breaches a contract due to a third person's reason shall bear default liability to the other party in accordance with law. The dispute between the breaching party and the third person shall be handled in accordance with the provisions of law or their agreement.
11	729	因不可归责于承租人的事由,致使租赁物部分或者全部毁损、灭失的,承租人可以请求减少租金或者不支付租金;因租赁物部分或者全部毁损、灭失,致使不能实现合同目的的,承租人可以解除合同。	Where the leased property is damaged or lost in part or in whole due to any reason not attributable to the lessee, the lessee may request reduction in rent or refuse to pay rent; where the purpose of the contract cannot be achieved due to damage to or loss of the leased property in part or in whole, the lessee may rescind the contract.	Where a leased object is partially or wholly destructed, damaged, or lost due to a cause not attributable to the lessee, the lessee may request a reduction or exemption of the rent, and the lessee may rescind the contract if the purpose of the contract is unable to be achieved owing to such destruction, damage, or loss.
12	1257	因林木折断、倾倒或者果实坠落等造成他人损害,林木的所有人或管理人不能证明自己没有过错的,应当承担侵权责任。	Where any harm is caused to another person by a broken or fallen tree, a fallen fruit, or the like, the owner or manager of the tree shall assume the tort liability if it cannot prove that it is not at fault.	Where a breaking or falling tree or a falling fruit causes damage to another person, the owner or manager of the tree shall bear tort liability if he cannot prove that he is not at fault.

续表

序号	出处(条)	原文	北大法宝译文(法宝版译文)	国家法规总库译文(总库版译文)
13	922	……因情况紧急,难以和委托人取得联系的,受托人应当妥善处理委托事务,但是事后应当将该情况及时报告委托人。	...in an emergency where the mandatary has difficulty in contacting the mandator, the mandatary shall properly handle the affair under the mandate but shall, in a timely manner, report it to the mandator thereafter.	... where the situation is emergent and it is difficult to obtain the principal's consent, the agent shall properly handle the entrusted matter, and shall, afterwards, promptly inform the principal of the situation.
14	611	标的物毁损、灭失的风险由买受人承担的,不影响因出卖人履行义务不符合约定,买受人请求其承担违约责任的权利。	Where the risk of damage to or loss of the subject matter is borne by the buyer, it shall not affect the buyer's claim of liability of the seller for breach of contract because the seller's performance of its obligations is not in conformity with the agreement.	Where a seller's performance is not in conformity with the agreement, the assumption of the risks of destruction, damage, or loss of the subject matter by the buyer does not affect the buyer's right to request the seller to bear default liability.

4.3 译文分析

汉语"因"字的使用具有普遍性和含义不确定性,加之英语中表示因果关系的表达方式众多,造成两个译本在翻译"因"字结构时差别甚大。表4.1所列例句仅为少数代表,入选标准为符合前文分析的运用情况,且译文表达方式出现频率较高。以下我们对比分析两版译文,探讨更为可取的翻译方法。

4.3.1 作介词的"因"的翻译

(1)O是V/VP的凭借、依据

这种情况下,两个版本最常用的表达方式是arising from,通常表述为

"因……产生的……(权利或关系)"。arising from 意味着某个事件或行为是另一个事件或行为的直接或间接结果,并且可能会导致一系列相关问题或争议,强调来源和衍生。在例句 1 中,用以指人身权利演变生成于婚姻家庭关系,非常贴切。但是并非所有的"因……而产生"都要译成 arising from,比如例句 2,源语条文指物的归属关系衍生于"加工、附合、混合"过程,但在法宝版译文中,arising from 的逻辑主语是 the attribution of the property,attribution 据《韦氏词典》和《牛津词典》的释义为"the act of saying what the origin or cause of something is",指的是归属行为,而非归属关系。行为可以是某事的结果,但不能是某事的衍生,故此,不如改为 resulting from 更合适。总库版译文做了意译处理,用 as a result of 表达"物"是"加工、附合、混合"过程的结果,把"归属"译为动词,也是可取的方法。

例句 3 中,法宝版用 in accordance with 表示"人民法院、仲裁机构的法律文书或者人民政府的征收决定等"是"物权设立、变更、转让或者消灭"的依据,总库版用 as a result of 表示"物权设立、变更、转让或者消灭"是"人民法院、仲裁机构的法律文书或者人民政府的征收决定等"的结果,在语义上没有太大差别,不过是译者理解的倾向不同,对意思表达没有影响。由此也可见,"因"字结构中"因"字含义的不确定性。

当 O 是 V/VP 的凭借方式时,如第 230 条中的"因继承取得物权的",两个版本都译为"Where a real right is acquired through succession",而对于第 779 条规定的"定作人不得因监督检验妨碍承揽人的正常工作",法宝版译为"The ordering party may not obstruct the normal work of the contractor with the supervision and inspection",总库版译为"The client may not disturb the normal work of the contractor by such supervision and inspection"。不同介词的选用,一方面取决于语境,一方面取决于译者的表达习惯,盖因英语中此类表达方式太多,而在某些语境中又可以互换,比如第 779 条中的 with 和 by,都是可取的。

(2)O 是 V/VP 的目的

英语中表示目的的方式也很多,两版译文中多用 for sth./doing sth.和

to do sth.结构来表达。例句 4 中，法宝版译文使用 for，总库版译文使用 for the purpose of，考虑到简明英语的要求，法宝版更可取。例句 5 中，法宝版译为 to do sth.，总库版译为 in doing sth.。法宝版认为“防止损失扩大”是支出“合理费用”的目的，而总库版认为“合理费用”是在“防止损失扩大”的行动中“支出”的，虽然对“因”字的理解不同，但对于法条意思的传达没有影响。本例再次验证了“因”字含义的不确定性。

(3) O 是 V/VP 的时间、时机

这种情况下，通常译为表示时间的表达方式。例句 6 中，法宝版使用“in case of”“under”表示“突发事件等紧急情况”是“监护人暂时无法履行监护职责，被监护人的生活处于无人照料状态”的时间；总库版用“owing to”表示“突发事件等紧急情况”是“监护人暂时无法履行监护职责”的原因(reason)，之后又用“thus”表示“监护人暂时无法履行监护职责”的结果，即导致“被监护人的生活处于无人照料状态”。两版在意思上没有差别。但法宝版译文没有表现出“监护人暂时无法履行监护职责，被监护人的生活处于无人照料状态”是后文“被监护人住所地的居民委员会、村民委员会或者民政部门应当为被监护人安排必要的临时生活照料措施”的条件，仅简单复制汉语条文中的外观句式结构，是错误的中式英语。汉语“意合”的特点是多散句，小句间的关系隐含在字里行间；英语“形合”的特点表现为句式完整，小句间的关系用标记词进行明示。法宝版的译文不妨改为：In case of emergency or under any other emergency circumstance <u>where</u> the guardian is temporarily unable to perform the duty of guardianship, <u>leaving</u> the ward unattended, the urban residents' committee, villagers' committee, or civil affairs department of the place of the ward's domicile shall arrange for necessary daily care for the ward.。

例句 7 中，“抚育子女、照料老年人、协助另一方工作”不是“负担较多义务”的目的。在婚姻中，一方负担较多义务的目的有可能是表达对另一方的爱意。因此，法宝版译文用“in doing”表示时间，即在“抚育子女、照料老年人、协助另一方工作”中“负担较多义务”，是可取译法。

(4) O 是 V/VP 的内容

例句 8 中,两版译文都用 over 和 dispute 搭配,表示"物权的归属、内容"是争议的内容,没有问题。例句 9 中,诉讼或仲裁的内容是"国际货物买卖合同和技术进出口合同争议",法宝版译为 for 引导的介宾短语,置于句首,表示 concerning"关于";总库版用 on 表示 about"关于",跟在"lawsuit or arbitration"之后作后置定语。通过在数据库中检索 arbitration 的用法,发现 arbitration 搭配 on 或 in respect of 都可以表示仲裁的内容,如"arbitration in respect of the restoration of confiscated quota"和"arbitration on the interpretation of the June 2003 agreement between the Fire Brigades Union and the local authority fire service employers"出自英国立法数据库,"arbitration on attorneys' fees and costs"出自美国法典库。可见,选择哪个介词翻译,还取决于行文中的词语搭配。

(5)O 是 V/VP 的直接原因

这种情况下,两版译文使用最多的表达方式是 due to,其次是 as a result of,其他还有 because of、owing to、result in/from 等。例句 10 中,"因第三人的原因",法宝版译为"because of a third party",总库版翻译为"due to a third person's reason"。在数据库中检索 due to 搭配 reason 的使用情况,香港法例库和美国联邦法规库中没有此种搭配,而英国立法数据库和美国法典库中出现的都是"due to a reason for which..."或"due to a reason other than...",可见 reason 在搭配中指的是某种具体的原因,而非总库版的没有实际意义的原因(汉语条文的意思是:原因是第三人),因此,总库版的译文像是中式英语,而法宝版译文此处更可取。

例句 11 中,"因不可归责于承租人的事由",两版译文都使用 due to 分别搭配 any reason 和 a cause,此处的 reason 和 cause 都指向某种具体原因,符合 due to 的规范用法。"因租赁物部分或者全部毁损、灭失",法宝版译为 due to,总库版译为 owing to。自 18 世纪以来,对 due to 和 owing to 的正确用法一直存在争议,有的认为 due to 只能用于修饰名词或作表语,owing to 可修饰动词作状语,如 Kernerman English Multilingual Dictionary 的注解。但《韦氏词典》认为,经过几十年来语言的发展和实践,due to 和 owing to 的用法已经趋于一致。但有学者发现,在表示原因时,内地译文倾向使用 due to,而香港立法语篇倾向使用 as a result of。香港的法律法规是以英语制定的,其表原因词组的使用应该是准确的(高雅蓉、钟玲俐,2022),因此,当 V/VP 可以看作 O 的直接结果时,不妨多使用 as a result of,一方面避开 due to 的正确用法之争;另一方面,鉴于 due to 和 owe to 本身含义多样,在法律语境中还可以表示"应该""欠""应得的""应负的"等,尽量少用它们表示原因,而选用词义单一的同义词组,以避免歧义。

例句 12,对于"因……造成他人损害",法宝版译为被动句,总库版译为主动句,前者用 by 引出原因,后者用原因作主语省译"因"字,都是可取做法。

4.3.2 作连词的"因"的翻译

"因"字作连词的情况在《民法典》中出现较少,因为汉语中的小句和短语有时很难分辨,如例句 13 中的"情况紧急",法宝版认为是一种紧急情况,因此译成"an emergency",总库版却译为小句"the situation is emergent",与"难以和委托人取得联系"同作"受托人应当妥善处理委托事务"的条件。但是细分析之,总库版译文各小句之间关系较松散,"and"在句中的连接作用较弱,而法宝版译文的句式更紧凑,更符合英语"形合"的特点。

例句 14 中,两版译文的差别较大。法宝版更贴近源语法条的语序,把"因"字翻译成连词 because。而总库版做了较大调整,把"因"字结构中的 O,即"出卖人履行义务不符合约定",用连词 where 译为整句的条件,把"标的物毁损、灭失的风险由买受人承担"译成一个名词性词组作"不影响"的主语。两版译文传达的意思一致,但是总库版句式更紧凑,更符合英语的表达习惯。

小 结

“因”字结构在《民法典》中可以分为“因”字作介词和连词两种情况。①作介词时，其基本结构为“因＋O＋V/VP”。根据 O 和 V/VP 的关系，大致又可分成表示凭借或依据、表示目的、表示时间或时机、表示内容、表示直接原因等五种类型。②“因”字作连词时，多数情况表示原因，少数情况表示条件。汉译英时“因”字译为相应的介词或连词。但是由于汉语法条表述的概括性，“因”字的含义具有不确定性，有些情况下，可做两种解释，但更多情况下，只有一种合理解释，译者应当根据语境体会出最合适的含义，译为相应的英语表述。但是鉴于英语中同义表述数量很多，选择哪一个，还须取决于语境和行文中的词语搭配。在高下难辨的情况下，建议选用词义单一的词语，以避免歧义。

5 “由”字结构的翻译

5.1 结构特点及其在《民法典》中的运用

5.1.1 结构特点

“由”字结构是介词“由”后跟宾语，置于句子谓语中心词之前作状语，可以表示为“A＋由＋O＋V/VP”。A 为受事，一般为名词或名词短语，少数也可以是主谓短语或动宾短语；A 有时省略，有时移到 V/VP 后面，这时“由”字结构出现在句首，可以表示为“由＋O＋V/VP”或“由＋O＋V/VP＋A”。“由”后的宾语 O 可以是施事，也可以是方式、起点、原因、依据、来源等。V/VP 是谓语中心词，可以是动词短语或形容词短语。根据《现代汉语虚词词典》(朱景松，2007)，“由”的意义是“归”时，引进动作的施事或相关对象；“由”的意义是“因为”时，引进原因或理由；“由”的意义是“用、通过”时，引进凭借对象；“由”的意义是“从”时，引进时间或空间的起点、事物的来源、行为或动作经由的路线。法律文本中，“由”字结构在多数情况下用于介绍动作行为的发出者，即施事。

5.1.2 在《民法典》中的运用

在《民法典》中该结构一共出现了 209 次，通常情况下“由”的意义是“归”，个别情况下，“由”的意义是“因为”或“从”。

(1)意义是“归”的“由”字结构

“由”字结构出现在句中,是最常规的情况,如第 604 条中,“标的物毁损、灭失的**风险**,在标的物交付之前**由**出卖人**承担**,交付之后**由**买受人**承担**”,本条规定了风险承担的分配,其中 A 是“风险”,是受事;O 是“出卖人”“买受人”,是施事;V 是“承担”,是动作。

“由”字结构出现在句首,可分成两种情况:

①A 移到 V 后作 V 的宾语。如第 768 条规定,“应收账款债权人就同一应收账款订立多个保理合同,致使多个保理人主张权利的……均未登记的,**由**最先到达应收账款债务人的转让通知中载明的**保理人取得应收账款**”,“由”后的 O 是“……保理人”,V 是“取得”,“应收账款”是“取得”的宾语,但也可以看作是 A 移到 V 后,所以此句是常规结构“**应收账款由**最先到达应收账款债务人的转让通知中载明的**保理人取得**”的变形。

②A 缺失。如第 42 条第二款规定:“代管有争议,没有前款规定的人,或者前款规定的人无代管能力的,**由**人民法院指定的人**代管**。”本款中“由”字结构的 A 缺失,但是根据第一款“失踪人的财产由其配偶、成年子女、父母或者其他愿意担任财产代管人的人代管”,可知 A 是省略的“失踪人的财产”,是“代管”的受事。又如第 1079 条规定:“夫妻一方要求离婚的,可以**由**有关组织**进行调解**或者直接向人民法院提起离婚诉讼。”“调节”此处是不及物动词,没有受事。

(2)意义是“因为”的“由”字结构

本结构可表示为“A+由+O+V”,O 表示 V 的原因,V 一般由“引起”“造成”等动词充当。如第 1203 条中规定:“产品缺陷**由**生产者**造成**的,销售者赔偿后,有权向生产者追偿。”“生产者”是导致“产品缺陷”的原因。

(3)意义是“从”的“由”字结构

本结构只出现一次,第 1216 条中“……机动车不明、该机动车未参加强制保险或者抢救费用超过机动车强制保险责任限额,需要支付被侵权人人身伤亡的抢救、丧葬等费用的,**由道路交通事故社会救助基金垫付**”,“道路交通事故社会救助基金”不是“垫付”的施事,而是垫付费用的来源。

5.2 译文对比

表 5.1 《民法典》中"由"字结构的翻译对比

序号	出处（条）	原文	北大法宝译文（法宝版译文）	国家法规总库译文（总库版译文）
1	32	没有依法具有监护资格的人的，监护人由民政部门担任，也可以由具备履行监护职责条件的被监护人住所地的居民委员会、村民委员会担任。	Where there is no person legally qualified for guardianship, the civil affairs department may or the urban residents' committee or villagers' committee of the place of the ward's domicile satisfying the conditions for performing the duty of guardianship may act as the guardian.	Where there is no person legally qualified to be a guardian, the civil affairs department shall act as the guardian, and the residents' committee or villagers' committee in the place where the ward's domicile is located may also act as the guardian if they are competent in performing the duties of guardian.
2	1234	……侵权人在期限内未修复的，国家规定的机关或者法律规定的组织可以自行或者委托他人进行修复，所需费用由侵权人负担。	… If the tortfeasor fails to do so, the authority specified by the state or the organization specified by law may conduct remediation, by itself or through any other party authorized by it, at the expense of the tortfeasor.	… Where the tortfeasor fails to restore it within the time limit, the State authorized agencies or the organizations authorized by law may initiate the restoration on its own or entrust it with others, and any expenses thus incurred shall be borne by the tortfeasor.
3	210	不动产登记，由不动产所在地的登记机构办理。……	An immovable shall be registered at the registration authority at the place where the immovable is located. …	The registration of immovable property shall be handled by the registration authority at the place where the immovable property is located. …

续表

序号	出处（条）	原文	北大法宝译文（法宝版译文）	国家法规总库译文（总库版译文）
4	19	**八周岁以上的未成年人**为限制民事行为能力人，**实施民事法律行为由**其法定代理人**代理**或者经其法定代理人同意、追认……	**A minor attaining the age of eight** is a person with limited capacity for civil conduct, **who shall be represented by** his or her statutory agent **in performing juridical acts** or whose performance of juridical acts shall be consented to or ratified by his or her statutory agent...	**A minor aged eight or above** has limited capacity for performing civil juristic acts and **may perform a civil juristic act through** or upon consent or ratification of his legal representative...
5	31	对监护人的确定有争议的，**由**被监护人住所地的居民委员会、村民委员会或者民政部门**指定监护人**……	In case of any dispute over the determination of guardian, the urban residents' committee, villagers' committee, or civil affairs department of the place of the ward's domicile **may designate the guardian**...	Where a dispute arises over the determination of a guardian, **the guardian shall be appointed by** the residents' committee, the villagers' committee, or the civil affairs department in the place where the ward's domicile is located...
6	1015	**自然人**应当随父姓或者母姓，但是有下列情形之一的，可以在父姓和母姓之外选取姓氏： …… （二）因**由**法定扶养人以外的人**扶养**而选取扶养人姓氏； ……	A natural person shall take the surname of either the father or mother. Under one of the following circumstances, he may adopt a surname other than that of the father or mother: ... (2) Adoption of the surname of a supporter, since **the citizen is supported by** a supporter other than the statutory one. ...	A natural person shall take the surname of either his father or mother, and may take a surname other than his father's or mother's in any of the following situations: ... (2) taking the surname of a foster parent, other than the legal care provider, **who provides care to him**; and ...

续表

序号	出处（条）	原文	北大法宝译文（法宝版译文）	国家法规总库译文（总库版译文）
7	1128	被继承人的子女先于被继承人死亡的，**由**被继承人的子女的直系晚辈血亲**代位继承**。 被继承人的兄弟姐妹先于被继承人死亡的，**由**被继承人的兄弟姐妹的子女**代位继承**。 ……	Where a decedent survived his child, the direct lineal descendants of the child who has predeceased the decedent **shall inherit in subrogation**. Where a decedent survived his brother or sister, the children of the brother or sister who has predeceased the decedent **shall inherit in subrogation**. …	Where a decedent is predeceased by a child of his, the lineal descendants of the predeceased child **shall inherit in subrogation**. Where a decedent is predeceased by a sibling of his, the children of the predeceased sibling **shall inherit in subrogation**. …
8	182	…… **危险由**自然原因**引起**的，紧急避险人不承担民事责任，可以给予适当补偿。 ……	… Where the danger **arises from** any natural cause, the person acting to avoid the danger shall not assume civil liability, but may make appropriate indemnification. …	… Where the peril **is caused by** natural forces, the person who causes harm to others when seeking to avoid the peril bears no civil liability, but may make appropriate compensation. …
9	516	…… 可选择的标的发生不能履行情形的，享有选择权的当事人不得选择不能履行的标的，但是**该不能履行的情形是由**对方**造成**的除外。	… If any of the alternative subject matters of an obligation becomes impossible to perform, the party having the choice shall not choose the subject matter, unless **the performance is made impossible by** the other party.	… Where one of the objects available for selection becomes impossible to perform, the party with the right of choice may not select such object to perform, unless **the impossibility to perform is caused by** the other party.

续表

序号	出处（条）	原文	北大法宝译文（法宝版译文）	国家法规总库译文（总库版译文）
10	1216	……机动车不明、该机动车未参加强制保险或者抢救费用超过机动车强制保险责任限额，需要支付被侵权人人身伤亡的抢救、丧葬等费用的，由道路交通事故社会救助基金垫付……	...or if the motor vehicle cannot be identified or is not covered by the mandatory insurance, or rescue expenses exceed the liability limit of the mandatory motor vehicle insurance, and the expenses for the death of or personal injury to the victim, such as rescue and funeral fees, need to be paid, the advances shall be made out of the Social Assistance Fund for Road Traffic Accidents...	...Where the motor vehicle cannot be located, is not covered by the compulsory insurance, or the rescue expenses exceed the limit of liability of the compulsory motor vehicle insurance, and payment needs to be made against the rescue, funeral, and other expenses incurred as a result of the death or bodily injury of the infringed person, such payment shall be paid from the Social Assistance Fund for Road Traffic Accidents...

5.3 译文分析

我们针对《民法典》中“由”字结构的使用情况，分别对比分析两个版本的对应译文，探讨更为可取的翻译方法。

5.3.1 意义是“归”的“由”字结构的翻译

①当“由”字结构出现在句中，基本结构为“A＋由＋O＋V/VP”，如例句1—4，O是施事，A是受事，翻译时根据具体情况可以译为主动句“O＋V＋A”，也可以译为被动句“A＋be V-ed＋by＋O”。

例句1中，两个版本都译为主动句。但是总库版在翻译“由民政部门担任”时，使用了情态动词shall，shall表示“必须”，是一种命令（mandatory duty)。而源语中民政部门担任监护人是一种许可，因为监护人"也可以由具备履行监护职责条件的被监护人住所地的居民委员会、村民委员会担任"，由此可见，法宝版使用情态动词 may 才是正确的。

例句 2 中，法宝版进行了意译，但是根据《韦氏词典》，at the expense of 意思是 in a way that harms (something or someone)，对应汉语的"以……为代价"，显然与源语条文的意思不同。总库版译为被动句，但译成主动句"the tortfeasor shall pay any expenses thus incurred"更好。主动语态强调主语或动作的执行者，被动语态强调动作或动作的接受者，本句"所需费用由侵权人负担"，规定的不是费用，而是费用的负担人，即动作的执行者，因此使用主动语态更简洁、直接。

例句 3 中，"办理"的施动者不明确且不重要，因此应当译为被动句。但是总库版译文轻率了，源语条文看似在规定办理登记的机构，实则规定的是办理登记的地点，因此，法宝版译文看似与源语不一致，其实忠实地传达了源语的真正意思。

例句 4 中，受事 A 是动宾短语"实施民事法律行为"，其逻辑主语是"八周岁以上的未成年人"。法宝版将"由"字结构译为非限制性定语从句，先行词是"八周岁以上的未成年人"，定语从句中使用被动语态"被代理"，A 译成表示时间的介宾短语 in doing sth.。总库版直接用"八周岁以上的未成年人"作主语，将两个句子合而为一，把 A 译成主要谓语，用情态动词 may 表示许可，把"由……代理"译成介宾短语 through sb.，应当说两版译文都没问题，但是总库版更简洁、更直接。

②"由"字结构出现在句首时，有两种情况：一种是 A 移到 V 后作 V 的宾语，如例句 5；一种是 A 缺失，如例句 6 和例句 7。

例句 5 中，就语态的选择而言，总库版的被动语态要优于法宝版的主动语态，因为法宝版句式有些头重脚轻。此外，被动语态可以在多个句子中保持相同的关注点，总库版译文将关注点集中在 guardian 上，语意顺畅。就情态动词的选择而言，法宝版使用 may 是正确的，因为监护人不光可以"由被监护人住所地的居民委员会、村民委员会或者民政部门指定"，也可以由有关当事人直接向人民法院申请指定，此处的指定是“许可”不是“命令”。

例句 6 中，根据前文语境可以推断，A 指的是“自然人”。法宝版使用被动语态，用“the citizen”指代“自然人”作主语，但这种翻译有歧义，“the citizen”有可能被误解为逗号前的“supporter”，被动结构中“by a supporter”所说的“supporter”一定指逗号前的“supporter”吗？也不一定。表述不严谨，歧义由此产生。总库版将整款译为逻辑主语是“自然人”的动名词结构，将“由”字结构译为 who 引导的非限制性定语从句，先行词是“a foster parent”，使用主动语态，“抚养”的宾语顺势译为 him，指代“自然人”。应当说，总库版译文没有歧义，更可取。

例句 7 中 A 是缺失的，而且 V 的宾语不言即明，也就是说“代位继承”的宾语是且只能是遗产，这种情况下，两版译文一致，都使用了主动语态，译为“O+V”结构，inherit 是不及物动词。

5.3.2 意义是“因为”的“由”字结构的翻译

“由”引出原因时，基本结构为“A+由+O+V”，V 通常由“引起”“造成”等词充当，总库版通常译为“A is caused by O”，如例句 8 和例句 9。

法宝版译文，在例句 8 中使用了 arise from，意思和 be caused by 没有差别。在例句 9 中，使用了意译，用“performance”作主语表示“履行”，performance 一词含义太多，此处容易产生歧义，任何任务或工作的履行都可用 performance 代替，第 516 条第一款中“当事人行使选择权”也是一种 performance。因此，总库版的译文“the impossibility to perform is caused by the other party”表述得更清晰。

5.3.3 意义是“从”的“由”字结构的翻译

这种情况下，“由”字结构通常译为被动语态句，“由”字根据搭配译成相应的介词。例句 10 中，因为“垫付”的施事者不好判断，也没有必要说明，两版译文都使用被动句，根据前文补充出了“垫付”的受事，即“被侵权人人身伤亡的抢救、丧葬等费用”，法宝版译为“the advances”，表示是垫付的预支款，总库版直接译为“such payment”呼应前句中的“payment”。“由”字分别译成介词“out of”和“from”，以搭配动词 make 和 pay。都是可取译文。

小　结

“由”字结构是介词“由”后跟宾语，置于谓语中心词之前作状语的结构。在《民法典》中，通常情况下“由”的意义是“归”；个别情况下，“由”的意义是“因为”或“从”。①意义是“归”时，如果出现在句中，基本结构可以表示为“A＋由＋O＋V/VP”，A 是受事，O 是施事，翻译时根据具体情况可以译为主动句“O＋V＋A”，也可以译为被动句“A＋be V-ed＋by＋O”。如果出现在句首，有两种情况：A 移到 V 后作 V 的宾语，此时可以看作是“A＋由＋O＋V/VP”结构的变形，翻译也同该结构；A 缺失时，根据语境可以补足 A 作主语，译为被动句，也可以译为主动句，尤其是 V 为不及物动词时。②意义是“因为”时，“由”引出原因，基本结构为“A＋由＋O＋V”，V 通常由“引起”“造成”等动词充当，可以译为“A is caused by O”，或者根据具体语境和行文译成其他表示原因的英语表达。③意义是“从”时，“由”字结构通常译为被动句，“由”引出事物的来源，根据与动词的搭配译成相应的介词。

6 “的”字结构的翻译

6.1 结构特点及其在《民法典》中的运用

6.1.1 结构特点

“的”字结构是法律汉语中最为常见的假定结构，其主要功能是表达条文适用的条件和情形。与普通的作定语的“的”字结构不同，本节所讨论的“的”字结构一般出现在句首，“的”后有逗号，其基本格式为“NP＋VP＋的”，NP＋VP构成主谓结构，该主谓结构可以是单个，也可以是多个。如“出卖人多交标的物的，买受人可以接收或者拒绝接收多交的部分”，“出卖人多交标的物的”是“的”字结构，其中“出卖人多交标的物”构成单个主谓结构；又如“监护人不履行监护职责或者侵害被监护人合法权益的，应当承担法律责任”，其中“监护人不履行监护职责或者侵害被监护人合法权益”是复句，构成两个主谓结构。很多时候，“的”字结构中的NP可以省略，“的”字前面形成动宾结构，如“依法需要办理法人登记的，应当……”立法文本中的“的”字结构具有类属意义，其表述不仅简洁，而且严谨，于严谨之中又有突出重点的效果(王洁，1999)。

6.1.2 在《民法典》中的运用

在《民法典》中该结构一共出现了1289次，可以分为以下几种情况：

(1)“的”字前是主谓结构

这种类型的数量最多。根据“的”字结构后面主句的构成情况,又可以分为两类:

①主句谓语前有主语,构成的句式为“NP1＋VP1＋的,NP2＋VP2”,如第44条规定的“人民法院变更财产代管人的,变更后的财产代管人有权请求原财产代管人及时移交有关财产并报告财产代管情况”。“的”字前后各有一个主谓完整的小句,“的”字结构相当于一个条件状语从句,表达假定条件,同时确定了法律条文适用的法律主体或对象。

②主句谓语前无主语,构成的句式为“NP1＋VP1＋的,VP2”。有时主句中VP2的逻辑主语就是NP1,此时,“VP1＋的”可以看作是NP1的限定成分,董秀芳(2003)将其视为后置关系小句修饰中心名词NP1。如第949条中的“原物业服务人违反前款规定的,不得请求业主支付物业服务合同终止后的物业费”,“违反前款规定”可以看作是“原物业服务人”的后置定语,如果改为前置定语,即“违反前款规定的原物业服务人”,意思不变。

还有的时候,主句中VP2的逻辑主语与“的”字结构中的NP1不同,如第498条规定:“格式条款和非格式条款不一致的,应当采用非格式条款。”

(2)“的”字前是动宾结构

基本句式为“VP1＋的,NP2＋VP2”,其中NP2有时省略。胡道华和蒋长刚(2016)认为,“VP＋的”可以表示自指和转指。表示自指时,指称条文规定的各种“情形”“条件”“行为”等,如第16条中,“涉及遗产继承、接受赠与等胎儿利益保护的,胎儿视为具有民事权利能力”,“涉及……胎儿利益保护的”,指称的不是具体的、个别的人或事物,而是一种情形或条件。表示转指时,指称法律主体,即实施了VP1行为的人,也就是缺省的NP1。

表示转指时,又可以分为两种类型:

①根据语境推断,NP1指某类特定的人或事物,如第949条规定:“原物业服务人违反前款规定的,不得请求业主支付物业服务合同终止后的物业费;造成业主损失的,应当赔偿损失。”“造成业主损失”的逻辑主语是违反前款规定的“原物业服务人”。

②NP1具有不定指意义,可以指任何人,如第999条中,“为公共利益

实施新闻报道、舆论监督等行为的，可以合理使用民事主体的姓名、名称、肖像、个人信息等”，此处法律规范调整的对象不是具体的、个别的人或物，而是“任何人”。

6.2 译文对比

表 6.1 《民法典》中“的”字结构的翻译对比

序号	出处（条）	原文	北大法宝译文（法宝版译文）	国家法规总库译文（总库版译文）
1	36	……前款规定的个人和民政部门以外的组织未及时向人民法院申请撤销监护人资格的，民政部门应当向人民法院申请。	…Where the individuals and organizations except the civil affairs department as prescribed in the preceding paragraph fail to apply for the disqualification of the guardian to the people's court in a timely manner, the civil affairs department shall file such an application with the people's court.	…Where the aforementioned individual and organization other than the civil affairs department, as stated in the preceding paragraph, fail to request the people's court to disqualify the guardian in a timely manner, the civil affairs department shall initiate such a request to the people's court.
2	51	被宣告死亡的人的婚姻关系，自死亡宣告之日起消除。死亡宣告被撤销的，婚姻关系自撤销死亡宣告之日起自行恢复……	The marital relationship of a person declared dead shall be extinguished from the date of declaration of death. If the declaration of death is revoked, the marital relationship shall resume automatically from the date of revocation of the declaration of death…	The marital relationship with a person declared dead ceases to exist from the date the declaration of his death is made. Where the declaration of death is revoked, the aforementioned marital relationship shall be automatically resumed from the date the declaration of death is revoked…

续表

序号	出处（条）	原文	北大法宝译文（法宝版译文）	国家法规总库译文（总库版译文）
3	120	民事权益受到侵害的，被侵权人有权请求侵权人承担侵权责任。	In case of infringement upon civil rights and interests, the victim shall have the right to request that the tortfeasor assume tort liability.	Where a person's civil-law rights and interests are infringed upon due to a tortious act, the person is entitled to request the tortfeasor to bear tort liability.
4	43	…… 财产代管人因故意或者重大过失造成失踪人财产损失的，应当承担赔偿责任。	... Where the property custodian causes damage to the absentee's property intentionally or with gross negligence, the custodian shall assume compensatory liability.	... A custodian who, intentionally or due to gross negligence, causes damage to the property of the missing person shall be liable for compensation.
5	726	出租人出卖租赁房屋的，应当在出卖之前的合理期限内通知承租人……	Where the lessor is to sell a leased property, it shall give the lessee a notice within a reasonable time limit before the sale...	A lessor intending to sell a leased house shall notify the lessee within a reasonable period of time prior to the sale...
6	10	处理民事纠纷，应当依照法律；法律没有规定的，可以适用习惯，但是不得违背公序良俗。	Civil disputes shall be resolved in accordance with the law; or if the law is silent, customs may apply, but not contrary to public order and good morals.	Civil disputes shall be resolved in accordance with law. Where the law does not specify, custom may be applied, provided that public order and good morals may not be offended.

续表

序号	出处(条)	原文	北大法宝译文(法宝版译文)	国家法规总库译文(总库版译文)
7	44	财产代管人不履行代管职责、侵害失踪人财产权益或者丧失代管能力**的**,失踪人的利害关系人可以向人民法院申请变更财产代管人。 ……	**Where** the property custodian fails to perform the duty of custody, infringes upon the absentee's property rights and interests, **or** becomes incapable of custody, an interested party for the absentee may apply to a people's court for replacement of the property custodian. …	**Where** a custodian fails to perform his duties of custodian, infringes upon the proprietary rights or interests of the missing person, **or if** the custodian becomes incompetent to be a custodian, an interested person of the missing person may request the people's court to replace the custodian. …
8	65	法人的实际情况与登记的事项不一致**的**,不得对抗善意相对人。	**The inconsistency** between the actual circumstances of a legal person and the registered information on the legal person shall not be set up against bona fide opposite parties.	**The actual situation** of a legal person, **which** is inconsistent with what is recorded upon registration, may not be asserted against a bona fide counterparty.
9	16	涉及遗产继承、接受赠与等胎儿利益保护**的**,胎儿视为具有民事权利能力……	**Where** the protection of the interests of a fetus is involved in, among others, a succession or acceptance of a gift, the fetus shall be presumed to have capacity for civil rights...	A fetus is deemed as having the capacity for enjoying civil-law rights **in** estate succession, acceptance of gift, and other **situations** where protection of a fetus' interests is involved...

续表

序号	出处(条)	原文	北大法宝译文(法宝版译文)	国家法规总库译文(总库版译文)
10	336	…… 因自然灾害严重毁损承包地等特殊情形,需要适当调整承包的耕地和草地<u>的</u>,应当依照农村土地承包的法律规定办理。	… <u>When</u> the contracted arable land or grassland needs to be adjusted appropriately due to special circumstances, such as serious damage to the contracted land or grassland caused by a natural disaster, the matter shall be handled in accordance with the provisions of laws on the contracting of rural land.	… <u>Under</u> special <u>circumstances</u> such as severe deterioration on the contracted land caused by natural disasters, appropriate adjustments shall be made in accordance with the provisions of laws on rural land contracting where necessary.
11	1220	因抢救生命垂危的患者等紧急情况,不能取得患者或者其近亲属意见<u>的</u>,经医疗机构负责人或者授权的负责人批准,可以立即实施相应的医疗措施。	<u>Where</u> the opinion of a patient or his close relative cannot be obtained in the case of an emergency such as rescue of a patient in critical condition, with the approval of the person in charge of the medical institution or an authorized person in charge, the corresponding medical measures may be taken immediately.	<u>In the case of</u> rescuing a terminally ill patient or in another emergency situation, where consent of the patient or his close relatives cannot be obtained, upon the approval of the person in charge of the medical institution or an authorized person in charge, the corresponding medical measures may be taken forthwith.

续表

序号	出处（条）	原文	北大法宝译文（法宝版译文）	国家法规总库译文（总库版译文）
12	259	履行国有财产管理、监督职责的机构及其工作人员，应当依法加强对国有财产的管理、监督，促进国有财产保值增值，防止国有财产损失；滥用职权，玩忽职守，造成国有财产损失<u>的</u>，应当依法承担法律责任。 ……	The institutions performing the duties of administration and supervision of state owned property and their staff members shall, in accordance with the law, strengthen the administration and supervision of state-owned property, promote the value preservation and increment of state-owned property, and prevent the loss of state-owned property; and <u>whoever</u> abuses power or neglects duty, causing any loss of state-owned property, shall assume legal liability in accordance with the law. …	Institutions and their staff with the duties of administration and supervision over the State-owned property shall strengthen the administration and supervision of the State-owned property in accordance with law, strive to preserve and increase the value of such property and prevent any loss thereof; they shall assume legal liabilities in accordance with law <u>if</u> losses are caused to the State-owned property as a result of their abuse of powers or dereliction of duties. …
13	316	拾得人在遗失物送交有关部门前，有关部门在遗失物被领取前，应当妥善保管遗失物。因故意或者重大过失致使遗失物毁损、灭失<u>的</u>，应当承担民事责任。	Lost property shall be properly kept by the finder before it is handed over to the relevant department and by the relevant department before it is taken back. <u>Whoever</u> causes any damage to or loss of the lost property intentionally or for gross negligence shall assume the civil liability.	A finder shall well keep a lost thing before it is delivered to the relevant department, and the relevant department shall well keep it before it is collected. <u>A person who</u>, intentionally or by gross negligence, causes the lost thing under his custody destructed, damaged, or lost shall bear civil liability.

续表

序号	出处(条)	原文	北大法宝译文(法宝版译文)	国家法规总库译文(总库版译文)
14	1228	…… 干扰医疗秩序，妨碍医务人员工作、生活，侵害医务人员合法权益的，应当依法承担法律责任。	… Anyone who interrupts the order of the medical system, or obstructs the work or life of medical staff, or infringes upon the lawful rights and interests of medical staff shall be subject to legal liability.	… Anyone, who interferes with the order of a medical institution, obstructs the work or life of the medical staff, or infringes upon the lawful rights and interests of the medical staff, shall bear liability in accordance with law.

6.3 译文分析

我们针对《民法典》中“的”字结构的使用情况，分别对比分析两个版本的对应译文，探讨可取的翻译方法。

6.3.1 “的”字前是主谓结构的翻译

①主句谓语前有主语时，“的”字前后是两个主谓完整的小句，“的”字结构通常译为条件状语从句或条件状语，表示法律主体实施法律行为需要满足的条件或情形，译文中经常使用表示假设关系的连词 if、where，或者介词短语 in case of。

where-条件句的使用频率最高，其次是 if-条件句。“where 引导的条件内容一般更趋于‘状/情况’性质，If/if 引导的是较严格意义上的‘条件’或‘限制’。”(李克兴，2013：94)例句 1 中，“的”字结构规定的是情形，即在此种情形下，民政部门应当向人民法院提出申请，两个版本都使用了 where-条件句，恰到好处。例句 2 中，“死亡宣告被撤销的”不是充分条件句:“死亡宣告”宣告的是什么或谁的死亡,需要依靠上文才能得出,法宝版译为 if-条件句,符合李克兴(2013)对 if 使用规则的分析。总库版使用 where 替代 if,大概是为了让译文更显正式、庄重,体现法律语言的文体特征。

介词短语 in case of 也常常用于表示假设,尤其是包含时间的语境。例句 3 中,“民事权益受到侵害的”既可以看作情形,也可以看作时间,即当民事权益受到侵害时。法宝版因此使用 in case of 后加名词的表达,比总库版译文更简洁。

②主句谓语前无主语时,构成的句式为“NP1＋VP1＋的,VP2”。如果主句中 VP2 的逻辑主语就是 NP1,翻译时,可以把 NP1 当作全句主语,VP2 作谓语,“VP1＋的”译成 NP1 的限定成分。例句 4 和例句 5 的总库版译文即为如此,例句 4 的“VP1＋的”译成 NP1 的定语从句,例句 5 译成现在分词短语修饰 NP1;法宝版译文仍然使用 where-条件句,主句中补出了缺省的主语“the custodian”和“it”,语法和语意都正确,但是从句重复主句的主语,比之总库版译文,稍显啰唆。

如果主句中 VP2 的逻辑主语不是 NP1,翻译时可以使用表示假设关系的连词 if、where,或者介词短语 in case of,这与主句谓语前有主语的译法一致。如例句 6 中,法宝版用“or if”强调“的”字结构是依赖语境的非充分条件句,总库版用“Where”凸显法律语体的正式和庄重,都是可取译文。

例句 7 中,两版译文都使用了 where-条件句,无可厚非。源语条文中“的”字前有三个主谓结构,具体而言,是一个标志为顿号和“或者”的选择复句,法宝版用逗号和“or”将三个主谓结构并列,是正常的英语表述方式;总库版在第三个主谓结构前使用了“or if”,实际等同于把 if 和 where 并列,用 if 替代 where。但是 where 和 if 出现在同句中时,where 引导的是起统辖作用的母条件,if 引导的是下位的子条件或次条件(李克兴,2013),可见同句中的 where 和 if 不是平等的,不能相互替换,总库版译文有误。

例句 8 中,主句“不得对抗善意相对人”的逻辑主语应当是“的”字结构所描述的情形,总库版译文用“法人的实际情况”作主语,曲解了源语条文。

如果用 where-条件句，可以译为"Where the actual circumstances of a legal person are inconsistent with what is recorded upon registration, it shall not be asserted against bona fide opposite parties."。"it"指代的是整个 where-条件句，相比之下，法宝版译文用"The inconsistency between... and ..."作主语，句式更为简洁。

6.3.2 "的"字前是动宾结构的翻译

这种情况的基本句式为"VP1＋的，NP2＋VP2"，NP2 有时省略。如果"的"字结构表示自指，即"VP1＋的"指称条文规定的各种"情形""条件""行为"等，翻译时，"的"字结构可以译成状语，最常见的是 where 和 if 引导的条件状语从句，如例句 9 的法宝版译文。如果强调法律行为发生的时间——将来某一天可能会去做或者会发生，可以译为 when 引导的时间状语从句，如例句 10 的法宝版译文。此外，根据语境和行文，也可以译为介词短语 in case of、in/under ... situation(s) /circumstances 等，如例句 9 和例句 10 的总库版译文。

如果"的"字结构表示转指，即"VP1＋的"指称条文规定的法律主体，也就是缺省的 NP1，翻译时可以分为以下两种情况：

① NP1 虽然缺省，但是根据前文推断，指某类特定的人或物。翻译时同"的"字结构表示自指的情况，如例句 11 中，法宝版译文使用 where-条件句表示情形，总库版译文使用介词短语 in the case of 和 in...situation，又用 where 引导非限制性定语从句对该情形作补充说明，两版译文都可取。

例句 12 中，根据前文可以推断出，"滥用职权，玩忽职守，造成国有财产损失的"，即"VP1＋的"，指称的是"履行国有财产管理、监督职责的机构及其工作人员"，又因为 VP1 和 VP2("应当依法承担法律责任")的逻辑主语相同，法宝版译为主语从句，但是 whoever 意指"任何人"，实则扩大了实施 VP1 行为的主体，与源语条文意思不符。总库版译文根据语意补出 VP2 的逻辑主语 they，用 if-条件句翻译"的"字结构，其中 VP1 的逻辑主语用 their 表示，语意明确、行文顺畅，没有歧义，是可取译文。

②当NP1指“任何人”时，可以采用林克难和籍明文(2002)提出的补出逻辑主语的多种翻译方法，包括whoever式、anyone who式、no one who式等。

例句13中，法宝版使用“Whoever”，总库版使用“A person who”，都可表达“任何人”的意思。

例句14中，两版译文都使用anyone who式，但是总库版中who引导的是非限定性定语从句。非限定性定语从句用于对先行词进行补充说明，如果省略，句意仍然清楚、完整。但是总库版译文不能省略掉who引导的非限定性定语从句，否则法理不完整，语意不合理，可见anyone who式中的定语从句是限定性的，总库版译文有误。

小结

在《民法典》中，“的”字结构用于句首，具有类属意义，是最常见的假定结构，构成的基本句式为“NP1＋VP1＋的，NP2＋VP2”，其中NP1和NP2可能会省略。

当“的”字前是主谓结构时，①如果主句谓语前有主语，“的”字前后是两个主谓完整的小句，“的”字结构通常译为条件状语从句或条件状语，常见的连词有if、where，介词短语in case of；②如果主句谓语前没有主语，构成的句式为“NP1＋VP1＋的，VP2”。倘若主句中VP2的逻辑主语就是NP1，翻译时，可以把NP1译作全句主语，VP2作谓语，“VP1＋的”译成NP1的限定成分，比如定语从句、分词或介词短语作后置定语等；倘若主句中VP2的逻辑主语不是NP1，翻译时与主句谓语前有主语的译法一致。

当“的”字前是动宾结构时，构成的基本句式为“VP1＋的，NP2＋VP2”，NP2有时省略。如果“的”字结构表示自指，指称的是条文规定的“情形”“条件”“行为”等，可以译成状语，最常见的是where和if引导的条件状语从句，也有时译为when引导的时间状语从句，或者译为介词短语in case of、in/under ... situation(s) /circumstances等。如果“的”字结构表示转指，指称的是法律主体，也就是缺省的 NP1，翻译时可以分为两种情况：①如果根据前文推断，NP1 指某类特定的人或物，翻译时同“的”字结构表示自指的情况；②如果 NP1 指“任何人”，可以补出逻辑主语，使用 whoever、anyone who、no one who、a person who 等主语从句或定语从句。

7 “下列”结构的翻译

7.1 结构特点及其在《民法典》中的运用

7.1.1 结构特点

“总分句”是立法文本中常见的表述方式，由总说句和分述句组成(邹玉华，2008)。总说句呈现法律条款的主干，包括法律主体、法律行为和情形、条件等要素，以冒号结束；分述句列举一系列事物、情形、要求等。“下列”结构即出现在总说句中，意思是“以下”，后接的名词是对分述句中所列各项的主题概括。

7.1.2 在《民法典》中的运用

“下列”结构在《民法典》中一共出现了88次，均与名词连用，其中有43次表述为“有下列情形之一的”。以下我们分两方面进行分析。

(1)普通情况

“下列＋名词”构成的词组在法律条款中可以作主语，也可以作宾语。如第395条规定“债务人或者第三人有权处分的**下列财产**可以抵押：(一)建筑物和其他土地附着物；(二)建设用地使用权……”“债务人或者第三人有权处分的下列财产可以抵押”是总说句，构成条款的主干，其中“下列财产”作句子主语；分述句中的(一)、(二)等项是对“财产”的列举。

又如第 1147 条规定："遗产管理人应当履行下列职责：(一)清理遗产并制作遗产清单；(二)向继承人报告遗产情况……"其中"下列职责"是总说句中主要动词"履行"的宾语。再如第 1127 条规定："遗产按照下列顺序继承：(一)第一顺序：配偶、子女、父母；(二)第二顺序：兄弟姐妹、祖父母、外祖父母。""下列顺序"与介词"按照"构成介宾短语，在总说句中作状语。

(2)"有下列情形之一的"

本结构适用于对符合某一法定资格、承担相同法律责任的情形或行为的列举(邹玉华，2008)，其目的是明确在哪些具体情形下法律规定将会适用，当事实情形符合这些列举的条件之一时，相关的法律规定就会生效。

根据在句中所处位置，可以分为三种情况：

①出现在总说句句首。如第 173 条规定："**有下列情形之一的**，委托代理终止：(一)代理期限届满或者代理事务完成；(二)被代理人取消委托或者代理人辞去委托……"其中，"有下列情形之一的"是"委托代理终止"的假定条件或情形。有时，"有下列情形之一"和"的"字之间还有其他成分，可以表示为"有下列情形之一，A 的"，A 可以是主谓结构，也可以是动宾结构，通常与"有下列情形之一"共同构成法律规定生效的条件。如第 1079 条："有下列情形之一，调解无效的，应当准予离婚。""准予离婚"需要满足两个条件：一是"有下列情形之一"，二是"调解无效"。

②"有下列情形之一的"前面有主语，通常是某类人。分述句中所列情形一般是该类人的行为，如第 36 条规定："**监护人有下列情形之一的**，人民法院根据有关个人或者组织的申请，撤销其监护人资格，安排必要的临时监护措施，并按照最有利于被监护人的原则依法指定监护人：(一)**实施**严重损害被监护人身心健康的**行为**；(二)**怠于履行**监护职责，或者**无法履行**监护职责**且拒绝**将监护职责部分或者全部委托给他人，导致被监护人处于危困状态；(三)**实施**严重侵害被监护人合法权益的其他**行为**。"有时分述句中不但列举该类人的行为，还有与其相关的情形，如第 748 条规定："**出租人有下列情形之一的**，承租人有权请求其赔偿损失：(一)无正当理由**收回**

租赁物;(二)无正当理由**妨碍、干扰**承租人对租赁物的占有和使用;(三)**因出租人的原因致使第三人对租赁物主张权利**。"(一)和(二)项属于出租人的行为,(三)项描述的是情形。

③"有下列情形之一的"出现在总说句的中部,前后有句号分隔,基本结构为"某人+A,有下列情形之一的"。如第1224条规定:"**患者在诊疗活动中受到损害,有下列情形之一的,**医疗机构不承担赔偿责任:(一)患者或者其近亲属不配合医疗机构进行符合诊疗规范的诊疗;(二)医务人员在抢救生命垂危的患者等紧急情况下已经尽到合理诊疗义务……"

7.2 译文对比

表7.1 《民法典》中"下列"结构的翻译对比

序号	出处(条)	原文	北大法宝译文(法宝版译文)	国家法规总库译文(总库版译文)
1	506	合同中的下列免责条款无效: (一)造成对方人身损害的; (二)因故意或者重大过失造成对方财产损失的。	The following exception clauses in a contract shall be void: (1) **Those** that cause personal damage to the other party. (2) **Those** that cause property damage to the other party intentionally or in gross negligence.	An exculpatory clause in a contract exempting the following liabilities are void: (1) **the liability** arising from physical injury inflicted on the other party; or (2) **the liability** arising from losses caused to the other party's property due to an intentional act or by gross negligence.

续表

序号	出处(条)	原文	北大法宝译文(法宝版译文)	国家法规总库译文(总库版译文)
2	152	<u>有下列情形之一的</u>,撤销权消灭: (一)当事人自知道或者应当知道撤销事由之日起一年内、重大误解的当事人自知道或者应当知道撤销事由之日起九十日内没有行使撤销权; ……	<u>Under any of the following circumstances</u>, the right of revocation shall be extinguished: (1) A party fails to exercise its right of revocation within one year from the day when the party knows or should have known the cause of revocation, or a party with gross misunderstanding fails to exercise its right of revocation within 90 days from the day when the party knows or should have known the cause of revocation. …	A party's right to revoke a civil juristic act is extinguished <u>under any of the following circumstances</u>: (1) the party has failed to exercise the right to revocation within one year from the date when it knows or should have known of the cause for revocation, or within 90 days from the date when the party who has performed the act with serious misunderstanding knows or should have known of the cause for revocation; …
3	549	<u>有下列情形之一的</u>,债务人可以向受让人主张抵销: (一)债务人接到债权转让通知时,债务人对让与人享有债权,且债务人的债权先于转让的债权到期或者同时到期; (二)债务人的债权与转让的债权是基于同一合同产生。	<u>Under any of the following circumstances</u>, a debtor may claim set-off against the assignee: (1) When the debtor receives a notice of assignment of the claim, the debtor is owed an obligation by the assignor, and the obligation is due before or at the same time as the claim assigned. (2) The obligation owed to the debtor and the claim assigned arise from the same contract.	A debtor may claim a set-off against the assignee <u>under either of the following circumstances</u>: (1) when the debtor receives the notice of assignment of a claim, the debtor has a claim against the assignor which becomes due prior to or at the same time of the due date of the assigned claim; or (2) the debtor's claim and the assigned claim are generated on the basis of the same contract.

续表

序号	出处（条）	原文	北大法宝译文（法宝版译文）	国家法规总库译文（总库版译文）
4	724	有下列情形之一，非因承租人原因致使租赁物无法使用的，承租人可以解除合同： （一）租赁物被司法机关或者行政机关依法查封、扣押； ……	Under any of the following circumstances, a lessee may rescind the contract if the leased property is rendered unusable not by the lessee: (1) The leased property is seized or impounded by the judicial or administrative authority according to the law. …	A lessee may rescind the contract under any of the following circumstances if the leased object cannot be used due to a reason not attributable to the lessee: (1) the leased object is sealed up or detained by the judicial authority or administrative authority in accordance with law; …
5	1079	…… 有下列情形之一，调解无效的，应当准予离婚： （一）重婚或者与他人同居； （二）实施家庭暴力或者虐待、遗弃家庭成员； ……	… A divorce shall be granted if mediation fails under any of the following circumstances: (1) Either spouse commits bigamy or cohabits with any third party. (2) There is domestic violence, or maltreatment or desertion of any family member. …	… A divorce shall be granted where any of the following circumstances exists and the mediation fails: (1) one spouse commits bigamy or cohabitates with another person; (2) one spouse commits domestic violence or maltreats or deserts a family member; …
6	1091	有下列情形之一，导致离婚的，无过错方有权请求损害赔偿： （一）重婚； （二）与他人同居； ……	Under any of the following circumstances which leads to a divorce, the no-fault party shall have the right to claim damages: (1) Bigamy. (2) Cohabitation of a married person with any third party. …	A no-fault spouse has the right to claim compensation where divorce is caused by one of the following acts done by the other spouse: (1) has committed bigamy; (2) has cohabitated with another person; …

续表

序号	出处(条)	原文	北大法宝译文(法宝版译文)	国家法规总库译文(总库版译文)
7	36	监护人有下列情形之一的,人民法院根据有关个人或者组织的申请,撤销其监护人资格,安排必要的临时监护措施,并按照最有利于被监护人的原则依法指定监护人: (一)实施严重损害被监护人身心健康的行为; (二)怠于履行监护职责,或者无法履行监护职责且拒绝将监护职责部分或者全部委托给他人,导致被监护人处于危困状态; ……	Where a guardian falls under any of the following circumstances, the people's court shall, upon application of the relevant individual or organization, disqualify the guardian, arrange necessary provisional guardianship measures, and designate another guardian in accordance with the law under the principle of most benefiting the ward: (1) Committing any conduct seriously detrimental to the ward's physical and mental health. (2) Being slack in performing the duty of guardianship, or being incapable of performing the duty of guardianship but refusing to delegate part or all of the duty of guardianship to another person, which causes distress of the ward. …	Where a guardian has performed any of the following acts, the people's court shall, upon request of a relevant individual or organization, disqualify the guardian, adopt necessary temporary measures, and appoint a new guardian in the best interest of the ward in accordance with law: (1) engaging in any act which severely harms the physical or mental health of the ward; (2) being indolent in performing the duties of guardian, or being unable to perform such duties but refusing to delegate all or part of the duties to others, thus placing the ward in a desperate situation; or …

续表

序号	出处(条)	原文	北大法宝译文(法宝版译文)	国家法规总库译文(总库版译文)
8	384	地役权人有下列情形之一的,供役地权利人有权解除地役权合同,地役权消灭: (一)违反法律规定或者合同约定,滥用地役权; (二)有偿利用供役地,约定的付款期限届满后在合理期限内经两次催告未支付费用。	Where the owner of the land to which the servitude is owed falls under any of the following circumstances, the owner of the servient land has the right to rescind the servitude contract, and servitude is extinguished. (1) Abusing servitude in violation of the provisions of any law or those agreed upon in the contract. (2) Failing to pay fees for the compensated use of the servient land after being urged to do so for two times within a reasonable period, after the expiration of the agreed term for payment.	Where a person entitled to an easement is under either of the following circumstances, the person who has the right in the servient land is entitled to rescind the easement contract to extinguish the easement: (1) abusing the right to easement in violation of the provisions of laws or the contract; or (2) in case of paid use of the servient land, failing to pay the relevant fees despite of receipt of two warning notices within a reasonable period of time after the payment is due according to the agreement.
9	748	出租人有下列情形之一的,承租人有权请求其赔偿损失: (一)无正当理由收回租赁物; (二)无正当理由妨碍、干扰承租人对租赁物的占有和使用; (三)因出租人的原因致使第三人对租赁物主张权利; ……	If a lessor has any of the following circumstances, the lessee shall have the right to request the lessor to make compensation for its loss: (1) Recovering the leased property without justification. (2) Obstructing or interfering with the lessee's possession and use of the leased property without justification. (3) A third party claims rights to the leased property because of the lessor. …	A lessee has the right to request the lessor to bear the liability for compensation where the lessor falls under any of the following circumstances: (1) the lessor takes back the leased object without just cause; (2) the lessor obstructs or interferes with the lessee's possession and use of the leased object without just cause; (3) a third person claims a right over the leased object due to a reason attributable to the lessor; or

续表

序号	出处（条）	原文	北大法宝译文（法宝版译文）	国家法规总库译文（总库版译文）
10	740	出卖人违反向承租人交付标的物的义务，**有下列情形之一的**，承租人可以拒绝受领出卖人向其交付的标的物： （一）标的物严重不符合约定； （二）未按照约定交付标的物，经承租人或者出租人催告后在合理期限内仍未交付。	Where a seller in breach of the obligation to deliver the subject matter to the lessee **has any of the following circumstances**, the lessee may refuse to accept the subject matter delivered to it by the seller: (1) The subject matter seriously does not conform to the agreement. (2) The subject matter fails to be delivered as agreed, and delivery fails to be made within a reasonable time limit after a demand from the lessee or the lessor.	A lessee may refuse to accept the subject matter delivered by the seller **where** a seller breaches his obligation of delivery of the subject matter to the lessee **and either of the following circumstances occurs**: (1) the subject matter is materially inconsistent with the agreement; or (2) the seller fails to deliver the subject matter as agreed by the parties, and still fails to deliver it within a reasonable period of time after being demanded by the lessee or the lessor.

7.3 译文分析

针对《民法典》中“下列”结构的运用情况，我们对比分析两个版本的对应译文，探讨可取的翻译方法。

7.3.1 普通情况的翻译

一般情况下，“下列＋名词”译成“the following＋名词”，该词组如果在源语条文中作主语，译文通常也相应地译作主语；如果在源语条文中作宾语，包括动词的宾语和介词的宾语，译文也都译作相应句子成分。

需要注意的是，“the following＋名词”中的“名词”是对分述句中所列各项的主题概括，有时与“下列＋名词”中的“名词”并不一致。如例句1，

“下列”后接的名词是“免责条款”，但是分述句中列举的各项并非这些条款本身，这点从(二)项的表述可以得到验证：免责条款不是人，怎么可能“因故意或者重大过失”而造成对方人身损害呢？可见，分项所列是这些条款内容中可能免除的责任。具体而言，如果该条款免除的是因造成对方人身损害而应当承担的责任，或因故意或者重大过失造成对方财产损失而应当承担的责任，那么这样的免责条款无效。法宝版译文在分述句各项中添加中心词“those”，后接定语从句，指代免责条款，是对源语条文理解错误。而总库版译文在总说句中用“exempting the following liabilities”作“an exculpatory clause”的后置定语，又在分述句所列各项中添加中心词“the liability”，正确地译出了分述句各项的主题类属，是“责任”而非“免责条款”。

此外，源语分述句使用“；”来分隔各项，而法宝版译文译为“.”，总库版译文译为“;”。其实分述句的各项既相对独立，又有密切的关系，它们之间相互并列，与总说句一起构成一个大的解说复句，因此总说句总是以“：”结束，分述句各项间应当使用“；”分隔。关于这一点，英语和汉语的用法相同。原生法律语料库也验证了我们的结论，如：“A U.S. vessel owner or operator shall only remotely reactivate a satellite buoy at sea that was activated in the IATTC Convention Area in the following circumstances: (1) To assist in the recovery of a beached FAD; (2) After a temporary deactivation during the closure period; or (3) Transfer of ownership while the FAD is at sea.”(Title 50, Chapter Ⅲ, Part 300, Subpart C, § 300.28, Code of Federal Regulations)。

7.3.2 “有下列情形之一的”结构的翻译

法宝版译文比较统一，通常译为“under any of the following circumstances”；总库版译文根据语境不同，译法多样。下面我们分三种情况，通过例句进行分析。

①“有下列情形之一的”出现在总说句句首时，如例句 2，法宝版译文译

为“Under any of the following circumstances”，置于句首；总库版译文译为“under any of the following circumstances”，置于总说句句末。根据英、汉语的句法规则，英语句子的重心在前，汉语句子的重心在后，即英语习惯将重要内容放在句子前面，而汉语放在后面。就法律条文而言，重点应是法律主体和法律行为。因此，“有下列情形之一的”在汉语条文中出现在句首，而在英语译文中应当置于句末，故总库版译文更可取。

例句 3 也是置于句首的情况，除了该结构在译文中的位置不同外，两个版本对“之一”的翻译也不同，总库版译为“either of”，法宝版译为“any of”。首先，选择 either 还是 any，取决于列举项的数量：当列举两项时，通常使用 “either”来指“两者之一”，“有且只有一个”。然而，如果列举项超过两项或者预期可能有更多项，使用 “any” 会更合适，因为它指“任何一个”，不局限于“只有一个”，不排除符合条件的选项多于一的可能。例句 3 中的(一)和(二)不是非此即彼的关系，某些情况下，可能同时具备，因此，译为“under any of the following circumstances”置于总说句句末，更可取。

当出现“有下列情形之一，A 的”结构时，如例句 4—6，A 通常与“有下列情形之一”一样，都是法律规定生效的条件。也就是说，法律规定要生效，既要满足“有下列情形之一”，又要满足 A。例句 4 中，法宝版将“under any of the following circumstances”置于句首，不符合英语的行文习惯；总库版译文将“under any of the following circumstances”置于主句之后，后接用 if-条件句翻译的 A，表明两个条件都要满足，较为可取。

例句 5 中，法宝版将“under any of the following circumstances”置于 if-条件句后，但该译文有歧义，读者也许会理解成：调解无效是由“下列情形之一”造成的。总库版将“有下列情形之一”和“调解无效”译为两个并列句，统一由连词“where”引导。如果 where 引导条件句，两个句子并列，正好可以表达出“既……又……”的要求，但是 where-条件句一般都放在段首(李克兴，2013)，不如改为 if 作引导词，更可取。

例句 6 中，法宝版把 A 翻译成 circumstances 的定语从句，定语从句也可以表示条件。但是，将 under 介宾短语及其定语从句移到主句之后，更符合英语习惯。总库版译文认为分述句所列各项是过错方的行为，离婚正是由于其中某个行为造成的。这种思路是可取的，但在具体措辞上还需商榷。首先，把“one of the following acts”改为“any of the following acts”更忠实源语条文，“one of”强调“其中之一”，排除了两个或多个的可能性，而“any of”不局限于“只有一个”。其次，英语句子中主语不可缺，但是分述句译文各分项都没有主语，建议改为动名词短语，“(1) committing bigamy; (2) cohabitating with another person; (3) committing domestic violence; (4) maltreating or deserting a family member; or (5) acting with other serious faults.”。

②“有下列情形之一的”前面用某人作主语时，法宝版通常译为“sb. falls under any of the following circumstances”或“sb. has any of the following circumstances”；总库版的译文有“sb. has performed any of the following acts”，“sb. is under any/either of the following circumstances”，或者“sb. falls under any of the following circumstances”。在原生法律数据库中检索 circumstances 和 acts 各自的搭配和词频，发现除 circumstances 和动词 exist 或 occur 搭配，以及“perform/commit (any of) the following acts”外，其他表述出现频次都为零。(见表 7.2)

表 7.2 “有下列情形之一的”的英文表达方式及检索频次

表达方式	国内	国外		
	香港法例库	英国立法库	美国联邦法规库	美国法典库
fall under (any of) the following circumstances	0	0	0	0
be under (any of) the following circumstances	0	0	0	0
have (any of) the following circumstances	0	0	0	0
circumstances+exist/occur	66	>200	385	40393

续表

表达方式	国内	国外		
	香港法例库	英国立法库	美国联邦法规库	美国法典库
perform/commit (any of) the following acts	21	>200	23	12563

据此，如果分述句所列各项为行为，其施动者往往是“某人”，即“有下列情形之一”的主语，如例句7和例句8，译文可仿照例句7总库版的思路，译为“Where sb. has performed any of the following acts”。如果分述句各项既包括“某人”的行为，也包括与“某人”有关的情形，如例句9，不妨用circumstances和动词exist或occur搭配，译为“if any of the following circumstances exists/occurs”。分述句各项采取总库版的译法，明确译出行为的施动者。

③“有下列情形之一的”出现在总说句的中部，基本结构为“某人＋A，有下列情形之一的”时，如例句10，法律规定要想生效，需要满足A和“有下列情形之一”的两个条件；分述句所列各项有可能是某种情形，如(一)项，也可能是“某人”的行为，如(二)项。总库版译文的思路较好，将“某人＋A”和“有下列情形之一”译为两个并列的条件句置于主句之后，但是，最好将译文中的引导词where改为if，将either of改为any of。在分述句中，译文需要给表示“行为”的项添加施动者，即用“某人”作其主语。

小　结

“下列”结构通常出现在“总分句”中，适用于对符合某一法定资格、承担相同法律责任的情形、行为、事物、要求等进行列举。一般情况下，“下列＋名词”译成“the following＋名词”。但有时“下列”后接的名词与“the following”后接的名词并不对应，后者是对分述句中所列各项的主题概括，翻译时需要判断出所列各项的类属，译为正确的主题名词。

“有下列情形之一的”是最常见的“下列”结构的表述方式，可以分为三种情况：①出现在源语条文总说句句首时，通常译为“under any of the following circumstances”，按照英语习惯置于译文总说句句末。对于“有下列情形之一，A 的”这种结构，可以译为“under any of the following circumstances if A”置于主句之后，或者“if any of the following circumstances exists and A”，表示法律规定要生效，“有下列情形之一”和 A 两个条件都需要满足。②“有下列情形之一的”前面用“某人”作主语时，分述句所列各项可能是“某人”的行为，也可能是与“某人”有关的情形。如果是行为，可以译为“Where sb. has performed any of the following acts”；如果既包括行为，也包括情形，不妨译为“if any of the following circumstances exists/occurs”并置于总说句句末，分述句各项需明确译出行为的施动者。③“有下列情形之一的”出现在总说句的中部，基本结构为“某人＋A，有下列情形之一的”。这种结构与“有下列情形之一，A 的”情况相似，建议译为“if A and any of the following circumstances exists/occurs”，分述句中表示“行为”的项也需明确译出施动者。

8 “不得”结构的翻译

8.1 结构特点及其在《民法典》中的运用

8.1.1 结构特点

法律文本中的“不得”源于古汉语用法，意思是“禁止”或“不准”，其后接表示违法行为的内容，表述哪种法律行为不被允许，属于禁止性规范，具有权威性和强制性。“不得”结构一般用于有主语或者有明确的被规范对象的句子中，主语既可以是人，也可以是物。但有时，“不得”的主语隐含在句意里，并未明确指出。

8.1.2 在《民法典》中的运用

在《民法典》中“不得”结构一共出现了195次，多数情况有明确的“禁令承受者”，如第132条规定：“民事主体不得滥用民事权利损害国家利益、社会公共利益或者他人合法权益。”少数情况，没有明确的“禁令承受者”，其逻辑主语要么暗含在前文中，要么不言而喻，如第244条规定：“国家对耕地实行特殊保护，严格限制农用地转为建设用地，控制建设用地总量。不得违反法律规定的权限和程序征收集体所有的土地。”法律规定，集体土地的征收主体只能是市、县级人民政府，本法条虽然没有指明“不得”的主语，但禁令的承受者不言而喻。

“不得”结构可分为三种情况：

(1)用被规范对象作主语

本结构呈现的基本句式为“A 不得 B”。B 为行为动词或动词短语，A 为禁令承受者，可以是人，如第 350 条中的“建设用地**使用权人**应当合理利用土地，不得改变土地用途”；也可以是物，如第 241 条规定“对重婚导致的无效婚姻的**财产处理**，不得侵害合法婚姻当事人的财产权益”，此处禁令规范的对象是财产处理行为，而非财产处理人。

“不得”结构也会用于规范某个公权力机构，如第 193 条规定：“**人民法院**不得主动适用诉讼时效的规定。”

有时，“不得”结构的被规范对象不是具体的禁令承受者。为了更大程度地体现对行为的否定性评价，立法者用“任何组织或者个人”作主语，对法律主体进行最大化描述，如第 3 条规定：“民事主体的人身权利、财产权利以及其他合法权益受法律保护，**任何组织或者个人**不得侵犯。”

(2)无主语或主语并非被规范对象

如第 293 条规定：“建造建筑物，不得违反国家有关工程建设标准，不得妨碍相邻建筑物的通风、采光和日照。”禁令的承受者显然不是“建造建筑物”，而是“建造建筑物”的人或单位。

(3)“不得”结构作定语

这种情况下，“不得”没有构成禁令，只是客观描述某种事实、条件或情形。如第 545 条规定：“当事人约定非金钱债权**不得**转让的，**不得**对抗善意第三人。当事人约定金钱债权**不得**转让的，**不得**对抗第三人。”本条涉及四个“不得”，但是第一和第三并非表达禁止，而是客观描述当事人约定的内容。

8.2 译文对比

表 8.1 《民法典》中"不得"结构的翻译对比

序号	出处(条)	原文	北大法宝译文(法宝版译文)	国家法规总库译文(总库版译文)
1	8	民事主体从事民事活动,不得违反法律,不得违背公序良俗。	The parties to civil legal relations shall not conduct civil activities in violation of the law, nor contrary to public order and good morals.	When conducting a civil activity, no person of the civil law may violate the law, or offend public order or good morals.
2	350	建设用地使用权人应当合理利用土地,不得改变土地用途;需要改变土地用途的,应当依法经有关行政主管部门批准。	The holder of the right to use land for construction shall make rational use of the land, and shall not change the use of the land; and if the use of the land needs to be changed, it shall be subject to the approval of the relevant administrative department in accordance with the law.	A person who has the right to use a lot of land for construction purposes shall make reasonable use of the lot and may not change its planned use. Where it is necessary to change the planned use of the lot, approval shall be obtained from the competent administrative department in accordance with law.
3	648	…… 向社会公众供电的供电人,不得拒绝用电人合理的订立合同要求。	… A power supplier who supplies power to the public shall not reject a user's reasonable request for contracting.	… A supplier providing electricity to the public may not refuse a reasonable request of a consumer to conclude such a contract.

续表

序号	出处（条）	原文	北大法宝译文（法宝版译文）	国家法规总库译文（总库版译文）
4	1110	收养人、送养人要求保守收养秘密的，其他人应当尊重其意愿，不得泄露。	Where the adopter and the person placing out the child for adoption wish to keep the adoption confidential, others shall respect their wish and shall not make a disclosure thereof.	Where an adopter or a party placing a child for adoption requires that the adoption be kept confidential, the other persons shall respect their will and may not disclose it.
5	193	人民法院不得主动适用诉讼时效的规定。	A people's court shall not apply the provisions on extinctive prescription of its own motion.	The people's court may not apply the provisions on limitation periods on its own initiative.
6	213	登记机构不得有下列行为： (一)要求对不动产进行评估； ……	The registration authority may not commit any of the following conduct: (1) Requiring the assessment of the immovable.	A registration authority may not engage in the following acts: (1) to require an appraisal of the immovable property; …
7	243	…… 任何组织或者个人不得贪污、挪用、私分、截留、拖欠征收补偿费等费用。	… No organization or individual may embezzle, misappropriate, privately divide, withhold, or default on the payment of indemnities for expropriation and other expenses.	… No organization or individual may embezzle, misappropriate, secretly distribute, intercept, default on the payment of the expropriation compensation fees, or the like.

续表

序号	出处（条）	原文	北大法宝译文（法宝版译文）	国家法规总库译文（总库版译文）
8	1151	存有遗产的人，应当妥善保管遗产，任何组织或者个人不得侵吞或者争抢。	Whoever has in his possession the estate of the decedent shall take good care of such estate and no organization or individual is allowed to misappropriate it or contend for it.	Anyone who has in his possession the property of a decedent shall properly keep such property, and no organization or individual may misappropriate or contend for it.
9	991	民事主体的人格权受法律保护，任何组织或者个人不得侵害。	The personality rights of parties to civil legal relations are protected by law and shall not be infringed upon by any organization or individual.	The personality rights of persons of the civil law are protected by law and free from infringement by any organization or individual.
10	1035	处理个人信息的，应当遵循合法、正当、必要原则，不得过度处理，并符合下列条件： ……	The personal information of a natural person shall be processed under the principles of lawfulness, justification and necessity, shall not be excessively processed, and shall meet the following conditions: …	The processing of personal information shall be in compliance with the principles of lawfulness, justification, and within a necessary limit, and may not be excessively processed; meanwhile, the following conditions shall be satisfied: …
11	1122	…… 依照法律规定或者根据其性质不得继承的遗产，不得继承。	… The estate that is not allowed to be inherited according to the law or based on its nature shall not be inherited.	… An estate not inheritable according to the provisions of law or based on the nature of the estate may not be inherited.

续表

序号	出处（条）	原文	北大法宝译文（法宝版译文）	国家法规总库译文（总库版译文）
12	160	民事法律行为可以附期限，但是根据其性质不得附期限的除外。	A juridical act may be subject to a term, unless such a term is not allowed according to the nature of the juridical act.	A term may be attached to a civil juristic act, unless the nature of such act denies such an attachment.

8.3 译文分析

我们针对《民法典》中"不得"结构的三种运用情况，分别对比分析两个版本的对应译文，同时探讨更为可取的翻译方法。

8.3.1 用被规范对象作主语时的翻译

在法宝版译文中，多数情况下，如例句1—5，这一结构译为"A＋shall not＋B"，例句9使用了被动语态。有些情况下，shall not用may not替换，如例句6中，这一结构译为"A＋may not＋B"。例句7和例句8把否定词提前，前者译为"no＋A＋may＋B"，后者译为"no＋A＋is allowed to＋B"。

在总库版译文中，多数情况下，如例句1—6，这一结构译为"A＋may not＋B"。例句7和例句8将否定词提前，译为"no＋A＋may＋B"。例句9根据前文句式，译为"free from＋B＋by＋A"。

两版译文的主要区别在于，"不得"译为"shall not"还是"may not"。shall和may是立法文本中使用频率最高的情态动词，通常用于表达强制、授权、禁止的意思。具体而言，肯定形式的shall和may分别属于法律语言中的强制词和授权词，否定形式shall not和may not又均属于禁止词。肯定式may在法律文本中的含义、用法和译法与其在普通英文中相同；而shall在立法文本中的作用相当于"must""have to""be to""be required to”,含有“本条款具有法律规定的指令性或强制性”之意。

关于 shall not 和 may not 在立法语篇中的区别,陶博(2004)认为 shall not 具有指示性施为性作用,具有防止预期行为发生的内涵;may not 具有和协议条款相同的宣布性的施为性作用,隐含的意思为相关的许可在同类文件中得到了承认。李奉栖(2017)总结了“权利(权力)受限”还是“法定禁止”两个标准,具体而言,may not 意味着对权利、权力或特权的限制,违反的后果是该行为无效;shall not 意味着以禁止的方式规定义务,违反的后果是当事人将受到惩罚。以中、英两种语言立法的香港更多地使用 shall not 来表达禁止之意,以强调内心的自省认同,而非外在的权力约束(王子颖,2013)。以上学者的研究结论是可取的。在翻译“不得”结构时,首先必须明确“不得”一词的真实内涵,在“权利(权力)受限”和“法定禁止”之间做出选择,分别译为 may not 和 shall not,或者二者的变体形式。但是很多时候,“权利(权力)受限”和“法定禁止”较难区分,法律在限制权利(权力)的同时,也以禁止的形式规定了义务,违法的后果不仅包括行为无效,也会面临惩罚。因此,这种情况最好译为 shall not,一方面可以体现强制力和自制力的结合(王子颖,2013),另一方面可以避免因 may 的词义过多[①]而造成读者对法律规范的含义和意图出现理解偏差。

例句 1 属于“法定禁止”,遵守法律和遵守公序良俗是民事主体的义务,违背的后果是将面临惩罚或者法律的制裁,因此符合 shall not 的使用特征,法宝版译文比较可取。

例句 2 中,《民法典》第 344 条规定了建设用地使用权人的具体权利,即依法“享有占有、使用和收益的权利,有权利用该土地建造建筑物、构筑物及其附属设施”,本条以禁止性条款的形式对其权利进行了明确限制,即“不得改变土地用途”。但是保持土地的原有用途也是建设用地使用人的义务,违背此义务,使用权可能会被收回,同时对违建进行拆除,可见此处很难区分是

① 在香港法例库里,may not 在不同语境中表述的意思有所不同。例如,可以表达可能性,像“或许不”“可能不”“可能不会”“可能并非”等。no...may...可以表示语气强烈的“禁止”。

法定禁止还是权利受限，最好译为 shall not。因此，法宝版译文更可取。

例句 3 同样是权利限制，如果供电人违反此项规定，其后果是该“拒绝”无效，因此，使用 may not 的总库版译文较妥当。

例句 4 与例句 1 类似，应收养人、送养人的要求保守秘密，是“其他人”的义务，而非权利，因此“不得泄露”是法定禁止，应当使用 shall not，法宝版译文更可取。

如果禁止性条款规范的是某个公权力机构或行政机关，如例句 5 和例句 6，禁令实质上是对公权力或行政职责进行限制，违反的后果是依据法律宣布无效，符合 may not 的使用特征。因此例句 5 的法宝版译文有失妥当，应当改为“may not”。

例句 7—9 的主语都是“任何组织或者个人”。其中，例句 7 和例句 8 中“不得”结构所在的句子都相对独立，比如例句 7 是第 243 条中的第四款，例句 8 属于义务性条款加禁止性条款，首先规定了“存有遗产的人”的义务，随后用“不得”结构禁止任何组织或者个人侵吞或争抢遗产。两版译文都使用了“no organization or individual”作主语，no 置于句首的否定句，其否定或禁止的语气比标准的否定句强烈（李克兴，2011），此处用强烈的、绝对的、不容置疑的语气彰显法律的权威和威严，可以更大程度地体现对行为的否定性评价。但是例句 7 和例句 8 都属于“法定禁止”，并非对权利或权力的限制，违反的后果是比较严重的，势必受到法律制裁，因此应当使用 shall not 而非 may not。至于例句 8，法宝版使用了“is allowed to”，该短语可以传达禁止的意思，但是考虑到翻译的同一性原则，对同一概念保持同一措辞，建议改用 shall not。

例句 9 中，“不得”结构处于一个省略句中，其宾语正是前句的主语，因此法宝版将其译为被动句“shall not be...by any organization or individual”，总库版使用了 free from 结构，译为“free from infringement by any organization or individual”。在原生法律语料库中对“free from infringement”进行检索，发现香港法例库、英国立法库、美国联邦法规库均没有此种表述，美国法典库中显示有 24 例，表述为“free from infringement of”，但是 free from 描述的是状态,缺少 shall 的强烈修辞性色彩,无法传达禁止性条款的强制性和权威性。故此,法宝版译文更可取。

8.3.2 无主语或主语并非被规范对象时的翻译

这种情况下,禁令的承受者没有明示,要么隐含在句意中,要么不言而喻,译文一般使用被动语态,用违法行为指向的对象作主语。

例句 10 中,“处理个人信息的”是全句主语,但是对于其后的三个动词短语“遵循……原则”、“不得过度处理”和“符合……条件”而言,该主语的指代不同,前两者的主语是“处理个人信息的<u>人/单位</u>”,后者的主语是“处理个人信息的<u>行为</u>”。法宝版选择“个人信息”作主语,对前两个动词短语使用被动语态,因为“个人信息”是被处理的对象;但是“个人信息”并不是第三个动词短语“符合……条件”的主语,此处用主动语态的翻译并不合适。总库版选择“个人信息的处理”作主语,但是“不得过度处理”的对象应当是“个人信息”,因此译文逻辑也不合理。另外,两版译文的区别还在于对 shall not 和 may not 的选择。第 1035 条最后一款规定,“个人信息的处理包括个人信息的收集、存储、使用、加工、传输、提供、公开等”,可见处理个人信息不是一种权利或权力。该条禁令不是限制权利或权力,而是对义务行为的法定禁止,如果违反禁令,将会受到法律制裁,符合 shall not 的使用特征。鉴于此,译文可改为“The personal information of a natural person shall be processed under the principles of lawfulness, justification and necessity, and shall not be excessively processed; meanwhile, the following conditions shall be satisfied...”。

例句 11 中的主语是“……遗产”,同时也是“不得继承”的对象,适合使用被动语态。但是该禁令是对继承权的限制,违反禁令的后果是继承行为无效,并不会受到法律制裁,因此,总库版译文使用“may not be”更可取。

8.3.3 “不得”结构作定语时的翻译

这种情况下,“不得”表述的不是禁令,只是客观描述法条涉及的对象。

如例句 11 中，第一个“不得”结构是“遗产”的定语，用以说明禁令指向的对象。例句 12 本身就不是禁止性条款，“不得附期限”用在省略了中心词的“的”字结构中，用以描述属于例外情况的民事法律行为。

法宝版译文把两例都译为“is not allowed to”。根据《牛津词典》的释义“If you are allowed to do something, you are given permission to do it”，反之，be not allowed to do something 表达的是禁止含义，具有强制性意味。可见，法宝版译文并不符合法条原意。例句 11 中，总库版把“不得继承的”译为“not inheritable”，修饰限制“an estate”。例句 12 中，“但是根据其性质不得附期限的除外”可以转述为“除非根据其性质不得附期限”，总库版因此译为 unless 引导的条件从句，用 deny 表示“其性质使其不能附期限”，也就是《牛津词典》中的“refuse to grant”之意。因此，总库版译文更可取。

小　结

“不得”是《民法典》中最常见的禁止性规范词，翻译时必须首先理解该词的真实含义。如果属于“权利(权力)受限”，可译为 may not 及其变体；如果属于“法定禁止”，则译为 shall not 及其变体；如果遇到“权利(权力)受限”和“法定禁止”很难区分的情况，最好译为 shall not。以此为基础，“不得”结构的翻译可以分为三种情况：第一种情况用被规范对象作主语，如果被规范对象是某个公权力机构或行政机关，“不得”一般译为 may not；如果规范的对象最大化为“任何组织或者个人”，一般将否定词提前，译为“no organization or individual shall do”，以彰显法律的权威。第二种情况是无主语或者主语并非被规范对象，即没有明示禁令的承受者，译文一般使用被动语态，主语是违法行为指向的对象。第三种情况用“不得”结构作定语，“不得”表述的不是禁令，而是对法条涉及的某人或某事做客观描述，翻译时不必使用禁止性措辞。

9 “禁止”结构的翻译

9.1 结构特点及其在《民法典》中的运用

9.1.1 结构特点

“禁止”结构在法律文本中用于表达对某种行为的限制或约束，通常构成禁止性条款。与“不得”相比，“禁止”通常针对更为严重或重要的事项，语气更加强烈。根据《立法技术规范(试行)》(一)(法工委发〔2009〕62 号)，“禁止”一般用于无主语的祈使句。

9.1.2 在《民法典》中的运用

在《民法典》中该结构一共出现了 24 次。通常针对的是那些严重违法或具有较大社会危害性的行为，这些行为一旦发生，就可能对个人、社会或国家造成重大损害。因此，对于这类行为，法律必须采取最为严格的禁止措施来加以防范和打击。

“禁止”结构可分为三种情况：

(1)“禁止”+行为模式

本结构在《民法典》中出现了 10 次，并未直接指明被规范者，被规范者要么隐含在句意内，要么统指全体公民。其后的行为模式有可能是名词或名词短语，如第 1042 条规定，“禁止**家庭暴力**。禁止家庭成员间的**虐待和**

遗弃";也可能是动词短语,如第1007条中的"禁止以任何形式买卖人体细胞、人体组织、人体器官、遗体"。

(2)"禁止"+被规范者+行为模式

本结构在《民法典》中出现了8次。有时被规范者非常明确,如第791条中"禁止承包人将工程分包给不具备相应资质条件的单位。禁止分包单位将其承包的工程再分包";有时被规范者比较笼统,如第265条规定,"集体所有的财产受法律保护,禁止任何组织或者个人侵占、哄抢、私分、破坏","任何组织或者个人"是对被规范者的最大化描述,禁止意味更显强烈。

(3)"禁止"结构用于描述说明法条所涉的事物、事项或情形

本结构在《民法典》中共出现了6次,其中5次作定语,表现为"……禁止……的……""禁止"前的主语通常为法律、法规,如第426条规定:"法律、行政法规禁止转让的动产不得出质。"也可以省略主语"法律",如第1247条规定:"禁止饲养的烈性犬等危险动物造成他人损害的,动物饲养人或者管理人应当承担侵权责任。"

9.2 译文对比

表9.1 《民法典》中"禁止"结构的翻译对比

序号	出处(条)	原文	北大法宝译文(法宝版译文)	国家法规总库译文(总库版译文)
1	680	禁止高利放贷,借款的利率不得违反国家有关规定。	Usury shall be prohibited, and the interest rate on a loan shall not contravene the relevant provisions issued by the state.	Usurious loans are prohibited, and the interest rate for lending may not violate the relevant regulations of the State.
2	1007	禁止以任何形式买卖人体细胞、人体组织、人体器官、遗体。 ……	Trading in human cells, human tissues, human organs, and remains in any form is prohibited. …	Any form of purchase or sale of human cells, tissues, organs, or remains is prohibited. …

续表

序号	出处(条)	原文	北大法宝译文(法宝版译文)	国家法规总库译文(总库版译文)
3	1044	收养应当遵循最有利于被收养人的原则，保障被收养人和收养人的合法权益。 禁止借收养名义买卖未成年人。	Adoption shall follow the principle of serving the best interest of the adopted person, and protect the lawful rights and interests of the adopter and the adopted person. It is prohibited to buy or sell a minor under the cloak of adoption.	Adoption shall be in compliance with the principle of acting in the best interest of the adoptee, and the lawful rights and interests of both the adoptee and the adopter shall be protected. Trafficking minors in the name of adoption is prohibited.
4	791	…… 禁止承包人将工程分包给不具备相应资质条件的单位。禁止分包单位将其承包的工程再分包。建设工程主体结构的施工必须由承包人自行完成。	... The contractor is prohibited from sub-contracting any part of the project to an entity not appropriately qualified. A sub-contractor is prohibited from further sub-contracting its contracted work. The main structure of the construction project must be constructed by the contractor itself.	... A contractor is prohibited from subcontracting the contracted project to any entity without the corresponding qualifications. A subcontractor is prohibited from re-subcontracting the contracted project. The main structure of the construction project must be completed by the contractor itself.
5	1048	直系血亲或者三代以内的旁系血亲禁止结婚。	The marriage between lineal relatives by blood or between collateral relatives by blood up to the third degree of kinship is prohibited.	Persons who are lineal relatives by blood, or collateral relatives by blood up to the third degree of kinship are prohibited from being married.

续表

序号	出处(条)	原文	北大法宝译文(法宝版译文)	国家法规总库译文(总库版译文)
6	258	国家所有的财产受法律保护,禁止任何组织或者个人侵占、哄抢、私分、截留、破坏。	The property owned by the state shall be protected by law, and no organization or individual may embezzle, loot, privately divide, withhold, or destroy them.	The State-owned property is protected by law, and no organization or individual may misappropriate, loot, secretly distribute, intercept, or destroy such property.
7	267	私人的合法财产受法律保护,禁止任何组织或者个人侵占、哄抢、破坏。	An individual's lawful property shall be protected by law, and no organization or individual may encroach upon, loot, or destroy it.	The property lawfully owned by a private individual is protected by law, and no organization or individual may misappropriate, loot, or destruct such property.
8	1046	结婚应当男女双方完全自愿,禁止任何一方对另一方加以强迫,禁止任何组织或者个人加以干涉。	Marriage shall be based on the complete willingness of both man and woman, and compulsion used by either party on the other and interference by any organization or individual shall be prohibited.	A man and a woman shall enter into marriage freely and voluntarily. Neither party may compel the other party to enter into marriage against his will, and no organization or individual may interfere with the freedom of marriage.
9	395	债务人或者第三人有权处分的下列财产可以抵押: …… (七)法律、行政法规未禁止抵押的其他财产。 ……	The following property which the debtor or a third party has the right to dispose of may be mortgaged: ... (7) Any other property that is not prohibited from being mortgaged by any law or administrative regulation. ...	The following property, which the debtor or a third person is entitled to dispose of, may be mortgaged: ... (7) any other property not prohibited by laws or administrative regulations from being mortgaged. ...

续表

序号	出处(条)	原文	北大法宝译文(法宝版译文)	国家法规总库译文(总库版译文)
10	597	…… 法律、行政法规<u>禁止</u>或者限制转让<u>的</u>标的物，依照其规定。	… <u>Where</u> the transfer of a subject matter <u>is prohibited</u> or restricted <u>by</u> any law or administrative regulation, the law or administrative regulation shall prevail.	… <u>Where</u> there are laws or administrative regulations <u>prohibiting</u> or restricting the transfer of a subject matter, such provisions shall be followed.
11	1051	有下列情形之一的，婚姻无效： …… (二)有<u>禁止</u>结婚<u>的</u>亲属关系； ……	A marriage shall be invalid under any of the following circumstances: … (2) There is <u>prohibited degree of</u> kinship between the married parties. …	A marriage is void under any of the following circumstances: … (2) the parties to the marriage fall within the relative relations <u>prohibited by law from</u> marrying each other; or …

9.3 译文分析

我们针对《民法典》中“禁止”结构的三种运用情况，分别对比分析两个版本的对应译文，同时探讨更为可取的翻译方法。

9.3.1 “‘禁止’+行为模式”结构的翻译

法宝版译文，在多数情况下，如例句2—4，通常译为“... is prohibited”。有些情况下，如例句1，添加情态动词shall，译为“... shall be prohibited”。总库版译文比较统一，均译为“...is/are prohibited”。

这种结构省略了被规范者，译文使用被动语态很合理，一方面可以规避行为模式的施动者,另一方面被动语态能够凸显法律的严肃性和庄重性。但是是否需要使用情态动词 shall 呢?使不使用又有什么不同呢?在原生法律语料库中检索 prohibit 的用法和频次,可得到如下结果:两种用法都有使用,但是不使用情态动词的频次要远高于使用情态动词的频次。(见表 9.2)

表 9.2 “‘禁止’+行为模式”的英文表达方式及检索频次

表达方式	国内	国外		
	香港法例库	英国立法库	美国联邦法规库	美国法典库
shall be prohibited	9	>200	114	7609
is/are prohibited	195	>200	4035	162310

香港法例库里的很多法规是双语起草,有中英对照文本,便于对比,因此我们对香港法例库的检索结果逐一进行人工识别和分析,力图辨明两种用法的使用情景。最后,得出以下结论:

使用 shall 的情境包括:①具有严重危害性,损害人身权利、国家利益的行为;②语气强烈,中文标记词为“任何”“无论”,英文标记词为“only”“all”等。如:

“No one shall be held in slavery; slavery and the slave-trade in all their forms shall be prohibited.(Chapter 383 Section 8, Article 4)

任何人不得使充奴隶;奴隶制度及奴隶贩卖,不论出于何种方式,悉应禁止。(《香港人权法案》第四条第一款)”

人权是国家精神和人类正义的基石,本条对基本人权实施保护,语气极为强烈,从“不论出于何种方式”“悉”等字眼上可见一斑。

又如:

“...New installations of halogenated hydrocarbons systems shall be prohibited on all ships as from 1 October 1994. (L.N. 410 of 1995)

……由 1994 年 10 月 1 日起,禁止所有船舶有新装设的卤化烃系统。(1995 年第 410 号法律公告)”

不使用 shall 的情景包括：①与一般的生产生活实践相关；②对所涉事物、事项或情形进行描述。如：

"...Hold-back hooks not subject to central control station release are prohibited.(Chapter 369Y Regulation 80)

禁止使用不能从中央控制站释放的速脱钩。[《商船(安全)(防火)(1984 年 9 月 1 日或之后建造的船舶)规例》第 80 条]"

本条是对一般性生产生活的规制，危害性不严重，无须使用 shall。

又如：

"(6) Any person on board an aircraft who smokes in the aircraft or in any compartment of the aircraft—

(a) when smoking in the aircraft, or in that compartment of the aircraft, as the case may be, is prohibited; or

(b) when instructed not to smoke by a member of the crew of the aircraft,

commits an offence. (Chapter 494 Section 12B)

(6) 任何在飞机上的人在该飞机上或该飞机上的任何隔间内吸烟，而 ——

(a) 当时在该飞机上或该隔间内(视属何情况而定)**吸烟是被禁止的**；或

(b) 当时该飞机的机组成员指令不得吸烟，

该人即属犯罪。(《航空保安条例》第 12B 条)"

此处的"禁止"用于描述飞机上吸烟行为构成犯罪的条件，不属于禁止性条款。

基于以上分析，我们来逐一分析例文。

例句 1，所谓高利贷，是指索取特别高额利息的贷款行为。但是单纯的放高利贷只是一种违法行为，本身不触犯刑法，只有进行高利转贷的行为才构成犯罪。可见，一般的高利贷只是借贷纠纷，危害性不大。法宝版译文使用 shall 的原因无从考究，但显然这种情况下总库版译文更为恰当。

例句 2，本条所涉的买卖人体器官等行为严重破坏了国家对人体器官移植规范的正常秩序，严重损害他人的身体健康，侵犯了他人基本人权，具有严重的社会危害性，必须给予严厉打击。因此源语条文用“任何形式”进行语气强化，译文也应当使用严厉措辞，建议两个版本都改为 shall be prohibited。

例句 3，买卖未成年人，可能严重损害他人的生命权、健康权，同时涉嫌拐卖妇女、儿童罪，该罪起刑为五年，属于重罪，社会危害性较大。鉴于此，此处的“禁止”也应当是严厉禁止，建议两个译本都改为 shall be prohibited。

9.3.2 “‘禁止’＋被规范者＋行为模式”结构的翻译

这种情况下，通常译为“...（被规范者）be prohibited from...（行为模式）”，如例句 4，工程分包属于一般性生产实践，违反规定的社会危害性一般不大，两版译文都使用了“is prohibited from”，合情合理。

例句 5，禁止近亲结婚不仅是基于医学角度，更是站在人文角度制定的法律条文。但是近亲结婚不构成犯罪，这种婚姻关系在民事法律上是无效的，鉴于其社会危害性较小，不必使用 shall。需要注意的是，此句从句式上并非祈使句，但是可以转换为祈使句。“直系血亲或者三代以内的旁系血亲”不是“禁止”的施动者，而是被规范对象，“结婚”不是“步入婚姻”，而是“结为夫妇”的意思。因此转换为祈使句可以说：禁止直系血亲或者三代以内的旁系血亲结为夫妇。总库版译文正是基于这种分析，用被规范者作主语，谓语为“are prohibited from”，但是将“结婚”译为“being married”会产生歧义。“being married”指处于结婚状态（the ongoing state of being in a marriage），“结为夫妇”强调相互成为伴侣，两者不同义，建议改为“are prohibited from marrying each other”。法宝版译文用“marriage”作主语，意为“禁止这样的婚姻”，也是可取译法。

例句 6 和例句 7 都涉及财产的保护，对被规范者进行了最大化描述，实际是加强语气,强调禁令的权威性。根据韩礼德(Halliday,1994 /2000:362)的情态观,may not 属于高值否定,shall not 属于中值否定。也就是说,may not 比 shall not 语气强烈,shall not 常用于对应“不得”,那么 may not 或许可以对应“禁止”,尤其是 no 提到句首的句式,语气更为严厉,两版译文都译为“no organization or individual may...”,甚为可取。但是,例句 6 的法宝版译文用“them”指代“the property”,是语法错误。

例句 8 条文中有“任何”字样,也应当视为语气的强化。法宝版译文将原文转写为“禁止任何一方对另一方**的强迫**,禁止任何组织或者个人**的干涉**”,为了强化语气,使用了“shall be prohibited”;总库版译文采用否定词前移的句式“Neither party may... and no organization or individual may...”,二者都是可取译文。

9.3.3 用于描述说明的“禁止”结构的翻译

“禁止”结构用于描述说明时,通常在句中作定语,用以修饰和限制所描述的对象,在译文中也通常译为定语或定语从句,如例句 9—11。这种情况下,不需要加情态动词 shall。

例句 9 中,“禁止”结构修饰、限制“其他财产”,“禁止”的主语为“法律、行政法规”。法宝版译为 that 引导的定语从句,总库版译为过去分词短语作后置定语,prohibit 的用法为“be prohibited by... from doing sth.”,都是可取译文。

例句 10 中,“禁止”结构修饰、限制“标的物”,但是它们共同构成的偏正名词短语不是全句的主语,而是描述了后句“依照其规定”的条件,属于法律条款的条件要素。两版译文都译为 where-条件句,法宝版使用被动语态,总库版使用主动语态,都是可取译文。

例句 11 中,“禁止”结构修饰、限制“亲属关系”,与“有”字又构成偏正动宾词组,用以描述导致婚姻无效的情形。总库版译文把“亲属关系”译为“relative relations”,又用“prohibited by law from marrying each other”作后置定语,不但啰唆,而且有中式英语之嫌。相较之下,法宝版译文既简洁又专业，根据 Wikipedia.org.（2014）的释义：“In law, a prohibited degree of kinship refers to a degree of consanguinity (blood relatedness) and sometimes affinity (relation by marriage or sexual relationship) between persons that results in certain actions between them being illegal.”。可见，“prohibited degree of kinship”正是“禁止结婚的亲属关系”的相应译文。

小　结

在《民法典》中，“禁止”结构通常构成禁止性条款，与“不得”结构相比，语气更加强烈。由于“禁止”结构一般用于无主句的祈使句，译文通常使用被动语态，可以分为三种情况：如果“禁止”后直接跟行为模式，通常译为“…（行为模式）be prohibited”。如果“禁止”和“行为模式”之间有“被规范者”，通常译为“...（被规范者）be prohibited from...（行为模式）”。但有时“禁止”结构不构成禁令，而是描述说明法条所涉的事物、事项或情形，译文通常译为定语或定语从句。

“be prohibited”前面有时需要使用情态动词 shall，以强化语气，情景包括①被禁止的是具有严重危害性，损害人身权利、国家利益的行为；②源语条文语气强烈，中文标记词为“任何”“无论”，英文标记词为“only”“all”等。如果“禁止”结构中有被规范者，且用“任何”进行修饰，译文通常使用否定词前移的句式“no...（被规范者）may...（行为模式）”。

10 “致使”结构的翻译

10.1 结构特点及其在《民法典》中的运用

10.1.1 结构特点

本节讨论的“致使”结构是指以“致使”为标记的单纯致使结构，用于表述某种行为或某些事项的发生导致了另一种特定的结果或后果。其基本句式可以表示为：致使者＋“致使”＋被使者＋结果。当“致使者”是人或者事件时，“致使”是动词作谓语，“被使者＋结果”是兼语式宾语；当“致使者”是行为时，“致使”是连词，连接两个句子。

10.1.2 在《民法典》中的运用

在《民法典》中“致使”结构一共出现了 53 次，通常出现在“的”字结构中，用于表述条文适用的条件和情形，如第 768 条规定：“应收账款债权人就同一应收账款订立多个保理合同，<u>致使</u>多个保理人主张权利<u>的</u>，已经登记的先于未登记的取得应收账款……”

“致使”结构可分为两种情况：

(1)“致使”作谓语动词

本结构在《民法典》中出现了 23 次，表示因某种原因而导致某一结果的发生或持续状态,最常见的搭配为"因……致使……"。如第660条规定:"依据前款规定应当交付的赠与财产因赠与人故意或者重大过失致使毁损、灭失的,赠与人应当承担赔偿责任。""赠与人故意或者重大过失"是导致赠与财产"毁损、灭失"的原因。

(2)"致使"作连词

本结构在《民法典》中出现了30次,"致使"连接两个句子,表示前句的行为动作导致后句的结果或状态。多数情况下,"致使"前有逗号,如第857条规定:"作为技术开发合同标的技术已经由他人公开,致使技术开发合同的履行没有意义的,当事人可以解除合同。"少数情况下,"致使"前没有逗号,如第958条规定:"第三人不履行义务致使委托人受到损害的,行纪人应当承担赔偿责任,但是行纪人与委托人另有约定的除外。"

10.2 译文对比

表10.1 《民法典》中"致使"结构的翻译对比

序号	出处(条)	原文	北大法宝译文(法宝版译文)	国家法规总库译文(总库版译文)
1	459	占有人因使用占有的不动产或者动产,致使该不动产或者动产受到损害的,恶意占有人应当承担赔偿责任。	Where the possessor causes any damage to the possessed immovable or movable due to the use thereof, the possessor in bad faith shall assume compensatory liability.	Where damage is caused to immovable or movable property by its possessor as a result of use of the property, a mala fide possessor shall be liable for compensation.

续表

序号	出处（条）	原文	北大法宝译文（法宝版译文）	国家法规总库译文（总库版译文）
2	858	…… 当事人一方发现前款规定的可能**致使**研究开发失败或者部分失败的情形时，应当及时通知另一方并采取适当措施减少损失……	... Where a party discovers any circumstance **which may lead to** the failure of the development in whole or in part as described in the preceding paragraph, it shall, in a timely manner, notify the other party and take the appropriate measures to mitigate loss...	... Where a party finds that a situation specified in the preceding paragraph exists **which may cause** total or partial failure of the research and development, the party shall promptly notify the other party and take appropriate measures to mitigate the loss...
3	327	**因**不动产或者动产被征收、征用**致使**用益物权消灭或者影响用益物权行使的，用益物权人有权依据本法第二百四十三条、第二百四十五条的规定获得相应补偿。	Where an immovable or movable is expropriated or requisitioned, **which results in** the extinction of the usufruct or affects the use of usufruct, the usufructuary has the right to compensation according to Articles 243 and 245 of this Code.	Where a right to usufruct is extinguished or adversely affected **due to** expropriation or requisition of the immovable or movable property, the usufructuary has the right to compensation according to the provisions of Articles 243 and 245 of this Code.
4	801	**因**施工人的原因**致使**建设工程质量不符合约定的，发包人有权请求施工人在合理期限内无偿修理或者返工、改建。	Where the construction project fails to meet the prescribed quality requirements **due to** any reason attributable to the constructor, the employer is entitled to require the constructor to repair, re-construct or make alteration gratuitously within a reasonable time.	Where the quality of a construction project fails to conform to the contract **due to** a reason attributable to the constructor, the contract-offering party has the right to request the constructor to repair, rework, or reconstruct the project without further charge within a reasonable period of time.

续表

序号	出处(条)	原文	北大法宝译文(法宝版译文)	国家法规总库译文(总库版译文)
5	935	因委托人死亡或者被宣告破产、解散,**致使**委托合同终止将损害委托人利益的,在委托人的继承人、遗产管理人或者清算人承受委托事务之前,受托人应当继续处理委托事务。	Where the mandator is deceased, or is declared bankrupt or dissolved, **resulting in** the termination of the contract of mandate which will harm the mandator's interests, the mandatary shall continue to handle the affair under the mandate before the successor, administrator of estate, or liquidator of the mandator takes over the affair under the mandate.	Where termination of an entrustment contract **resulting from** the death, declared bankruptcy, or declared dissolution of the principal is to harm the interests of the principal, the agent shall continue to handle the entrusted matter until the heirs, administrator of estate, or the liquidator of the principal takes it over.
6	53	…… 利害关系人隐瞒真实情况,**致使**他人被宣告死亡而取得其财产的,除应当返还财产外,还应当对由此造成的损失承担赔偿责任。	… Where an interested party conceals facts, **causing** another person to be declared dead, and thus obtains any property of the person, the interested party shall, in addition to returning the property, assume compensatory liability for any loss so caused.	… Where an interested person conceals the true information **and causes** a natural person to be declared dead so as to obtain the latter's property, the interested person shall, in addition to returning the wrongfully obtained property, make compensation for any loss thus caused.

续表

序号	出处（条）	原文	北大法宝译文（法宝版译文）	国家法规总库译文（总库版译文）
7	412	债务人不履行到期债务或者发生当事人约定的实现抵押权的情形，**致使**抵押财产被人民法院依法扣押的，自扣押之日起，抵押权人有权收取该抵押财产的天然孳息或者法定孳息，但是抵押权人未通知应当清偿法定孳息义务人的除外。	Where the mortgaged property is detained by a people's court in accordance with law **since** the debtor fails to pay the due debt or falls under any circumstance where mortgage shall be exercised as agreed upon by the parties, from the date when the property is detained, the mortgagee has the right to collect the natural or legal fruits accrued from the mortgaged property, except that the mortgagee fails to notify the obligor to pay off the legal fruits.	Where a debtor fails to perform his obligation due or an event upon the occurrence of which a mortgage is to be enforced as agreed upon by the parties occurs, **resulting in** the seizure of the mortgaged property by the people's court in accordance with law, the mortgagee is entitled to collect the natural fruits or civil fruits accrued from the mortgaged property as of the date of the seizure, unless the mortgagee fails to notify the person who is obligated to pay off the civil fruits.
8	610	因标的物不符合质量要求，**致使**不能实现合同目的的，买受人可以拒绝接受标的物或者解除合同……	Where the quality of the subject matter does not conform to the quality requirements, **making it impossible to** achieve the purpose of the contract, the buyer may refuse to accept the subject matter or may rescind the contract...	Where a subject matter fails to meet the quality requirements **so that** the purpose of the contract cannot be achieved, the buyer may refuse to accept the subject matter or may rescind the contract...

续表

序号	出处（条）	原文	北大法宝译文（法宝版译文）	国家法规总库译文（总库版译文）
9	857	作为技术开发合同标的的技术已经由他人公开，致使技术开发合同的履行没有意义的，当事人可以解除合同。	Where the technology which is the subject matter of a technology development contract is made public by a third party, thereby making the performance of the technology development contract meaningless, the parties may rescind the contract.	Where a technology which is the object of a technology development contract is revealed to the public by others, thus rendering the performance of the contract meaningless, the parties may rescind the contract.
10	893	寄存人交付的保管物有瑕疵或者根据保管物的性质需要采取特殊保管措施的，寄存人应当将有关情况告知保管人。寄存人未告知，致使保管物受损失的，保管人不承担赔偿责任；保管人因此受损失的，除保管人知道或者应当知道且未采取补救措施外，寄存人应当承担赔偿责任。	Where the deposited property delivered by the depositor is defective or requires special deposit measures in light of its nature, the depositor shall inform the depositary of the relevant situation. **Where** the depositor fails to do so, thereby causing damage to the deposited property, the depositary shall be exempt from liability for compensation; **where** the depositary sustains any loss as a result, the depositor shall be liable for compensation, except where the depositary knows or should have known the situation and fails to take remedial measures.	Where an article delivered by the depositor to be kept under custody has defects or needs special safekeeping measures based on its nature, the depositor shall inform the custodian of the relevant information. **Where** the depositor fails to do so, **if** damage is thus caused to the article, the custodian does not bear the liability for compensation, and **if** losses are thus caused to the custodian, the depositor shall be liable for compensation unless the custodian knows or should have known the situation but fails to take remedial measures.

10.3 译文分析

针对《民法典》中“致使”结构的两种运用情况，我们对比分析两个版本的对应译文，探讨更为可取的翻译方法。

10.3.1 “致使”作谓语动词情况的翻译

当“致使”的主语是人或物时，两个版本通常译为“cause”，根据《朗文当代英语词典》，cause 指 to make something happen，especially something bad，而《民法典》中“致使”通常引出不好的结果，因此，cause 可以视为“致使”的标准翻译。如例句 1 中，“致使”的主语是“占有人”，“致使”的结果是“该不动产或者动产受到损害”，法宝版使用“cause”的主动语态，总库版使用被动语态，都是可取的。但是“因使用占有的不动产或者动产”不是其受损的直接原因，而是方式状语，法宝版的“due to”和总库版的“as a result of”都表示直接原因，建议改为“through”。

例句 2 中，“致使”结构作定语，修饰“情形”，实际上“情形”是“致使”的逻辑主语。两版译文都译为 which 引导的定语从句。“lead to”和“cause”的区别在于，首先，“lead to”的用法比较中性，引出的结果既可以正面也可以负面。其次，“lead to”表达的因果关系不如“cause”直接，“lead to”的主语可能只是导致结果的几个因素之一。在例句 2 语境中，“致使研究开发失败或者部分失败的情形”不一定直接导致“研究开发失败或者部分失败”，也许还掺杂其他因素，因此，法宝版使用 “lead to”也是可取的。

例句 3 和例句 4 都涉及“因……致使……”结构，“致使”前面没有逗号，“因”后面的宾语通常为名词短语，是“致使”结果的直接原因。这种情况下，“因”和“致使”的语义重叠，翻译时一般参照“因”字结构中“因”字引导直接原因的译法。例句 3 中，对于“因”字的宾语——“不动产或者动产被征收、征用”，法宝版译为句子，后面用 which 引导非限定性定语从句，“result in”表示直接结果，是可取的；总库版将其译为名词短语，作“due to”

的宾语，表示直接原因，但是为了避免 due to 和 owing to 的用法之争(参见"因"字结构)，改成"as a result of"更合适。例句 4 中，"因……人的原因致使……"，两版译文都译为"due to a/any reason attributable to somebody"，是可取译法。

10.3.2 "致使"作连词情况的翻译

"致使"作连词时，连接两个句子，表示前句的行为动作导致后句的结果或状态。两版译文通常译为现在分词短语作结果状语，常用的动词为 cause、render、result in；有时也会译为从句，如例句 7 的法宝版和例句 8 的总库版。

在"因……致使……"结构中，如果"致使"前有逗号，"因"通常为连词，后接句子，如例句 5。法宝版按照源语条文的语序，先因后果，使用 resulting in 作结果状语；总库版先果后因，使用 resulting from 作 termination 的后置定语，两个版本都是可取译文。

例句 6 中，法宝版译文前句"利害关系人隐瞒真实情况"是后句中"他人被宣告死亡"的原因，法宝版译文使用"causing"现在分词短语作结果状语，总库版译文用"an interested person"作主语，cause 是第二个小句的谓语动词，连词 and 表明两个小句在逻辑上具有因果关系，因此都是可取译法。但是考虑到整句条文的语境，法律制裁是基于法律主体的违法行为，违法行为又是出于一定的目的，"利害关系人隐瞒真实情况，致使他人被宣告死亡"的目的是"取得其财产"，总库版译文用 so as to 凸显了违法主体的目的，而法宝版译文的"thus"仅表明"取得其财产"是违法行为的结果，不能忠实地传达源语条文的全部意思，故此，总库版译文更可取。

例句 7 中，法宝版译文使用 since 连接两个句子，但是 since 作连词既可以表示较弱或间接的因果关系，也可以表示时间上的前后关系，而立法文本措辞必须严谨无疑义，因此需要谨慎使用 since，最大限度地减少歧义。总库版译文用 resulting in 现在分词短语作结果状语，更可取。

例句 8 中，总库版译文使用 so that，是同样的问题。so that 既可以表示目的,也可以表示结果,语义不单一,容易造成歧义,导致误解,应谨慎使用。法宝版使用现在分词短语没有问题,但是考虑到 making it impossible to do sth.较为口语化,建议改为更为正式的用词"rendering it impossible to do sth."。

例句 9 中,两版译文都使用现在分词短语作结果状语,并且用 thereby 和 thus 进行强调,都是可取的方法,但是法宝版的选词 making 较为口语化,不如像总库版一样改用 rendering。

例句 10 中,就"致使"结构本身的翻译而言,两版译文的译法都是可取的。但是,放在整句法条的大的语境中看,二者又有差异。源语条文中,"保管人不承担赔偿责任"的后面是";",说明前后两句并列,但是细分析之,并列的不是"寄存人未告知,致使保管物受损失"和"保管人因此受损失"两种情形及其处理方法。实际上,"寄存人未告知"是大的总的情形,"致使保管物受损失"和"保管人因此受损失"才是大情形下并列的两个小情形。因此总库版用 where 引导母条件句,用两个 if 引导子条件句,更符合法律语句的逻辑和表达习惯(李克兴,2013)。

小　结

在《民法典》中"致使"结构用于表述某种行为或某些事项的发生导致了另一种特定的不好的结果或后果,通常出现在"的"字结构中,说明法条适用的条件和情形。可以分为两种情况:①当"致使"作谓语动词时,如果"致使"的主语是人或物,cause 可以视为"致使"的标准翻译;如果涉及"因……致使……"结构,"致使"前面没有逗号,"因"后面的宾语通常为名词短语,是"致使"结果的直接原因,翻译时一般参照"因"字结构中"因"字引导直接原因的译法。②"致使"作连词时,连接两个句子,表示前句的行为动作导致后句的结果或状态,通常译为现在分词短语作结果状语,常用的动词为 cause、render、result in。

11 “不影响”结构的翻译

11.1 结构特点及其在《民法典》中的运用

11.1.1 结构特点

“不影响”结构在法律文本中通常用于表明某种法律效力，或者权利人的某种权利或行为，没有受到影响、干扰或损害。如果“不影响”的主体是一种假设的情形，该结构通常表示此种例外情况的出现并不对某种法律效力或者权利的拥有产生影响，如“合同不生效、无效、被撤销或者终止的，不影响合同中有关解决争议方法的条款的效力”；如果“不影响”的主体是某种客观行为，该结构通常表明该行为不会对另一种责任的承担或者义务的履行产生影响，如“承担行政责任或者刑事责任不影响承担民事责任”。

11.1.2 在《民法典》中的运用

在《民法典》中该结构一共出现了 16 次。根据“不影响”结构是否是条文阐述的核心内容，可以分为两种情况：

(1)“不影响”是核心动词

本结构在《民法典》中出现了 13 次。多数情况下，“不影响”的主体是一种假设的情形，用“的”字结构表示，如第 706 条规定：“当事人未依照法律、行政法规规定办理租赁合同登记备案手续**的**，**不影响**合同的效力。”少数情况下，“不影响”的主体是某种行为，如第 742 条规定：“**承租人对出卖人行使索赔权利**，**不影响**其履行支付租金的义务。”

（2）“不影响”是非核心动词

本结构在《民法典》中共出现了三次，分别是第 156 条、第 580 条和第 839 条。如第 580 条规定：“有前款规定的除外情形之一，致使不能实现合同目的的，人民法院或者仲裁机构可以根据当事人的请求终止合同权利义务关系，但是**不影响**违约责任的承担。”该款的核心内容是对“有前款规定的除外情形之一，致使不能实现合同目的的”情形提出救济，即“人民法院或者仲裁机构可以根据当事人的请求终止合同权利义务关系”，“不影响违约责任的承担”是对该救济的补充说明。

11.2 译文对比

表 11.1 《民法典》中“不影响”结构的翻译对比

序号	出处（条）	原文	北大法宝译文（法宝版译文）	国家法规总库译文（总库版译文）
1	49	自然人被宣告死亡但是并未死亡**的**，**不影响**该自然人在被宣告死亡期间实施的民事法律行为的效力。	**Where** a natural person declared dead is alive, the validity of the juridical acts performed by the natural person during the period of declared death **shall not be affected**.	The declaration of the death of a natural person who is still alive **does not affect** the effects of the civil juristic acts performed by the person during the period the death declaration is effective.

续表

序号	出处（条）	原文	北大法宝译文（法宝版译文）	国家法规总库译文（总库版译文）
2	215	当事人之间订立有关设立、变更、转让和消灭不动产物权的合同，除法律另有规定或者当事人另有约定外，自合同成立时生效；未办理物权登记的，不影响合同效力。	A contract entered into by the parties on the creation, modification, transfer, or extinction of the real right in an immovable shall become valid from the date when the contract is entered into, unless it is otherwise provided for by any law or agreed upon by the parties; and if the real right has not been registered, it shall not affect the validity of the contract.	A contract concluded by the parties on the creation, alteration, transfer, or extinguishment of a real right becomes effective upon its formation, unless it is otherwise provided by law or agreed upon by the parties, and the validity of the contract is not affected by the fact that the real right registration is not completed.
3	502	…… 依照法律、行政法规的规定，合同应当办理批准等手续的，依照其规定。未办理批准等手续影响合同生效的，不影响合同中履行报批等义务条款以及相关条款的效力；……	… With regard to contracts that are subject to approval as stipulated by relevant laws or administrative regulations, the provisions thereof shall be followed. If the approval and other procedures fail to be performed, precluding the contract from becoming effective, the validity of the terms regarding obligations such as the obligation to apply for approval and related terms of the contract is not affected...	… Where there are laws or administrative regulations providing that a contract shall be subject to approval or other procedures, such provisions shall be followed. Where failure to complete the approval or other procedures is to affect the effectiveness of the contract, the validity of the clauses concerning the performance of the obligation of filing for approval and the like procedures and the other relevant clauses in the contract are not affected...

续表

序号	出处(条)	原文	北大法宝译文(法宝版译文)	国家法规总库译文(总库版译文)
4	609	出卖人按照约定未交付有关标的物的单证和资料**的,不影响**标的物毁损、灭失风险的转移。	The failure of the seller to deliver the documents and information relating to the subject matter as agreed upon **shall not affect** the passing of the risk of damage to or loss of the subject matter.	A seller's failure to deliver the documents and information of the subject matter in accordance with the agreement **does not affect** the shift of the risks of destruction, damage, or loss of the subject matter.
5	611	标的物毁损、灭失的风险由买受人承担**的,不影响**因出卖人履行义务不符合约定,买受人请求其承担违约责任的权利。	Where the risk of damage to or loss of the subject matter is borne by the buyer, it **shall not affect** the buyer's claim of liability of the seller for breach of contract because the seller's performance of its obligations is not in conformity with the agreement.	Where a seller's performance is not in conformity with the agreement, the assumption of the risks of destruction, damage, or loss of the subject matter by the buyer **does not affect** the buyer's right to request the seller to bear default liability.
6	738	依照法律、行政法规的规定,对于租赁物的经营使用应当取得行政许可的,出租人未取得行政许可**不影响**融资租赁合同的效力。	Where any law or administrative regulation requires a lessee to obtain administrative license for the operation and use of the leased property, the failure of the lessor to obtain administrative license **does not affect** the validity of the financial leasing contract.	Where the operation or use of a leased object requires an administrative license in accordance with the provision of laws or administrative regulations, the failure of the lessor to obtain such administrative license **does not affect** the validity of the contract for financing lease.

续表

序号	出处(条)	原文	北大法宝译文(法宝版译文)	国家法规总库译文(总库版译文)
7	567	合同的权利义务关系终止，不影响合同中结算和清理条款的效力。	The termination of a relation of rights and obligations under a contract shall not affect the validity of clauses that related to settlement of accounts and winding-up.	Termination of the relationship of rights and obligations under a contract does not affect the validity of the contract clauses regarding settlement and liquidation.
8	187	民事主体因同一行为应当承担民事责任、行政责任和刑事责任的，承担行政责任或者刑事责任不影响承担民事责任……	Where a party to civil legal relations shall be held civilly, administratively, and criminally liable for the same act, the assumption of administrative liability or criminal liability does not affect the assumption of civil liability...	Where a person of the civil law has to concurrently bear civil, administrative, and criminal liabilities as a result of the same act performed by him, the assumption of administrative or criminal liabilities by the person may not affect the civil liability he should bear...
9	156	民事法律行为部分无效，不影响其他部分效力的，其他部分仍然有效。	Where the partial invalidity of a juridical act does not affect the validity of the other part, the other part shall remain valid.	If invalidation of a part of a civil juristic act does not affect the validity of the other part, the other part of the act remains valid.

续表

序号	出处（条）	原文	北大法宝译文（法宝版译文）	国家法规总库译文（总库版译文）
10	580	…… 有前款规定的除外情形之一，致使不能实现合同目的的，人民法院或者仲裁机构可以根据当事人的请求终止合同权利义务关系，但是不影响违约责任的承担。	… If any of the foregoing circumstances makes it impossible to achieve the purpose of contract, the people's court or arbitration institution may terminate the relation of contractual obligations and rights at the request of either party, without affecting the assumption of the liability for breach of contract.	… Where one of the situations specified in the preceding paragraph exists so that the purpose of the contract cannot be achieved, the people's court or an arbitration institution may terminate the contractual relationship of rights and obligations upon request by a party, but the default liability to be borne is not affected.
11	839	多式联运经营人可以与参加多式联运的各区段承运人就多式联运合同的各区段运输约定相互之间的责任；但是，该约定不影响多式联运经营人对全程运输承担的义务。	The multimodal carriage operator and the segment carriers may enter into agreements on their respective duties concerning each segment, provided that the obligations of the multimodal carriage operator with respect to the entire course of carriage are not affected by any such agreement.	An operator of multi-modal transport may agree with the carriers of the different sections of the multi-modal transport on their respective responsibilities for transport in each section under the multi-modal transport contract, except that such an agreement does not affect the obligations of the operator for the entire transport.

11.3 译文分析

针对《民法典》中“不影响”结构的两种运用情况，我们分别对比分析两个版本的对应译文，探讨更为可取的翻译方法。

11.3.1 “不影响”是核心动词时的翻译

多数情况下，“不影响”的主体用“的”字结构表示，指某种假设的情形，如例句1—5。法宝版通常将“的”字结构译为 where 或 if 引导的状语从句，如例句1—3；有时也将条件句中的主要动词转换为抽象名词，将整个情形译为以该抽象名词为核心的名词短语，如例句4和例句5。总库版译文略有不同，例句1、例句4和例句5使用以抽象名词为核心的名词短语，例句3译为 where 引导的条件句。一般情况下，这两种翻译方式都是可行的，都能够充分表达源语条文的含义。

对于“不影响”作为核心动词的翻译，两个版本译文的差异主要在于是否应当使用情态动词 shall。李克兴（2007：54）总结了 shall 在法律文本中的用法：通常搭配第二人称和第三人称，表示命令、义务、职责、权利、特权和许诺等。但是 shall 在法律英语和法律翻译中的失范和滥用现象，已经是国内外许多专家、学者的共识（如陈忠诚，1992；Wydick，1998；李克兴，2007；李晋、董晓波，2021）。英语国家的立法起草技术在过去几十年发生了巨大变化，在简明语言运动和简明英语运动的直接影响下，shall 的使用受到极大限制。根据《布莱克法律词典》（第十版）的释义，现代法律文本中 shall 的用法只有“has a duty to；more broadly，is required to”这一表示“命令”或者“义务”的意义才是标准的用法；在原生英语法律语料库中，与 shall 搭配的主语为有灵主语（各种义务承担者）和无灵主语（各种义务）（李晋、董晓波，2021）；在法律条文对内容进行客观阐述或客观定义时，无须使用 shall（王子颖，2013）。限制 shall 的使用既符合法律英语简明化运动的趋势，又能避免读者对 shall 含义的不同进行不必要的揣测，从而提高法律条文的精确度及其可操作性。

当“不影响”的主体是假设的情形时，该结构的宾语通常是某种法律效力，如例句1—3；或者权利，如例句5。此处的“情形”和“不影响”的宾语“效力”或者“权利”之间没有“要求”或“义务”关系，不符合shall的使用规则，因此总库版的译文更可取。例句3中，两版译文都把情形译为条件句，主句用“效力”作主语，谓语使用affect的被动语态，是可取译法，只是总库版译文出现了语法错误，“validity”作主语时，谓语系动词不应使用“are”。

例句4中，“不影响”的宾语不是“效力”或者“权利”，而是“风险的转移”。即一旦售卖，标的物毁损、灭失的风险便由买方承担，哪怕出卖人未按照约定交付有关标的物的单证和资料。“不影响”的主语并非义务的承担者，可见，本条不是对义务的规定，而是法律规定，法律规定无须使用shall。此外，shall not属于禁止词，通常用于禁止性规范，那么“不影响”结构属于禁止性规范吗？当然不是。禁止性规范的标志词通常为“不得”和“禁止”，《民法典》中涉及“不影响”结构的条文均是对法律规定的客观阐述，因此没有必要使用shall not。

例句6和例句7中，“不影响”的主体尽管没有使用“的”字结构，但是“出租人未取得行政许可”和“(结算和清理条款未履行完即终止)合同的权利义务关系”，同样是假设的情形，两个版本都译为以抽象名词为核心的名词短语，都是可取译法。但是“不影响”的主语是情形，宾语是“效力”，同例句1—3一样，无须使用shall，法宝版例句7译文又是对shall的滥用。

例句8中，两版译文的区别在于需不需要使用情态动词may。肯定式may在法律文本中的含义、用法和译法与其在普通英文中相同，但是may not属于高值否定(Halliday，1994/2000：362)，表达对某种行为的限制或约束时，比shall not的语气更强烈。前文已经谈到，涉及“不影响”结构的《民法典》条文只是对法律规定的客观阐述，不属于禁止性规范，无须使用shall not，更遑论否定阈值更高的may not。因此，法宝版译文更可取。

11.3.2 “不影响”是非核心动词时的翻译

例句 9—11 中，“不影响”结构不是源语条文阐述的主要内容，“不影响”均为非核心动词。

法律英语中有一个常用程式语，也可以表达“不影响”的意思，即 without prejudice to，如：

> “If the carrier carries out the instructions of the consignor for the disposition of the cargo without requiring the production of the part of the air waybill or the cargo receipt delivered to the latter, the carrier will be liable, without prejudice to its right of recovery from the consignor, for any damage which may be caused thereby to any person who is lawfully in possession of that part of the air waybill or the cargo receipt. (HongKong e-Legislation: Cap. 500 Carriage by Air Ordinance — Schedule 1A The Monreal Convention)
>
> 承运人按照托运人的指示处置货物，没有要求出示托运人所收执的那份航空货运单或者货物收据，给该份航空货运单或者货物收据的合法持有人造成损失的，承运人应当承担责任，但是**不影响**承运人对托运人的追偿权。（香港法例：第 500 章《航空运输条例》—附表 1A《蒙特利尔公约》）”

鉴于 without prejudice to 并非谓语动词，其表述的内容通常也并非条文的核心内容。根据 Collins 词典的解释，“if you take an action without prejudice to an existing situation, your action does not change or harm that situation”。可见，该程式语通常用于表示当事人的法律权利或特权未受损害或丧失。在汉语中，意思相当于“在不损害……的原则下”“在不影响……的情况下”“……不受影响”“不妨碍……”“不规限……”等等。without prejudice to 前后的内容并不直接构成明显的条件或转折关系（王芳、汤文华，2023）。

例句 9 中，两版译文将“不影响”结构都译为条件句中的主要动词“does not affect”，能够传达原文的意思，但如果使用 without prejudice to，不妨改为：If a part of a civil juristic act is invalid without prejudice to the validity of the other part, the other part remains valid。

例句 10 原文的主要内容是对“有前款规定的除外情形之一，致使不能实现合同目的的”情形提出救济，“不影响违约责任的承担”是对该救济的补充说明。总库版按照原文语序将“不影响”结构译为 but 引导的并列从句，但是原文并没有明显的转折意味；法宝版译为 without 复合结构，在句中作伴随状语，似乎更符合原文的语意。也可以考虑 without prejudice to，改为“without prejudice to the liability for breach of contract”。

例句 11 中，“多式联运经营人对全程运输承担的义务”不是签订“该约定”的条件、例外或限制，因为多式联运经营人对多式联运承担责任是多式联运合同责任承担的基本原则。经营人与托运人签订多式联运合同后，尽管各承运人都参与了这一合同关系，但对托运人而言，多式联运经营人仍然要承担全部责任。可见原文“；”后，“但是”引导的内容是对前文的补充说明。然而，法宝版译文用“provided that”、总库版译文用“except that”，表达的都是条件或者例外。因此，可以改为“without prejudice to the obligations of the multimodal carriage operator for the entire course of carriage”。without prejudice to 结构传达的静态意味更符合英语读者的阅读习惯。

小　结

在《民法典》中，根据“不影响”结构是否为条文阐述的核心内容，可以分为两种情况：①“不影响”是核心动词。“不影响”的主体通常为某个假定的情形或某种行为，根据行文和语境，译文可将主体译为 where 或 if 引导的条件句，也可译为以抽象名词为核心的名词短语，主要动词“不影响”译为 does not affect 或其被动语态，无须使用 shall 或 may。②“不影响”为非核心动词。翻译时需要结合语境判断逻辑关系，如果“不影响”的主体和其宾语之间并不直接构成明显的条件或转折关系，可以考虑使用常用程式语 without prejudice to。

12 “发生效力”结构的翻译

12.1 结构特点及其在《民法典》中的运用

12.1.1 结构特点

在法律文本中,“发生效力”结构通常用于描述法律文件或法律行为在满足一定条件后,具有法律约束力和执行力。该结构的主语可以是合同或某个法律文件,也可以是民事法律行为、权利或权利的设立、变更、转让等。“发生效力”在某些条文中会缩略为“生效”,意思无差别。

12.1.2 在《民法典》中的运用

在《民法典》中该结构一共出现了 54 次,其中 20 次表述为“发生效力”,34 次表述为“生效”。

(1)“发生效力”

“发生效力”通常用作《民法典》条文的主要谓语,其前文描述发生效力的条件,如第 209 条规定:“不动产物权的设立、变更、转让和消灭,**经依法登记,发生效力;未经登记,不发生效力**……”一般情况下,本结构用“对”字表明需要接受或服从法律约束力的对象,如第 520 条规定:“债权人对部分连带债务人的给付受领迟延的,**对其他连带债务人**发生效力。”此外,也会与“自……时”连用,表明发生效力的时间,如第 230 条规定:“因继承取得物权的,自继承开始时发生效力。”

(2)“生效”

多数情况下,“生效”在《民法典》条文中用作谓语动词,意思是发生效力;少数情况下用作定语,与其搭配的名词通常为“条件”“期限”“时间”或“地点”,如第 492 条规定:“承诺生效的地点为合同成立的地点。”

当“生效”用作主要谓语动词时,其前文内容往往规定产生法律约束力的条件或时间,如第 484 条规定:“承诺不需要通知的,根据交易习惯或者要约的要求作出承诺的行为时生效。”

有时,“生效”结构也会出现在状语中,用以明确条文规定的法律事项的时间、条件或情形,如第 940 条规定:“建设单位依法与物业服务人订立的前期物业服务合同约定的服务期限届满前,业主委员会或者业主与新物业服务人订立的物业服务合同生效的,前期物业服务合同终止。”

12.2 译文对比

表 12.1 《民法典》中“发生效力”结构的翻译对比

序号	出处(条)	原文	北大法宝译文(法宝版译文)	国家法规总库译文(总库版译文)
1	157	民事法律行为无效、被撤销或者确定不发生效力后,行为人因该行为取得的财产,应当予以返还……	After a juridical act is void, revoked, or determined as having no binding force, the property obtained by the actor as a result of the act shall be restituted...	Where a civil juristic act is void, revoked, or is determined to have no legal effect, the property thus obtained by a person as a result of the act shall be returned...

续表

序号	出处（条）	原文	北大法宝译文（法宝版译文）	国家法规总库译文（总库版译文）
2	209	不动产物权的设立、变更、转让和消灭，经依法登记，发生效力；未经登记，不发生效力，但是法律另有规定的除外。	The creation, modification, transfer, or extinction of a real right in an immovable shall become valid after it is registered in accordance with the law; it shall have no binding force if it is not registered in accordance with the law, except as otherwise provided for by any law.	The creation, alteration, transfer, or extinguishment of a real right in immovable property shall become effective upon registration in accordance with law, and does not take effect without registration, unless otherwise provided by law.
3	224	动产物权的设立和转让，自交付时发生效力，但是法律另有规定的除外。	The creation or transfer of the real right in a movable shall become valid upon delivery, except as otherwise provided for by any law.	The creation or transfer of a real right in movable property shall take effect upon delivery, unless otherwise provided by law.
4	231	因合法建造、拆除房屋等事实行为设立或者消灭物权的，自事实行为成就时发生效力。	Where a real right is created or extinguished due to such factual behavior as lawful construction and demolition of buildings, it shall have binding force at the time when the factual behavior is committed.	Where a real right is created or extinguished as a result of a *de facto* act such as lawful construction or demolition of a house, the creation or extinguishment of the real right becomes effective when the *de facto* act is accomplished.

续表

序号	出处（条）	原文	北大法宝译文（法宝版译文）	国家法规总库译文（总库版译文）
5	136	民事法律行为**自**成立**时生效**，但是法律另有规定或者当事人另有约定的除外……	A juridical act **shall become valid upon** its formation, except as otherwise provided for by any law or agreed upon by the parties...	Unless otherwise provided by law or agreed by the parties, a civil juristic act **takes effect at the time** it is accomplished...
6	215	当事人之间订立有关设立、变更、转让和消灭不动产物权的合同，除法律另有规定或者当事人另有约定外，**自**合同成立**时生效**；未办理物权登记的，不影响合同效力。	A contract entered into by the parties on the creation, modification, transfer, or extinction of the real right in an immovable **shall become valid from the date when** the contract is entered into, unless it is otherwise provided for by any law or agreed upon by the parties; and if the real right has not been registered, it shall not affect the validity of the contract.	A contract concluded by the parties on the creation, alteration, transfer, or extinguishment of a real right **becomes effective upon** its formation, unless it is otherwise provided by law or agreed upon by the parties, and the validity of the contract is not affected by the fact that the real right registration is not completed.
7	170	执行法人或者非法人组织工作任务的人员，就其职权范围内的事项，以法人或者非法人组织的名义实施的民事法律行为，**对**法人或者非法人组织**发生效力**。	Where a person who performs tasks for a legal person or an unincorporated organization conducts juridical acts related to matters within his or her scope of powers in the name of the legal person or the unincorporated organization, such acts **shall have binding force on** the legal person or unincorporated organization.	A civil juristic act performed by a person for fulfilling his responsibilities assigned by a legal person or an unincorporated organization, within the scope of authority and in the name of the legal person or the unincorporated organization, **is binding on** the legal person or unincorporated organization.

续表

序号	出处（条）	原文	北大法宝译文（法宝版译文）	国家法规总库译文（总库版译文）
8	504	法人的法定代表人或者非法人组织的负责人超越权限订立的合同，除相对人知道或者应当知道其超越权限外，该代表行为有效，订立的合同对法人或者非法人组织发生效力。	Where the legal representative of a legal person or the person in charge of an unincorporated organization enters into a contract ultra vires, the representation shall be effective, and the contract **shall be effective against** the legal person or unincorporated organization, unless the other party knows or should have known that he or she acts ultra vires.	Where the legal representative of a legal person or the responsible person of an unincorporated organization concludes a contract *ultra vires*, such an act is effective and the contract **is binding on** the legal person or the unincorporated organization unless the other party knows or should have known that the legal representative or the responsible person acts *ultra vires*.
9	1060	夫妻一方因家庭日常生活需要而实施的民事法律行为，对夫妻双方发生效力，但是夫妻一方与相对人另有约定的除外。	A juridical act performed by one of the spouses to meet the needs of the family's daily life **shall be binding on** both of them, except as otherwise agreed between one spouse and an opposite party.	A civil juristic act performed by one of the spouses to meet the daily needs of the family **is binding on** both spouses unless otherwise agreed between the third person and the spouse performing the act.
10	171	行为人没有代理权、超越代理权或者代理权终止后，仍然实施代理行为，未经被代理人追认的，对被代理人不发生效力。	Where an actor still performs an act of agency without a power of attorney, beyond his or her power of attorney, or after his or her power of attorney terminates, the act **shall not be binding on** the principal without the principal's ratification.	An act performed by a person without authority, beyond the authority, or after the authority is terminated **is not effective against** the principal who has not ratified it.

续表

序号	出处（条）	原文	北大法宝译文（法宝版译文）	国家法规总库译文（总库版译文）
11	546	债权人转让债权，未通知债务人的，该转让对债务人不发生效力。	Where a creditor assigns its claim without giving the debtor notice, such assignment will have no effect on the debtor.	Where a creditor assigns his claim but fails to notify the debtor, the assignment is not effective against the debtor.
12	765	应收账款债务人接到应收账款转让通知后，应收账款债权人与债务人无正当理由协商变更或者终止基础交易合同，对保理人产生不利影响的，对保理人不发生效力。	Where after an accounts receivable debtor receives a notice of assignment of accounts receivable, the accounts receivable creditor and debtor negotiate the modification or termination of the underlying transaction contract without justification, which adversely affects the factor, the modification or termination shall be without effect against the factor.	Where, after a debtor of an account receivable receives the notice of assignment thereof, the creditor and the debtor of the account receivable agree to modify or terminate the underlying contract without just cause, if it has an adverse impact on the factor, such modification or termination is not effective against the factor.
13	226	动产物权设立和转让前，权利人已经占有该动产的，物权自民事法律行为生效时发生效力。	Where the right holder has possessed a movable before the real right in the movable is created or transferred, the real right shall have binding force when the juridical act becomes valid.	Where a right holder is already in possession of a movable property before a real right in the movable property is created or transferred, the real right in the movable property becomes effective at the time when the civil juristic act is effected.

续表

序号	出处（条）	原文	北大法宝译文（法宝版译文）	国家法规总库译文（总库版译文）
14	341	流转期限为五年以上的土地经营权，自流转合同生效时设立……	The land operating right with a circulation period of five years or more shall be created when the circulation contract becomes valid...	The right to management of land which is transferred for a term of five years or longer is created when the contract for the transfer enters into force...
15	403	以动产抵押的，抵押权自抵押合同生效时设立；未经登记，不得对抗善意第三人。	Where a movable is mortgaged, mortgage is created at the time when the mortgage contract becomes valid; and if it is not registered, it shall not be set up against a bona fide third party.	A mortgage on movable property shall be created at the time when the mortgage contract enters into effect; without registration, such a mortgage may not be asserted against a bona fide third person.
16	510	合同生效后，当事人就质量、价款或者报酬、履行地点等内容没有约定或者约定不明确的，可以协议补充……	Where, after the contract becomes effective, there is no agreement in the contract between the parties on such content as quality, price or remuneration, place of performance etc., or such agreement is ambiguous, the parties may agree upon supplementary terms through consultation...	After a contract becomes effective, where the parties have not agreed on such contents as the quality, price or remuneration, or the place of performance, and the like, or the relevant agreement is unclear, the parties may make a supplementary agreement...

12.3 译文分析

我们针对《民法典》中本结构的使用情况，分别对比分析两个版本的对应译文，探讨更为可取的翻译方法。

12.3.1 “发生效力”或“生效”结构用作主要谓语时的翻译

“发生效力”在《民法典》条文中一般用作主要谓语，只有例句1除外。例句1中，“不发生效力”是“确定”的宾语，根据各自行文，法宝版译为动名词结构“having no binding force”，总库版译为不定式结构“to have no legal effect”。

①作为主要谓语动词，当“发生效力”或“生效”的前文内容是需要满足的条件或时间时，法宝版译文通常译为“shall become valid”，如例句2、例句3、例句5和例句6；“shall have binding force”，如例句4和例句13；“不发生效力”则译为“shall have no binding force”，如例句2。

总库版译文包括例句2的“shall become effective”、例句3的“shall take effect”，例句4、例句6和例句13的“becomes effective”，例句5的“takes effect”；“不发生效力”则译为例句2的“does not take effect”。

由此可见，不但两版译文不统一，两版译文内部的译法也不统一。根据《布莱克法律词典》，valid意思是“legally sufficient; binding”，通常指某个法律文件、协议、合同或行为符合法律要求，受到法律保护，并具有法律约束力。binding意思是“(of an agreement) having legal force to impose an obligation; (of an order) requiring obedience”，通常用于指协议、合同等具有施加义务的法律效力，或法律、判决等具有要求服从的约束力。take effect意思是“to be in force; to go into operation”，强调发生效力的动作。effective指“being in effect”，与become连用也体现发生效力的动态性。综上，以上各种表达方式都可以表达“发生效力”或“生效”的意思。

但是，美国法律起草之父瑞德·迪克逊(Reed Dickerson)指出，法律起草必须遵守"表达一致"原则，即"用同一种方式表达相同的意义，用不同的方式表达不同的意义，保证在重复使用同一个词或术语时其意义一致，避免用同一个词表达一个以上的意义"(转引自李晋、董晓波，2021)。因此，当几种表达方式都可以表述同一概念时，我们需要在同一文本中保留一种方式；考虑到译本的读者受众，尽量选择符合目的语读者表达习惯的方式。在此，我们不妨考察一下几个短语在原生英语法律语料库中的使用情况。(见表 12.2)

表 12.2 "(不)发生效力"的英文表达方式及检索频次

表达方式	国内	国外		
	香港法例库	英国立法库	美国联邦法规库	美国法典库
have binding force	0	2	0	81
take effect	456	>200	610	147973
become effective	36	>200	1170	116328
become valid	0	45	0	1189
have no binding force	0	3	0	239
have no legal effect	0	16	5	988
not take effect	56	>200	52	13246
not become effective	1	9	86	7233

* 对否定式的检索统计结果都去除了 not...until 结构的影响。

如表 12.2 所示，原生英语法律语料库中使用频次较高的表示肯定意义的表达方式为"take effect"和"become effective"，而表示否定意义时，较多使用"not take effect"的否定式。

对于谓语动词是否应当使用 shall，两个版本也有不同倾向。法宝版每个相关例句都使用了 shall，而总库版除例句 2 和例句 3 外，都没有使用 shall。对于 shall 在法律英语和法律翻译中的失范和滥用现象，国内外学者和专家都诟病已久，shall 用法及含义的多样化，与"表达一致"原则背道而驰，几十年来，法律英语简明化运动导致在主要英语国家中 shall 的使用率快速下降，《布莱克法律词典》(第十版)也注明，现代法律文本中 shall 的标准用法是“has a duty to; more broadly, is required to”这一表示“命令”或者“义务”的意义。在《民法典》条文中，“发生效力”的主语通常是某个法律文件、合同、民事法律行为、权利或权利的设立、变更、转让等，“发生效力”并不是它们的“责任”或“义务”，不符合 shall 在现代法律文本中的标准用法。因此，本结构中不使用 shall 才符合简明英语的国际趋势。

②作为主要谓语动词，“发生效力”也会与“对”字结构连用，表明需要接受或服从法律约束力的对象。对此，法宝版译文较为多样，包括“shall have binding force on”，如例句 7；“shall be effective against”，如例句 8；“shall be binding on”，如例句 9。总库版则统一译为“is binding on”，如例句 7—9。

当把某人排除在发生效力针对的对象之外时，条文中使用的结构为“对……不发生效力”，法宝版的译文包括“shall not be binding on”，如例句 10；“will have no effect on”，如例句 11；“shall be without effect against”，如例句 12。总库版统一译为“is not effective against”，如例句 10—12。

显然，这些涉及“对……(不)发生效力”结构的法条不属于义务条款，法宝版译文对情态动词 shall 的倾向实属对 shall 的滥用；总库版译文使用一般现在时，表示条文是一般性的法律规定，更为恰当。

在数据库中对两版译文中的各表达方式进行词频统计，可见，原生英语法律语料库中使用频率最高的为“be binding on”的肯定式和否定式；“have no effect on”也常用来表示某人不在效力针对的对象范围内。(见表12.3)

表 12.3 “对……(不)发生效力”的英文表达方式及检索频次

表达方式	国内	国外		
	香港法例库	英国立法库	美国联邦法规库	美国法典库
have binding force on	0	0	0	3
be binding on	148	＞200	669	77601
be effective against	1	31	17	3945

续表

表达方式	国内	国外		
	香港法例库	英国立法库	美国联邦法规库	美国法典库
be not binding on	4	80	76	24708
have no effect on	1	>200	0	21610
be not effective against	0	2	3	472
be without effect against	0	0	0	5

尽管"be effective against"的肯定式和否定式都有一定的使用频次，但该短语通常表达的是"具有对抗……的效力"，如：

"The assessment required by paragraph (1) shall include

(a)...

(b) the definition of the characteristics which personal protective equipment must have in order to be effective against the risks referred to in sub-paragraph (a), taking into account any risks which the equipment itself may create. [Personal Protective Equipment at Work Regulations (Northern Ireland) 1993]

"第(1)款要求的评估应包括

(a)……

(b)个人防护设备必须具备的特性的定义，以便**有效应对**第(a)项中提到的风险，同时考虑到设备本身可能造成的任何风险。[工作场所个人防护设备条例(北爱尔兰)1993]"

然而，汉语中"对……(不)发生效力"结构只是对"发生效力"的对象进行明确，效力和对象之间并非一定具有对抗性。因此，译文使用短语 be (not) effective against 并不合适。

12.3.2 "生效"结构在条文中作状语时的翻译

这种情况下，汉语法条通常表述为"自……生效时"和"……生效后"，两版译文都处理成 when 或 after 引导的状语从句,但是对于"生效"的翻译不同。法宝版译为"become valid",如例句 13—15;或"become effective",如例句 16。总库版译文包括例句 13 的"be effected"、例句 14 的"enter into force"、例句 15 的"enter into effect"、例句 16 的"become effective"。

根据《韦氏法律词典》,effect 作为动词,意思是"1. to cause to come into being; 2. to bring about often by surmounting obstacles; 3. to put into operation",并没有"发生效力"的意思,因此总库版例句 13 的译文当属误译。

我们已经检索过 become valid 和 become effective 的词频,后者在原生英语法律语料库中较为常用,此处追加检索 enter into effect 和 enter in force 的词频,结果显示 enter into force 更受青睐。(见表 12.4)

表 12.4 "生效"的英文表达方式及检索频次

表达方式	国内	国外		
	香港法例库	英国立法库	美国联邦法规库	美国法典库
enter in effect	0	25	4	637
enter into force	172	>200	7	6097

小　结

在《民法典》中,"发生效力"结构也会表述为"生效"结构,两者意思无差。"发生效力"或"生效"的主语通常是某个法律文件、合同、民事法律行为、权利或权利的设立、变更、转让等。多数情况下,该结构在条文中用作主要谓语,少数情况下,"生效"结构用作状语。用作主要谓语时,条文规定的不是"义务"规则,不需要使用 shall;作为一种法律规定,使用一般现在时即可。用作状语时,同样需要使用一般现在时。

"发生效力"或"生效"在英语中的对应表达方式呈现多样化,但是根据法律起草和法律翻译的“表达一致”原则，在同一文本中应当保留一种方式，避免使读者揣测不同词语的差别，从而影响法律条文的精确度和可操作性。考虑到译本的读者受众，应当尽量选择符合目的语读者表达习惯的方式。因此，根据原生英语法律语料库的检索结果，当该结构呈现为“……发生效力”“……自……时发生效力/生效”或“……生效后”时，优先使用的表达方式为“become effective”“take effect”或“enter into force”，否定式使用“not take effect”。当该结构为“对……（不）发生效力”时，优先使用“be binding on”的肯定式和否定式，另外，否定式也可以使用“have no effect on”。

13 “不能确定”结构的翻译

13.1 结构特点及其在《民法典》中的运用

13.1.1 结构特点

“不能确定”结构在法律文本中通常用于表明与前文内容有所不同的一种情况。如果前文是“可以确定”的情形，该结构可表明一种与之相对的“不能确定”的情形。如果前文内容是一种“不能确定”的情形，该结构也可表明另一种“不能确定”的情形。

13.1.2 在《民法典》中的运用

在《民法典》中该结构一共出现了28次，均与“……的”结构连用。多数情况表示被动意义，其逻辑主语暗含在前文中，如第603条规定：“当事人没有约定交付地点或者约定不明确，依据本法第五百一十条的规定仍不能确定的，适用下列规定。”“不能确定”指的是前文所说的“交付地点”不能（被）确定。少数情况下，“不能确定”的宾语紧随其后，如第309条规定：“按份共有人对共有的不动产或者动产享有的份额，没有约定或者约定不明确的，按照出资额确定；不能确定出资额的，视为等额享有。”

“不能确定”结构可分为两种情况：

（1）“……仍不能确定”

本结构在《民法典》中出现了25次。这种情况下，本结构与其前文的内容一般是递进关系。如第976条规定：“合伙人对合伙期限没有约定或者约定不明确，依据本法第五百一十条的规定仍不能确定的，视为不定期合伙。”相对于“……没有约定或者约定不明确”导致的不确定，与“依据本法第五百一十条的规定仍不能确定的”从意义上形成了递进关系。

(2)“……不能确定”

本结构中没有“仍”字，在《民法典》中共出现了 3 次，分别是第 309 条、第 842 条和第 1170 条。这种情况下，本结构相对独立，与本条中前文的内容是并列关系。如第 1170 条规定：“二人以上实施危及他人人身、财产安全的行为，其中一人或者数人的行为造成他人损害，能够确定具体侵权人的，由侵权人承担责任；不能确定具体侵权人的，行为人承担连带责任。”在该条中，“；”前后的两个部分是并列关系：前者是“确定具体侵权人的”情况，后者是“不能确定具体侵权人的”情况。

13.2 译文对比

表 13.1 《民法典》中“不能确定”结构的翻译对比

序号	出处(条)	原文	北大法宝译文(法宝版译文)	国家法规总库译文(总库版译文)
1	582	对违约责任没有约定或者约定不明确，依据本法第五百一十条的规定**仍不能确定的**，受损害方根据标的的性质以及损失的大小，可以合理选择请求对方承担修理、重作、更换、退货、减少价款或者报酬等违约责任。	Where there is no agreement in the contract on the liability for breach of contract or such agreement is not clear, **nor can it be determined** in accordance with the provisions of Article 510 of this Code, the aggrieved party may, in light of the nature of the subject matter and the degree of loss, reasonably choose to request the other party to bear the liability for breach of contract by repairing, remaking, replacing, returning the goods, reducing the price or remuneration, etc.	Where there is no agreement between the parties on the default liability or the relevant agreement is unclear, **and if it cannot be determined** according to the provisions of Article 510 of this Code, the aggrieved party may, by virtue of the nature of the object and according to the degree of the losses, reasonably request the other party to bear the default liability such as repair, redoing, replacement, return of the subject matter, decrease in price or remuneration, and the like.

续表

序号	出处（条）	原文	北大法宝译文（法宝版译文）	国家法规总库译文（总库版译文）
2	603	当事人没有约定交付地点或者约定不明确，依据本法第五百一十条的规定**仍不能确定的**，适用下列规定。	Where there is no agreement between the parties as to a place for delivery, or such agreement is not clear, **nor can it be determined** according to the provisions of Article 510 of this Code, the following provisions shall apply.	Where there is no agreement between the parties on the place of delivery or the relevant agreement is unclear, **if it cannot be determined** according to the provisions of Article 510 of this Code, the following provisions shall be applied.
3	675	对借款期限没有约定或者约定不明确，依据本法第五百一十条的规定**仍不能确定的**，借款人可以随时返还。	Where the loan term is not agreed or the agreement is not clear, **nor can it be determined** in accordance with Article 510 of this Code, the borrower may repay at any time.	Where there is no agreement between the parties on the time limit of repayment of the loan, or the relevant agreement is unclear, **if it cannot be determined** according to the provisions of Article 510 of this Code, the borrower may repay the loan at any time.
4	730	当事人对租赁期限没有约定或者约定不明确，依据本法第五百一十条的规定**仍不能确定的**，视为不定期租赁。	Where the term of a lease is not agreed or the agreement is not clear, **nor can it be determined** in accordance with Article 510 of this Code, such lease is deemed an indeterminate-term lease.	Where there is no agreement between the parties on the term of the lease, or the relevant agreement is unclear, **if it cannot be determined** according to the provisions of Article 510 of this Code, the lease is deemed a lease with an indefinite term.

续表

序号	出处（条）	原文	北大法宝译文（法宝版译文）	国家法规总库译文（总库版译文）
5	782	对支付报酬的期限没有约定或者约定不明确，依据本法第五百一十条的规定仍不能确定的，定作人应当在承揽人交付工作成果时支付。	Where the time limit of payment is not agreed or the agreement is not clear, nor can it be determined in accordance with Article 510 of this Code, the ordering party shall pay it at the time when the contractor delivers the work results.	Where there is no agreement between the parties on the time limit for paying remuneration or the relevant agreement is unclear, if it cannot be determined according to the provisions of Article 510 of this Code, the client shall make payment at the time of delivery of the work product.
6	861	没有约定或者约定不明确，依据本法第五百一十条的规定仍不能确定的，在没有相同技术方案被授予专利权前，当事人均有使用和转让的权利。	Where such matters are not agreed or the agreement is not clear, nor can they be determined in accordance Article 510 of this Code, each party is entitled to use and transfer the technology, before a patent is granted on the same technical solution.	Where there is no such an agreement between the parties or the relevant agreement is unclear, if it cannot be determined according to the provisions of Article 510 of this Code, all the parties have the right to use and transfer the said work product, as long as no patent right has been granted on a same technological solution.
7	976	合伙人对合伙期限没有约定或者约定不明确，依据本法第五百一十条的规定仍不能确定的，视为不定期合伙。	Where partners fail to agree or fail to clearly agree on the term of the partnership, and the term cannot be determined according to the provisions of Article 510 of this Code, the partnership shall be treated as being with an indeterminate term.	Where there is no agreement between or among the partners on the term of the partnership, or the relevant agreement is unclear, if the term cannot be determined according to the provisions of Article 510 of this Code, the partnership is deemed as a partnership with an indefinite term.

续表

序号	出处（条）	原文	北大法宝译文（法宝版译文）	国家法规总库译文（总库版译文）
8	309	按份共有人对共有的不动产或者动产享有的份额，没有约定或者约定不明确的，按照出资额确定；<u>**不能确定出资额的**</u>，视为等额享有。	Where the co-owners in divided co-ownership fail to agree on the shares of the co-owned immovable or movable or such an agreement is ambiguous, the shares shall be determined based on their amount of investment. <u>**If the amount of investment cannot be determined,**</u> it shall be deemed that they have equal shares.	The share of a co-owner by shares in the immovable or movable property shall be determined according to his capital contribution where there is no agreement or the relevant agreement is unclear. <u>**Where it is impossible to determine the amount of capital contribution,**</u> each co-owner by shares shall be entitled to an equal share.
9	842	货物的毁损、灭失发生于多式联运的某一运输区段的，多式联运经营人的赔偿责任和责任限额，适用调整该区段运输方式的有关法律规定；<u>**货物毁损、灭失发生的运输区段不能确定的**</u>，依照本章规定承担赔偿责任。	Where damage to or loss of the cargo occurred within a particular segment of the course of a multimodal carriage, the multimodal carriage operator's liability for damages and any limitation thereon are governed by the applicable transportation law of the jurisdiction which such segment is under. <u>**Where the segment in which the cargo is damaged or lost cannot be determined,**</u> the liability for compensation shall be borne in accordance with the provisions of this Chapter.	Where destruction, damage, or loss of goods occurs in one section of the multi-modal transport, the provisions of the relevant laws regulating the transport modes of the section shall apply to the liability for compensation to be assumed by the operator of multi-modal transport and the limit of the liability. <u>**Where the section of transport in which such destruction, damage, or loss has occurred cannot be determined,**</u> liability for compensation shall be borne in accordance with the provisions of this Chapter.

续表

序号	出处（条）	原文	北大法宝译文（法宝版译文）	国家法规总库译文（总库版译文）
10	1170	二人以上实施危及他人人身、财产安全的行为，其中一人或者数人的行为造成他人损害，能够确定具体侵权人的，由侵权人承担责任；<u>不能确定具体侵权人的</u>，行为人承担连带责任。	Where two or more persons engage in conduct that endangers the personal or property safety of another person, if only the conduct of one or several of them causes harm to another person and the specific tortfeasor can be determined, the tortfeasor shall be liable; <u>or if the specific tortfeasor cannot be determined</u>, all of them shall be liable jointly and severally.	Where two or more persons commit acts that endanger another person's personal or property safety and the damage is caused only by acts of one or several of them, if the specific tortfeasor(s) can be identified, the tortfeasor(s) shall bear liability, <u>and if the specific tortfeasor(s) cannot be identified</u>, all of the actors shall assume joint and several liability.

13.3 译文分析

我们针对《民法典》中"不能确定"结构的两种运用情况，分别对比分析两个版本的对应译文，同时探讨更为可取的翻译方法。

13.3.1 "……仍不能确定"结构的翻译

法宝版译文中，在多数情况下，如例句 1—6，这一结构译为"…，nor can it be determined"。有些情况下，如例句 7，受到前半句结构的影响，该结构译为"...can not be determined"，可看作"…，nor can it be determined"的变通用法。

总库版译文中，在多数情况下，如例句 2—7，这一结构译为"…，if…cannot be determined"。在有些情况下，如例句 1，译为"…，and if it cannot be determined"。

基于对于“……仍不能确定”结构在《民法典》中的运用情况分析，本结构与前面的部分不是简单的并列关系而是递进关系。如果把该结构译为“...，nor can it be determined”或者“...， and if it cannot be determined”，虽然也可解释为二者含有递进的意义，但很容易让读者理解为二者是并列关系。如果把该结构译为“...， if it cannot be determined”，表明该结构是在前文条件之下的第二个层次上的条件，更明确地表明两部分内容是递进关系，因此，更为可取。

13.3.2 “……不能确定”结构的翻译

在例句 8、例句 9、例句 10 中，“……不能确定”结构在原文中都是一个并列分句，用“；”与前面的部分分开。但是，例句 8、例句 9 与例句 10 不同。在例句 8、例句 9 中，该结构与本句前面的全部内容是并列关系，而在例句 10 中，该结构是在一个母条件下，与前面一部分形成并列关系。两个译本都体现出了这一差别。在例句 8、例句 9 的译文中，两个译本都将本结构译为一个独立的句子；而在例句 10 的译文中，两个译本都译为与前一个 if 从句并列的从句。

在例句 8 中，“……不能确定”结构的法宝版译文使用了连词“If”，而译文句首用的是“where”，看似不能准确体现本结构与前面的部分的并列关系，改为“Where”更好。但是，还需要进一步分析例句 8 原文中的逻辑关系。实际上，“；”前后两个部分并不是完全并列的，其后面的部分省略了一个母条件，即“按份共有人对共有的不动产或者动产享有的份额，没有约定或者约定不明确的”。如果将“；”之后的部分翻译成独立的句子，用 If 更好。对此，李克兴（2013）对 “Where-句”与“If-句”作了对比研究，认为：以 where 为段首（并非句首）引导词的复杂条件句中，where 引导母条件，其后可跟多个 If/if 引导的子条件句，子条件句须受母条件句的统辖。基于同样的原因，总库版对该条的译文，第一句，将“where”从句置于段首，并将第二句开头的“Where”改为“if”更好。当然，也可以将本条内容翻译成一个长句，使用“Where...， if...， and if...”结构。

在例句 10 原文中，因为本结构与前文是并列而非选择关系，总库版译文“and if”比法宝版译文“or if”更为可取；又因为本结构是与前面的一小部分而非整个部分并列，与前一部分之间的标点符号，总库版译文用“,”，比法宝版译文“;”更为可取。在例句 10 中，“……不能确定”结构的法宝版译文使用的动词“determine”，而总库版译文使用的是“identify”。根据《布莱克法律词典》，identify 指 to prove the identity of (a person or thing)。例句 10 表达的意义是：“不能确定”谁是具体侵权人，意义有差别。首先在词义范围上，determine 指 to discover the facts about sth.; to calculate sth. exactly，“确定”的方法可以包括调查、测量、计算等多种手段；而 identify 多用于“确认”某人的身份或某样东西，如：The witness identified the weapon。可见，determine 适用的情形更广。此外，在四大数据库中检索两词的使用频次和情境，也验证了我们的结论。(见表 13.2)“determine”的出现频次比较高；除美国法典外，其被动形式更为常用；identify 的宾语多为某(类)人。因此 determine 更适合用作汉语语境中“确定”一词的普适性翻译。

表 13.2 “……不能确定”的英文表达方式及检索频次

表达方式	国内	国外		
	香港法例库	英国立法库	美国联邦法规库	美国法典库
cannot be determined	49	>200	249	22620
cannot determine	3	72	123	36623
cannot be identified	13	>200	97	5071
cannot identify	2	44	44	9867

小 结

在《民法典》中，“不能确定”结构一般与“的”字结构连用，表示条件，动词“确定”多有被动意义，有两种情况。一是“……仍不能确定”结构，表示递进关系，可译为“..., if...cannot be determined...”。二是“……不能确定”结构，表示并列关系，如果与所在句子前面的整个部分并列，可将本结构及后面的部分翻译成独立的句子，译为“Where...cannot be determined...”；如果在一个母条件下，与前面的部分内容并列，可翻译为并列分句，译为“..., and if...cannot be determined...”。这一结构，根据具体语境适当调整词语和语序后，可用主动语态翻译。

14 “另有规定”结构的翻译

14.1 结构特点及其在《民法典》中的运用

14.1.1 结构特点

法律用语中的“另有规定”是指在某个法律、法规、合同或其他具有法律约束力的文件中明确指出，在所说法律条款之外还有其他法律条款对同一事项作出规定。它表示在特定情况下，适用的规定与通常情况下的规定不同或有所变化。“另有规定”的主语通常为法律、法规；如果主语是合同或当事人，则使用“另有约定”。

14.1.2 在《民法典》中的运用

“另有规定”或“另有约定”在《民法典》中一般与“的”字连用，写为“另有规定的”或“另有约定的”，表示条件或情形。通常本结构与“但是……除外”或“除……外”结构连用，在《民法典》共计出现 87 次。此种情况下，本结构依附主条款而存在，又对主条款进行限制性否定（邢伟星，2022）。如第 136 条规定，“民事法律行为自成立时生效，**但是**法律**另有规定**或者当事人**另有约定的除外**”，其中“民事法律行为自成立时生效”是作为一般规定的主条款，“但是法律另有规定或者当事人另有约定的除外”是对主条款的限制性否定。又如第 87 条规定：“事业单位法人设理事会的，**除法律另有**

规定外，理事会为其决策机构。”“事业单位法人设理事会的，理事会为其决策机构”是主条款，“除法律另有规定外”是对主条款的补充说明。

少数情况下，呈现的句式为“……另有规定的，依照其规定”和“……另有约定的，按照其约定”。尽管在形式上没有“但是”或者“除外”等字眼，在内容上仍然是针对法条中的一般规定作出例外、限制、附加等特殊规定。具体可分为两种情况：

（1）“另有规定/约定”句式紧密依附于主条款语句

这种情况共计出现24次。主条款语句在前，对某一事项进行原则性、普适性规定，“另有规定/约定”句式紧随其后，在限制否定主条款的基础上，将该事项的适用规范引致其他法律、法规或约定。这种情况与“但是……除外”“除……外”结构连用的情况，在意思上一般无二。

“另有规定”的主语通常为法律、法规，如第70条规定：“法人的董事、理事等执行机构或者决策机构的成员为清算义务人。**法律、行政法规另有规定的，依照其规定**。”如果将“法律、行政法规另有规定的，依照其规定”改为“但是法律、行政法规另有规定的除外”，意思没有任何差异。

“另有约定”的主语通常为“当事人”，如第389条规定：“担保物权的担保范围包括主债权及其利息、违约金、损害赔偿金、保管担保财产和实现担保物权的费用。**当事人另有约定的，按照其约定**。”同样，“当事人另有约定的，按照其约定”可以改为“但是当事人另有约定的除外”。

（2）“另有规定/约定”句式独立于主条款语句

此种情况较少，共计出现5次，主要标志为用“对”字引出“另有规定”或“另有约定”的规范事项，即主条款指向的同一事项，因此可相对独立于主条款，既可以紧跟主条款之后，也有时呈现为一个独立条款，或某条款中的独立一款。如第833条规定：“货物的毁损、灭失的赔偿额，当事人有约定的，按照其约定；没有约定或者约定不明确，依据本法第五百一十条的规定仍不能确定的，按照交付或者应当交付时货物到达地的市场价格计算。**法律、行政法规对赔偿额的计算方法和赔偿限额另有规定的，依照其规定**。”其中，第一个句号之前是主条款，指向的事项为货损赔偿额的确定，该句号之后,"法律、行政法规对赔偿额的计算方法和赔偿限额另有规定的,依照其规定"中,用"对"字引出"另有规定"的规范事项——"赔偿额的计算方法和赔偿限额",这与主条款的指向事项为同一事项。又如"电子合同当事人**对交付商品或者提供服务的方式、时间**另有约定的,按照其约定",是第512条的第三款规定,其对主条款的依附并不紧密。

14.2 译文对比

表 14.1 《民法典》中"另有规定"结构的翻译对比

序号	出处(条)	原文	北大法宝译文(法宝版译文)	国家法规总库译文(总库版译文)
1	204	期间的计算方法依照本法的规定,但是法律另有规定或者当事人另有约定的除外。	Time periods shall be calculated in methods specified by this Code, except as otherwise provided for by any law or agreed upon by the parties.	The counting of a time period shall be governed by the provisions of this Code, unless otherwise provided by law or agreed by the parties.
2	604	标的物毁损、灭失的风险,在标的物交付之前由出卖人承担,交付之后由买受人承担,但是法律另有规定或者当事人另有约定的除外。	The risk of damage to or loss of a subject matter shall be borne by the seller prior to the delivery of the subject matter and by the buyer after delivery, except as otherwise stipulated by law or agreed upon by the parties.	The risks of destruction, damage, or loss of the subject matter shall be borne by the seller prior to the delivery and by the buyer after the delivery, unless otherwise provided by law or agreed by the parties.

续表

序号	出处(条)	原文	北大法宝译文(法宝版译文)	国家法规总库译文(总库版译文)
3	1016	自然人决定、变更姓名,或者法人、非法人组织决定、变更、转让名称的,应当依法向有关机关办理登记手续,<u>但是法律另有规定的除外</u>。	A natural person deciding or changing his own name, or a legal person or unincorporated organization deciding, changing, or transferring its own name shall undergo the registration formalities with the relevant authority according to the law, <u>except as otherwise prescribed by law</u>.	A natural person who decides to take or change his name, or a legal person or an unincorporated organization who decides to take, change, or transfer its entity name, shall file registration with the relevant authorities in accordance with law, <u>unless otherwise provided by law</u>.
4	590	当事人一方因不可抗力不能履行合同的,根据不可抗力的影响,部分或者全部免除责任,<u>但是法律另有规定的除外</u>。	Where a party is unable to perform the contract due to a force majeure, the party shall be exempt from liability in part or in whole based on the impact of force majeure, <u>except as otherwise provided by the law</u>.	Where a party is unable to perform the contract due to force majeure, it shall be exempted from liability in whole or in part according to the impact of the force majeure, <u>unless otherwise provided by law</u>.
5	720	在租赁期限内因占有、使用租赁物获得的收益,归承租人所有,<u>但是当事人另有约定的除外</u>。	During the lease term, any benefit accrued from the possession or use of the leased property belongs to the lessee, <u>except otherwise agreed by the parties</u>.	Any proceeds accrued from the possession or use of the leased object during the term of the lease shall belong to the lessee, <u>unless otherwise provided by the parties</u>.

续表

序号	出处（条）	原文	北大法宝译文（法宝版译文）	国家法规总库译文（总库版译文）
6	491	当事人一方通过互联网等信息网络发布的商品或者服务信息符合要约条件的，对方选择该商品或者服务并提交订单成功时合同成立，**但是当事人另有约定的除外**。	If the information on goods or service released by one party on an information network such as the Internet meets the conditions for an offer, the contract is formed when the other party selects the goods or service and successfully submits the order, **unless the parties agree otherwise**.	Where the information about goods or services published by a party via information network, such as internet, satisfies the conditions for an offer, **unless otherwise agreed by the parties**, a contract is formed at the time when the other party selects such product or service and successfully submits the order.
7	888	寄存人到保管人处从事购物、就餐、住宿等活动，将物品存放在指定场所的，视为保管，**但是当事人另有约定**或者另有交易习惯**的除外**。	If a depositor engages in activities such as shopping, dining, and accommodation at the depositary and deposit its property in the designated place, deposit shall be treated as taking place, **subject to the agreement between the parties** or usage of trade.	Where a depositor conducts shopping, dining, lodging, or other activities in the custodian's place and deposits an article at a designated area, the article is deemed to be placed under the custodian's custody **unless otherwise agreed by the parties** or required by the course of dealing.
8	977	合伙人死亡、丧失民事行为能力或者终止的，合伙合同终止；**但是，合伙合同另有约定**或者根据合伙事务的性质不宜终止**的除外**。	Where a partner is deceased, incapacitated, or terminated, the contract of partnership is terminated, **unless the contract of partnership otherwise stipulates**, or the termination is inappropriate based on the nature of partnership business.	Where a partner dies, loses capacity for performing civil juristic acts, or is terminated, the partnership contract is terminated, **unless otherwise provided in the partnership contract** or it is inappropriate to terminate the contract due to the nature of the partnership affairs.

续表

序号	出处（条）	原文	北大法宝译文（法宝版译文）	国家法规总库译文（总库版译文）
9	199	法律规定或者当事人约定的撤销权、解除权等权利的存续期间，**除法律另有规定外**，自权利人知道或者应当知道权利产生之日起计算，不适用有关诉讼时效中止、中断和延长的规定。	**Except as otherwise provided for by any law**, the duration of rights such as the right of revocation and the right of rescission as granted by laws or agreed upon by the parties shall be calculated from the day when a right holder knows or should have known that such a right has arisen, and the provisions on the suspension, interruption, and extension of extinctive prescription shall not apply to the above duration.	The time period within which a right holder may exercise certain rights, such as the right to revocation and the right to rescission, which are provided by law or agreed by the parties shall begin, **unless otherwise provided by law**, from the date when the right holder knows or should have known that he has such a right, and the provisions on the suspension, interruption, or extension of the limitation period are not be applicable.
10	188	向人民法院请求保护民事权利的诉讼时效期间为三年。**法律另有规定的，依照其规定**。 诉讼时效期间自权利人知道或者应当知道权利受到损害以及义务人之日起计算。**法律另有规定的，依照其规定**……	An action instituted in a people's court for protection of civil rights is prescribed by three years, **except as otherwise prescribed by any law**. The prescriptive period shall be calculated from the day when the obligee knows or should have known that his or her right has been infringed upon and who the obligor is, **except as otherwise provided for by any law** ...	The limitation period for a person to request the people's court to protect his civil-law rights is three years, **unless otherwise provided by law**. **Unless otherwise provided by law**, the limitation period begins from the date when the right holder knows or should have known that his right has been harmed and that who is the obligor ...

续表

序号	出处(条)	原文	北大法宝译文(法宝版译文)	国家法规总库译文(总库版译文)
11	441	以汇票、本票、支票、债券、存款单、仓单、提单出质的,质权自权利凭证交付质权人时设立;没有权利凭证的,质权自办理出质登记时设立。**法律另有规定的,依照其规定**。	Where a bill of exchange, promissory note, check, bond, certificate of deposit, warehouse receipt or bill of lading is pledged, pledge is created at the time when the right certificate is delivered to the pledgee; in the absence of such a right certificate, pledge is created at the time when pledge is registered, except as otherwise provided for by any law.	Unless otherwise provided by law, a pledge on a bill of exchange, promissory note, check, bond, certificate of deposits, warehouse receipt, or bill of lading is created at the time when the certificate of such a right is delivered to the pledgee, or, in the absence of such a certificate, at the time when the pledge is registered.
12	835	货物在运输过程中因不可抗力灭失,未收取运费的,承运人不得请求支付运费;已经收取运费的,托运人可以请求返还。**法律另有规定的,依照其规定**。	Where the cargoes are lost in the course of carriage due to force majeure, if the freight has not been collected, the carrier may not request the payment thereof; if the freight has been collected, the consignor may request the refund of the freight, except as otherwise provided by the law.	Where the goods are lost in the course of transport due to force majeure, unless otherwise provided by law, the carrier may not request the payment of the freight if the freight has not yet been paid, and the consignor may request for a refund if the freight has already been paid.
13	321	天然孳息,由所有权人取得;既有所有权人又有用益物权人的,由用益物权人取得。**当事人另有约定的,按照其约定**。	Natural fruits shall be obtained by the owner; if there are both the owner and the usufructuary, natural fruits shall be obtained by the usufructuary. If it is otherwise agreed upon by the parties, their agreement shall prevail.	Unless otherwise agreed by the parties, the natural fruits of a thing shall be acquired by the owner of the thing, or by a usufructuary if there are both an owner and a usufructuary of the thing.

续表

序号	出处（条）	原文	北大法宝译文（法宝版译文）	国家法规总库译文（总库版译文）
14	492	采用数据电文形式订立合同的，收件人的主营业地为合同成立的地点；没有主营业地的，其住所地为合同成立的地点。**当事人另有约定的，按照其约定**。	In the case of contracting in the form of a data message, the place of formation of the contract shall be the main business place of the recipient, or absent a main business place, the place of its domicile, unless the parties agree otherwise.	Where a contract is concluded in the form of data message, unless otherwise agreed by the parties, the recipient's principal place of business is the place where the contract is formed; in the absence of a principal place of business, the recipient's domicile is the place where the contract is formed.
15	691	保证的范围包括主债权及其利息、违约金、损害赔偿金和实现债权的费用。**当事人另有约定的，按照其约定**。	The scope of suretyship covers the principal obligation and its interest, liquidated damages, damages, and the cost of realizing the obligation, unless otherwise agreed by the parties.	The scope of suretyship covers the principal claim and the interest thereof, the liquidated damages, compensatory damages, and the expenses for enforcing the claim, unless otherwise agreed by the parties.
16	833	**……法律、行政法规对**赔偿额的计算方法和赔偿限额**另有规定的，依照其规定**。	...Where a law or administrative regulation provides otherwise for the measures for the calculation of damages and of the ceiling of the amount of damages, these provisions shall be applied.	... If there are laws or administrative regulations providing otherwise concerning the calculation method and the limit of the compensation amount, such provisions shall be followed.

续表

序号	出处（条）	原文	北大法宝译文（法宝版译文）	国家法规总库译文（总库版译文）
17	877	法律、行政法规对技术进出口合同或者专利、专利申请合同另有规定的，依照其规定。	Where the relevant laws or administrative regulations provide otherwise in respect of technology import or export contracts or in respect of patent contracts or contracts for patent application, such provisions shall prevail.	Where there are laws or administrative regulations providing otherwise on contracts for technology import and export, or on contracts for patents and application of patents, the relevant provisions shall be followed.
18	137	……当事人对采用数据电文形式的意思表示的生效时间另有约定的，按照其约定。	... If the parties have otherwise agreed upon the time when a declaration of will made in the form of data message becomes valid, such an agreement shall apply.	... Where the parties have agreed otherwise on the effective time of the expression of intent made in the form of an electronic data message, such an agreement shall prevail.
19	512	电子合同当事人对交付商品或者提供服务的方式、时间另有约定的，按照其约定。	If the parties to an electronic contract otherwise agree on the method and time of delivering goods or providing services, such agreement shall prevail.	Where the parties to the said electronic contract agree otherwise on the mode and time of delivery of goods or provision of services, such an agreement shall be complied with.

14.3 译文分析

以下，通过对比两个版本中“另有规定（约定）”结构的对应译文，分析探讨更为可取的翻译方法。

14.3.1 与“但是……除外”或“除……外”结构连用时的翻译

关于标志词“但是……除外”“除……外”的翻译：法宝版较多使用的英语结构为“except as＋过去分词”（如例句1—4、例句9），其他还有少量“except＋过去分词”结构（如例句5）、unless从句（如例句6和例句8），以及“subject to＋名词”结构（如例句7）。总库版则统一使用省略了“it is”的unless从句（如例句1—9）。

关于法律“有规定”的翻译：法宝版通常翻译为provided for by any law（如例句1、例句9），此外还有stipulated by law（如例句2）、prescribed by law（如例句3）、provided by the law（如例句4）。总库版一般译为provided by law（如例句1—4、例句9）。

关于当事人/合同“有约定”的翻译：法宝版通常译为agreed upon by the parties（如例句1—2），此外还有agreed by the parties（如例句5）、the parties agree（如例句6）、the agreement between the parties（如例句7）、the contract...stipulates（如例句8）。总库版通常译为agreed by the parties（如例句1、例句2、例句6、例句7），个别译为provided by the parties（如例句5）、provided in the contract（如例句8）。

第一，关于标志词“但是……除外”“除……外”的翻译。除了法宝版例句5的“except＋过去分词”结构外，其他句式结构选择都合乎语法规范，都是常见的法律英语结构。“except as otherwise provided/agreed...”可以解构为except（介词）＋[as（关系副词）＋过去分词]（关系副词引导的介词短语），整个结构作为状语，修饰主条款语句，说明在什么情况下不适用主条款的一般性规定。“unless [illegible]条件状语从句，“unless otherwise provided/agreed...”省略了“it is”，表示“除……另有……外”，在法律文件中非常常见，用于确保条款的灵活性和适应性，允许法律对某些事项有优先权或例外规定。

但是，except通常后跟完整、明确的表达，以便明确指代特定情境或条件，法宝版例句5使用“except otherwise agreed...”虽然能够传达基本意思,但不是最佳选择,因为没有"as"强调特殊情况下的约定,读者可能会心存疑问:"otherwise"是指什么?在什么情况下被认为是"另有约定"?

subject to 表示受某些条件、协议或法规的约束,适用于表明条款的依赖性或受约束的情况,法宝版例句 7 译文"subject to the agreement between the parties or usage of trade"应当译为"依照双方约定或贸易惯例"。也就是说,遵循双方约定或贸易惯例是主条款规定实施的前提,意思严重偏离原文。

第二,关于法律"有规定"的翻译。provide、prescribe 和 stipulate 这三个动词虽然都有"规定"的意思,但 provide 侧重于"提供、给予"某种规定或条款,prescribe 注重强制性的法律规定,stipulate 更强调在合同或协议中的明确约定。原文"法律另有规定"只是指出了"另有规定"的存在状态,并未强调规定的"强制性",因此 provide 更具普适性。

"provided by (the) law"和"provided for by (any) law"都可用于表示法律对某项内容的规定,但在用法和侧重点上也略有不同:"provided by law"强调法律对某项内容的一般性规定或要求,具有不特定的广泛性,适用于需要强调法律对某项内容**有**规定的情况;"provided by **the** law" 更强调**某项具体法律**的要求或规定,通常后面有限定成分,比如,The fee can be set in any manner **provided by the law of the State in which such EFS is filed**.(§205.205 Fees. Code of Federal Regulation);"provided for by law" 强调法律对某项内容的详细安排或具体规定,适用于需要突出法律对某项内容有**明确安排或具体规定**的情况;而"provided for by **any** law" 更强调任何法律或法规中对特定事项的特别规定,适用于需要明确指出**任何**法律或法规中可能存在的**例外情况或特别规定**。可见除"provided by the law"外,其他三种措辞的差别并不大,均为可取选择,译文的不同主要反映了译者表述的侧重点稍有不同。

为进一步区分,可以考察原生法律英语数据库中相关搭配的词频,结果如表 14.2 和表 14.3 所示。

表 14.2 “法律有规定”的英文表达方式及检索频次

表达方式	国内	国外		
	香港法例库	英国立法库	美国联邦法规库	美国法典库
provided by law	8	56	536	77759
provided for by law	3	45	45	8825
provided by any law	0	9	0	148
provided for by any law	0	0	0	155

表 14.3 “法律另有规定”的英文表达方式及检索频次

表达方式	国内	国外		
	香港法例库	英国立法库	美国联邦法规库	美国法典库
unless otherwise provided by law	0	5	51	2372
except as otherwise provided by law	0	1	112	8110
except otherwise provide by law	0	0	0	0
except as otherwise provided for by any law	0	0	0	0
except otherwise provided (by/in+具体法律法规)	1	6	1	76
except as otherwise provided (by/in+具体法律法规)	129	>200	3014	65963
unless otherwise provided (by/in+具体法律法规)	49	>200	859	15837

如表 1 所示，在英美原生法律语料库中，“provided by law”的使用频次最高，表述更侧重强调法律对某项内容<u>有</u>规定。此外，“provided by any law”是在语料库中检索时发现的新表达方式，但频次并不高，列于表中，以供参考。

如表2所示,当"另有规定"的主语为某种具体的法律法规时,"except as otherwise provided (by/in+具体法律法规)"和"unless otherwise provided (by/in+具体法律法规)"都是高频法律英语表达方式,其中前者频次更高;当"另有规定"的主语为非具体法律法规时,香港和英国法律语料库中鲜见此种表述,而美国法律语料库中,"unless otherwise provided by law"和"except as otherwise provided by law"两者均可,但后者频次更高。

由此可见,在英美原生法律语料库中,"但是法律另有规定的除外""除法律另有规定外"的高频对应表达方式为"except as otherwise provided by law"。

第三,关于当事人/合同"有约定"的翻译。在原生英语法律语料库中,如表14.4所示,"agreed upon by the parties"与"agreed by the parties"均较为常见,只不过美国法律文本更倾向于使用前者,而香港和英国法律文本更倾向于后者。但在unless从句中,"agreed upon by the parties"出现的频次相对较低。根据二项式检验(Binomial test)[①],"unless otherwise agreed by the parties"的词频显著高于"unless the parties agree otherwise"($p \approx 0.0000$, $p < 0.05$)。另外,对于"但是当事人另有约定的除外",使用unless从句的频率远高于使用except介词短语作状语。因此,"但是当事人另有约定的除外"或"除当事人另有约定外"可以译为"unless otherwise agreed by the parties"。

表14.4 "当事人有约定"的英文表达方式及检索频次

表达方式	国内	国外		
	香港法例库	英国立法库	美国联邦法规库	美国法典库
agreed upon by the parties	15	58	115	11400
agreed by the parties	41	>200	50	4833
unless otherwise agreed upon by the parties	0	0	7	388

① 二项式检验用于检验一个变量的两个类别之间的比例是否显著不同,如果 $p < 0.05$,则存在显著差异。

续表

表达方式	国内	国外		
	香港法例库	英国立法库	美国联邦法规库	美国法典库
unless otherwise agreed by the parties	38	>200	35	3620
unless the parties agree otherwise	2	73	28	1089
except as otherwise agreed upon by the parties	0	0	2	15
except as otherwise agreed by the parties	0	1	3	194

当“有约定”的主语为“合同”时，“合同”并非“约定”的动作发出者，而是“约定”的载体。原生英语法律语料库的词频检索显示(见表 14.5)，香港法例库中的数据可以忽略不计，英国法律中“agreed in the contract”的词频最高，但是根据二项式检验，其词频与“stipulated in the contract”($p\approx0.1146$)和“provided by the contract”($p\approx0.0584$)没有存在显著差异，但显著高于“provided in the contract”($p\approx0.0027$)。而美国法律中更倾向于使用“provided in the contract”，根据二项式检验，美国法典中“provided in the contract”的词频均显著高于其他表达方式($p<0.05$)。

表 14.5 “合同有约定”的英文表达方式及检索频次

表达方式	国内	国外		
	香港法例库	英国立法库	美国联邦法规库	美国法典库
provided by the contract	3	14	8	706
provided in the contract	0	13	60	2897
stipulated by the contract	0	6	0	70
stipulated in the contract	2	18	6	1292
agreed in the contract	0	26	1	199

综上,“但是合同另有约定的除外”或“除合同另有约定外”既可以译为“unless otherwise agreed in the contract”,也可以译为“unless otherwise provided in the contract”,两种表达方式在英美法律语料库中都有出现,只是不同国家倾向不同。另外,需注意同一译本应使用统一措辞。

此外,“但是……另有……除外”和“除……另有……外”尽管句式意思相近,但在语气上似乎存在差别。前者用转折词“但是”引出“另有”这一例外情况,使例外情况的语气更显突出;后者则侧重于强调一般规则,给人一种先立规矩,再提例外的感觉。例句 9 中,法宝版译文将“除法律另有规定外”置于句首,似乎在强调例外情况,与原文语气不符。建议当原文出现“除……另有……外”句式时,英语译文应根据行文,将其置于句中或句末,以突出一般规则。

14.3.2 “另有规定/约定”句式紧密依附于主条款语句

(1)“法律另有规定的,依照其规定”的翻译

本句式在形式上独立成句,但在意思上无法脱离主条款语句的语境,翻译中两个译本都将其处理为主条款语句的附属成分,汉语意思相当于“但是……另有规定的除外”。其中,法宝版通常使用 except as otherwise provided for by any law,置于句末,如例句 10—11,例句 12 译为“except as otherwise provided by the law”;总库版译文倾向于使用 unless otherwise provided by law,有时置于句末,如例句 10(第一款),有时置于句首,如例句 10(第二款)和例句 11,还有时置于句中,如例句 12。

根据前文对“但是法律另有规定的除外”译文的分析,可以借鉴国际法律语言惯例,统一译为“except as otherwise provided by law”。如果译为“unless otherwise provided by law”,也无不可,但需注意,同一版本必须保持统一措辞。另外,unless 从句放置的位置也应慎重考虑。一般而言,英语句式重心在前,即用主句表述重要信息,而将从句置于主句之后,提供次要信息。总库版例句 10 第二款中,将 unless 从句置于句首,强调意味甚浓,但此款的主要信息应为主条款的内容,即对诉讼时效期间计算的一般

规定,“法律另有规定”只是特殊情况,因此放在句末作补充说明更为合适。

总库版例句 11 中 unless 从句同样在句首,却很合适,因为此处主条款的一般规定分为两种情况:有权利凭证和没有权利凭证。如果 unless 从句放在句末,有可能导致理解歧义,读者可能会认为“法律另有规定”的特殊情况针对的只是没有权利凭证的规定。总库版例句 12 出于同样的考虑,将 unless 从句置于句中,避免了对主条款规定的两种情况“顾此失彼”。

(2)“当事人另有约定的,按照其约定”的翻译

法宝版译文出现三种表达方式:“If it is otherwise agreed upon by the parties, their agreement shall prevail”,如例句 13;“unless the parties agree otherwise”,如例句 14;“unless otherwise agreed by the parties”,如例句 15。总库版译文较统一,一般译为“unless otherwise agreed by the parties”,见例句 13—15。

本句式与“法律另有规定的,依照其规定”一样,在形式上独立成句,但在意思上无法脱离主条款语句的语境。如果译为独立句,如法宝版例句 13,固然无妨,但相较之下,译为 unless 引导的条件从句,语言简洁,结构紧凑,更符合简明法律英语的要求。

结合前文分析,“当事人另有约定的,按照其约定”句式可以译为“unless otherwise agreed by the parties”。如果原文主条款规定的内容单一,只涉及一种情况,建议将 unless 从句放在句末,如总库版例句 15;如果主条款涉及多种情况,可酌情将 unless 从句置于句首(如总库版例句 13)或句中(如总库版例句 14),以避免读者产生误解。

14.3.3 “另有规定/约定”句式独立于主条款语句

此种情况下,两个版本均译为独立句,将“……对……另有规定/约定的”译为条件从句,“依照其规定”和“按照其约定”译为主句,是为可取方法。

对于“……对……另有规定的”,法宝版通常译为“Where ... provide(s) otherwise for/ in respect of ...”,如例句 16—17。总库版有时译为“If there are ... providing otherwise concerning ...”，如例句16；有时译为“Where there are ... providing otherwise on ...”，如例句17。对于“……对……另有约定的”，如例句18—19，法宝版通常译为“If the parties otherwise agree upon/on ...”；总库版通常译为“Where the parties agree otherwise on ...”。

比较两版译文，差别主要表现在：(1)条件句的引导词使用where还是if；(2)如何翻译介词“对”。

根据李克兴(2013:89)对where和if的辨析，where主要引导充分法律条件句，if引导依赖语境条件句。尽管此种情况下，“……对……另有规定的，……”句式独立于主条款语句，但还构不成充分法律条件句，比如例句16中提到的“赔偿额的计算方法和赔偿限额”，这是针对什么情况的赔偿额？对此的一般性规定是什么？不依赖前文就无法获知。故此，用if作引导词更可取。总库版例句16译文使用的there be句型强调“存在”法律或行政法规，清楚地表明了条件，语言自然流畅，更契合法律文本的严谨性和逻辑性。同理，“……对……另有约定的，……”句式也无法构成充分法律条件句，无论是例句18还是例句19，不依赖前文，读者因为不明了前文所提的一般性规定，都会对“另有约定”不知所云。因此法宝版译文使用的if-条件句更可取。

至于介词“对”的翻译，在“……对……另有规定的”中，译为in respect of(如法宝版例句17)较为合适。首先，in respect of是法律英语中常用的短语，符合法律语言的专业性和严谨性；其次，in respect of能够明确地指向特定的内容或方面，强调法律条款或规定所涉及的具体领域或事项，有助于避免歧义和误解，确保法律文本的准确性和可操作性。而for(法宝版例句16)与provide搭配，在逻辑连贯性上稍弱一些，没有in respect of具有的强调“关于……方面”的效果；concerning(总库版例句16)和on(总库版例句17)虽也能表达“关于”的意思，但多用于日常英语，在某些情况下，存在语义的潜在模糊性，且缺少in respect of的正式度和专业性。

在“……对……另有约定的”中，agree on和agree upon在意思上基本相同，前者更自然、简洁，后者更正式，但也略显过时。尽管两者均是法律英语高频用词,agree on 更符合简明法律英语的发展趋势。对原生英语法律语料库的检索结果也验证了此分析,见表 14.6。

表 14.6 “对……有约定”的英文表达方式及检索频次

表达方式	国内	国外		
	香港法例库	英国立法库	美国联邦法规库	美国法典库
agree on	75	>200	400	93193
agree upon	10	>200	215	40788

对于主句“依照其规定”和“按照其约定”,法宝版分别译为“these provisions shall be applied”(例句 16),“such provisions shall prevail”(例句 17),“such an agreement shall apply”(例句 18),“such agreement shall prevail”(例句 19)。总库版则译为“such provisions shall be followed”(例句 16),“the relevant provisions shall be followed”(例句 17),“such an agreement shall prevail”(例句 18),“such an agreement shall be complied with”(例句 19)。

关于“其规定”的翻译,“the relevant provisions”更强调这些规定与特定情境直接相关,表述较为传统和正式;而“such provisions”指代前面提到的规定,语气正式,在某种程度上更加直接和简洁,在清晰度上稍占优势。此外,作为限定词,such 和 these 也略有差别:“such provisions” 显得更正式,指代上文提到的“相关规定”。这种用法在法律文书中比较常见,能有效地强调和确认已经提到的内容。“these provisions” 相对口语化,虽然表达意思清楚,但在法律语境下可能显得不够专业。

关于“其约定”的翻译,译为“such agreement”较为合适,因为“such an agreement”适用于强调某个具体的约定实例,而“such agreement”适用于泛指此类约定。《民法典》作为基本法律,“在内容上表现为以规定指导思想或基础准则的方式对具体法律规则作原则性、普适性表述”(邢伟星,2022:100)。因此“另有约定”涉及的约定并非特别明确和具体,翻译为

“such agreement”普适性更强。原生英语法律语料库中,“agreement”作为不可数名词的形式通常更为常见。(见表 14.7)

表 14.7 “其约定”的英文表达方式及检索频次

表达方式	国内	国外		
	香港法例库	英国立法库	美国联邦法规库	美国法典库
such agreement	113	>200	545	46202
such an agreement	27	>200	255	31968

至于“按照”或“依照”,此处都用作动词,尽管 be applied、apply、be followed、be complied with 都可以表示“实施”,都与规定或条款的执行相关,但 prevail 强调不同规定或条款相冲突时,哪种规定或条款具有优先权或决定性,因此与原文语义更相符。

小　结

《民法典》中,“另有规定”结构表示在特定情况下,适用的规定与通常情况下的一般规定不同。“另有规定”的主语通常为法律、法规;如果主语是合同或当事人,则使用“另有约定”。

多数情况下,本结构与“但是……除外”或“除……外”结构连用。结合对原生英语法律语料库的词频考察,“但是法律另有规定的除外”“除法律另有规定外”可以翻译为“except as otherwise provided by law”;“但是当事人另有约定的除外”或“除当事人另有约定外”可以翻译为“unless otherwise agreed by the parties”。“但是合同另有约定的除外”或“除合同另有约定外”既可以译为“unless otherwise agreed in the contract”,也可以译为“unless otherwise provided in the contract”,注意同一译本需保持措辞统一。“除……另有……外”句式对例外情况的强调语气较弱,英语译文最好将其置于句末或句中,以突出一般规则。

少数情况下，本结构呈现的句式为“……另有规定的，依照其规定”和“……另有约定的，按照其约定”。具体分为两种情况：①“另有规定/约定”句式紧密依附于主条款语句。“法律另有规定的，依照其规定”，建议统一译为介词短语作状语：“except as otherwise provided by law”；“当事人另有约定的，按照其约定”，可以译为“unless otherwise agreed by the parties”。②当“另有规定/约定”句式独立于主条款语句时，可译为独立句。“……对……另有规定的，依照其规定”，可译为“If there are ... providing otherwise in respect of ..., such provisions shall prevail”；“……对……另有约定的，按照其约定”，可译为：“If the parties otherwise agree on ..., such agreement shall prevail.”。

15 “没有约定”结构的翻译

15.1 结构特点及其在《民法典》中的运用

15.1.1 结构特点

“约定”是双方在某一特定交易或事项上达成的共识。在法律语境下，“约定”可以作名词，通常指在合同或协议中，由双方当事人达成的具体条款和条件；也可以作动词，后跟达成共识的具体事项。虽然这些约定本身并不是法律条款，但它们可以成为法律效力的基础。如《海商法》第 94 条规定：“本章其他有关合同当事人之间的权利、义务的规定，仅在航次租船合同没有约定或者没有不同约定时，适用于航次租船合同的出租人和承租人。”该条明确了在没有合同约定情况下的适用法律规范，确保当事人在任何情况下都能清楚自己的权利和义务，从而提高法律的实用性和有效性，有助于解决潜在的争议。

15.1.2 在《民法典》中的运用

《民法典》中“没有约定”结构一共出现了 59 次，通常与“……的”结构连用，表示条件或情形。一般而言，《民法典》先规定有约定的情况，之后使用“没有约定”结构，规定没有约定情况下的相关事项的解决方案，以确保法律的完整性和适用性。如第 620 条规定：“买受人收到标的物时应当在约定的检验期限内检验。没有约定检验期限的，应当及时检验。”

多数情况下，“没有约定”与“或者约定不明确”相连，用以描述在特定情境下，当事各方之间要么没有达成明确协议，要么已有的协议存在歧义或缺少清晰度。

根据句中是否呈现“约定”的对象，可以分为两种情况：

第一，呈现“约定”的对象，通常有三种句式：“没有约定……的，……”“没有约定……或者约定不明确的，……”“对/就……没有约定或者约定不明确的，……”。第一种句式，如第621条第二款：“当事人没有约定检验期限的，买受人应当在发现或者应当发现标的物的数量或者质量不符合约定的合理期限内通知出卖人……”第二种句式，如第602条规定：“当事人没有约定标的物的交付期限或者约定不明确的，适用本法第五百一十条、第五百一十一条第四项的规定。”第三种句式，如第976条规定：“合伙人对合伙期限没有约定或者约定不明确，依据本法第五百一十条的规定仍不能确定的，视为不定期合伙。”

第二，不呈现“约定”的对象，句式为“没有约定或约定不明确，……”如第875条规定：“当事人可以按照互利的原则，在合同中约定实施专利、使用技术秘密后续改进的技术成果的分享办法；没有约定或者约定不明确，依据本法第五百一十条的规定仍不能确定的，一方后续改进的技术成果，其他各方无权分享。”

15.2 译文对比

表 15.1 《民法典》中"没有约定"结构的翻译对比

序号	出处（条）	原文	北大法宝译文（法宝版译文）	国家法规总库译文（总库版译文）
1	423	…… （二）没有约定债权确定期间或者约定不明确，抵押权人或者抵押人自最高额抵押权设立之日起满二年后请求确定债权； ……	… （2）In the absence of an agreement on the term for determining the creditor's right or such an agreement is ambiguous, the mortgagee or the mortgagor claims the determination of the creditor's right after the lapse of two years from the date of creation of the maximum mortgage. …	… （2）where there is no agreement on the period of time for the claims to be ascertained or the relevant agreement is unclear, and the mortgagee or the mortgagor requests for ascertainment of the claims after the lapse of two years from the date of the creation of the mortgage; …
2	603	出卖人应当按照约定的地点交付标的物。 当事人没有约定交付地点或者约定不明确，依据本法第五百一十条的规定仍不能确定的，适用下列规定：……	The seller shall deliver the subject matter at the agreed place. Where there is no agreement between the parties as to a place for delivery, or such agreement is not clear, nor can it be determined according to the provisions of Article 510 of this Code, the following provisions shall apply: …	A seller shall deliver the subject matter at the agreed place of delivery. Where there is no agreement between the parties on the place of delivery or the relevant agreement is unclear, if it cannot be determined according to the provisions of Article 510 of this Code, the following provisions shall be applied: ...

续表

序号	出处（条）	原文	北大法宝译文（法宝版译文）	国家法规总库译文（总库版译文）
3	699	同一债务有两个以上保证人的，保证人应当按照保证合同约定的保证份额，承担保证责任；没有约定保证份额的，债权人可以请求任何一个保证人在其保证范围内承担保证责任。	Where there are not less than two sureties for the same obligation, the sureties shall assume suretyship liability in accordance with the share of suretyship agreed in the contract of suretyship; and absent agreement on the share of suretyship, the creditor may request any surety to assume suretyship liability to the extent of its suretyship.	Where there are two or more sureties guaranteeing one obligation, the sureties shall undertake the suretyship liability in proportion to their share of suretyship in accordance with the suretyship contract. In the absence of such an agreement, the creditor may request any of the sureties to undertake the suretyship liability within the scope of his liability.
4	626	买受人应当按照约定的数额和支付方式支付价款。对价款的数额和支付方式没有约定或者约定不明确的，适用本法第五百一十条、第五百一十一条第二项和第五项的规定。	The buyer shall pay the price according to the agreed amount and payment method. Where the price and payment method are not agreed or the agreement is not clear, the provisions of Article 510 and Article 511 (2)and (5) of this Code shall be applied.	A buyer shall make payment in accordance with the agreed amount and method of payment. Where there is no agreement between the parties on the amount of price or the method of payment, or the relevant agreement is unclear, the provisions of Article 510 and Subparagraphs (2) and (5) of Article 511 of this Code shall be applied.
5	309	按份共有人对共有的不动产或者动产享有的份额，没有约定或者约定不明确的，按照出资额确定；……	Where the co-owners in divided co-ownership fail to agree on the shares of the co-owned immovable or movable or such an agreement is ambiguous, the shares shall be determined based on their amount of investment. ...	The share of a co-owner by shares in the immovable or movable property shall be determined according to his capital contribution where there is no agreement or the relevant agreement is unclear. ...

续表

序号	出处（条）	原文	北大法宝译文（法宝版译文）	国家法规总库译文（总库版译文）
6	1022	当事人对肖像许可使用期限没有约定或者约定不明确的，任何一方当事人可以随时解除肖像许可使用合同，但是应当在合理期限之前通知对方。	Where the parties have not agreed on the time limit for licensed use of likeness or the agreement is undefined, either party may terminate the contract on the licensed use of a likeness at any time, but shall notify the other party prior to a rational time limit.	Where the parties have not agreed on the term of authorized use of an image, or the relevant agreement is unclear, either party may rescind the contract authorizing the use of the image at any time, provided that the other party shall be notified within a reasonable period of time.
7	886	技术咨询合同和技术服务合同对受托人正常开展工作所需费用的负担没有约定或者约定不明确的，由受托人负担。	Where a technical consulting contract or technical service contract is silent on, or is not clear in, the payment of the expenses necessary for the consultant or service provider to normally conduct work, the consultant or service provider shall pay the expenses.	Where there is no agreement in a technology consultation contract or a technology service contract on the bearing of the necessary expenses for the entrusted person to carry out the normal work, or the relevant agreement is unclear, the said expenses shall be borne by the entrusted person.
8	972	合伙的利润分配和亏损分担，按照合伙合同的约定办理；合伙合同没有约定或者约定不明确的，由合伙人协商决定；……	The allocation of the profits and sharing of losses of a partnership shall be governed by the contract of partnership; if the contract of partnership is silent or not clear, the partners shall negotiate a decision; ...	The sharing of the profits and allocation of losses of a partnership shall be in accordance with the partnership contract; where there is no such an agreement in the partnership contract or the relevant agreement is unclear, the partners shall make a decision through consultation. ...

续表

序号	出处（条）	原文	北大法宝译文（法宝版译文）	国家法规总库译文（总库版译文）
9	283	建筑物及其附属设施的费用分摊、收益分配等事项，有约定的，按照约定；**没有约定或者约定不明确的**，按照业主专有部分面积所占比例确定。	Where there is an agreement on such matters as the apportioning of expenses for a building and its ancillary facilities and the distribution of proceeds therefrom, such an agreement shall prevail; **in the absence of such an agreement or if such an agreement is ambiguous**, such matters shall be determined based on the proportion of the area of the owners' private portions to the total area of the building.	Where there is an agreement on matters such as allocation of expenses on and distribution of income gained from a building and its auxiliary facilities, such matters shall be determined in accordance with the agreement; **where there is no agreement or the relevant agreement is unclear**, such matters shall be determined in proportion to the area of each unit owner's exclusive unit to the total area.
10	322	因加工、附合、混合而产生的物的归属，有约定的，按照约定；**没有约定或者约定不明确的**，依照法律规定；……	Where there is an agreement on the attribution of the property arising from processing, attachment, or mixing, such an agreement shall prevail; **in the absence of such an agreement or if such an agreement is ambiguous**, the ownership shall be determined in accordance with the provisions of laws; ...	A thing, that is created as a result of processing, or combining or mixing with another thing or things, shall be owned as agreed if there is such an agreement, or in accordance with law **if there is no agreement or the relevant agreement is unclear**, or, ...

续表

序号	出处(条)	原文	北大法宝译文(法宝版译文)	国家法规总库译文(总库版译文)
11	1065	男女双方可以约定婚姻关系存续期间所得的财产以及婚前财产归各自所有、共同所有或者部分各自所有、部分共同所有。约定应当采用书面形式。**没有约定或者约定不明确的**，适用本法第一千零六十二条、第一千零六十三条的规定。	So far as the property acquired during the marriage and the prenuptial property are concerned, husband and wife may agree as to whether they should be in the separate possession, joint possession or partly separate possession and partly joint possession. The agreement shall be made in writing. **In the absence of such an agreement or of an express agreement**, the provisions of Articles 1062 and 1063 of this Code shall apply.	The spouses or a man and a woman in anticipation of marriage may agree that their premarital property and the property to be acquired by them during their marriage may be owned by them separately or jointly, or partially owned separately and partially owned jointly. The agreement shall be in writing. **Where there is no agreement or the relevant agreement is unclear**, Articles 1062 and 1063 of this Code shall apply.
12	692	债权人与保证人可以约定保证期间，但是约定的保证期间早于主债务履行期限或者与主债务履行期限同时届满的，视为没有约定；**没有约定或者约定不明确的**，保证期间为主债务履行期限届满之日起六个月。	A creditor and the surety may agree on a period for suretyship, but if the agreed period for suretyship precedes, or expires at the same time as, the time limit for performance of the principal obligation, the period shall be treated as having never been agreed; **and absent agreement, or if the agreement is not clear**, the period for suretyship shall be six months from the expiration of the time limit for performance of the principal obligation.	A creditor and a surety may agree on the term of suretyship. However, where the expiration date of the agreed term of suretyship is earlier than or the same as the expiration date of the period of performance of the principal obligation, it is deemed as there is no agreement on the term of suretyship. **Where there is no agreement** between the parties **on** the term of suretyship **or the relevant agreement is unclear**, the term of suretyship shall be six months from the expiration date of the period of performance of the principal obligation.

15.3 译文分析

我们针对《民法典》中“没有约定”结构的使用情况，分别对比分析两个版本的对应译文，探讨更为可取的翻译方法。

15.3.1 “没有约定”结构的翻译

（1）呈现“约定”对象的情况

法宝版译文中的处理方式非常多样，包括“in the absence of an agreement on ...”，如例句 1；“where there is no agreement ... as to ...”，如例句 2；“and absent agreement on ...”，如例句 3；“where ... are not agreed”，如例句 4；“where ... fail to agree on ...”，如例句 5；“where ... have not agreed on ...”，如例句 6；“where ... is silent on ...”，如例句 7。

总库版译文在多数情况下译为“where there is no agreement on ...”，如例句 1、例句 2、例句 4 和例句 7；例句 3 和例句 5 省略了“约定”对象，分别译为“in the absence of such an agreement”和“where there is no agreement”。例句 6 则译为“where ... have not agreed on ...”。

“where there is no ...”常用于法律文本中的否定或排除性规定，即用于明确说明在特定情境下缺乏某种条件、依据或资料时所适用的规则、程序或后果。“in the absence of”也是法律语境中的常见短语，通常用来指出缺乏某种必要条件，并明确在这种情况下将采取的行动或后果。“absent”在法律文本中也可用作介词，表明某种条件、同意、许可或指令的缺失。可见这三种用法都能用于指出缺失条件的情况，后加 agreement，都是“没有约定”的合适译文。但三者相比较，“absent”相对较为简洁，使用方便，适合直接表述缺乏的情况；“where there is no ...” 和 “in the absence of” 更加正式，适合详细阐述缺乏的情况及其后果。

“where ... are not agreed”“where ... fail to agree on ...”和“where ...

have not agreed on ...”虽然也都涉及协议或同意的缺失，但语义侧重点不同。“where ... are not agreed”表示在某些条款或事项上没有达成一致，可能暗示多个当事人对某个问题存在不同意见。“where ... fail to agree on ...”指当事各方在讨论或协商过程中未能达成一致或共识，强调努力协商但未能取得成功的结果。“where ... have not agreed on ...”使用现在完成时，强调至今未达成一致的状态。而汉语条文中“对……没有约定”或“没有约定……”表达的仅是各方之间存在协议缺失的状态，因此，作为译文，这三个短语在意思上不够准确，可能会导致译文读者理解偏差。

“where ... is silent on ...”在法律文本中也比较常见，用以指代某个条款、法律、规章或合约在某种情境、问题或事项上未提及或没有明确规定的情况。法宝版例句 7 译文用这个短语强调合同对费用支付问题没有相关的条款或指示，清楚地表达出合同在特定问题上协议的缺失，符合条文原义。

但是根据法律翻译同一性原则，对同一表述最好使用同一译文，以避免歧义。为此，可以考察原生英语法律语料库中的用法，结果如表 15.2 所示：

表 15.2 “没有约定”的英文表达方式及检索频次

表达方式	国内	国外		
	香港法例库	英国立法库	美国联邦法规库	美国法典库
in the absence of (such) agreement	26	323	5	454
in the absence of (such) an agreement	10	68	32	2842
(where/if) there is no agreement	6	75	9	919
absent agreement	0	0	5	2899
absent an agreement	0	0	5	0
is silent (on)	0	9	9	12590

如表 15.2 所示，“in the absence of”和“(where/if) there is no agreement”都有一定的使用频率，但是前者更占优势，其中我国香港和英国法律倾向于 agreement 作不可数名词的用法，美国更倾向于使用 agreement 作可数名词。absent 作介词和 agreement 连用，我国香港和英国立法数据库中未见其用法，美国法典倾向使用 absent agreement，盖其含义更加宽泛，适用于任何缺少协议的情境。用法律、规章或合约作“is silent (on)”的主语的情况，美国法典中出现的频率非常高，但是英国法律和美国联邦法规中屈指可数。

因此，为与国际法律语言惯例接轨，建议在翻译“没有约定……”和“对/就……没有约定”时，优先使用“in the absence of (an) agreement on ...”或“where/if there is no agreement on ...”，同一译本应使用统一表述。至于汉语条文中用“合同”作“没有约定”的主语的情况，如例句 7，“合同”其实是“约定”的出处，同样可以使用上述两个表述，译为“in the absence of (an) agreement in ...(合同) on ...”或“where/if there is no agreement in ...(合同) on ...”。

需要注意的是，在“where/if there is no agreement on ...”结构中，where 和 if 的用法应予以区别。where 主要引导充分法律条件句，一般置于句首；if 引导依赖语境条件句，离开它，该法律语段往往不能自圆其说或不可单独操作；当 where 引导条件句置于句中或句末时，if 可以取代 where，两者功能相同(李克兴，2013)。例句 1、例句 5—7，“没有约定”所在的语段意思完整，无须依赖其他语境或上下文即可独立存在，如果使用本结构，可用 where 引导，语气更显正式、客观、庄重。而例句 2—4 都是信息不充分的条件，不能单独与其主句构成一条法理充足的、可以独立存在或实施的法律条文，因此应当使用 if 作引导词。

有时，汉语条文语段先规定有约定情况下当事人的权利和义务，然后规定没有约定情况下的默认规则，如例句 3。通常译文会将此段处理为两个完整语句，“没有约定”结构作为第二句，其译文省略掉“约定”对象，变为“such an agreement”，也是可取译法，更显简洁、直接。

例句 5 的总库版译文，将 where 从句置于句末，相当于 if-条件句，“约定”的对象已经在主句中明示，也是不错的变通。

(2) 不呈现“约定”对象的情况

这种情况下，“没有约定”结构所在的语句都非法理充分、自圆其说的完整语段，需依赖前文予以明确“约定”的对象。

法宝版译文在多数情况下译为“in the absence of such an agreement”，如例句9—11。此外，例句8译为“if … is silent”，例句12译为“and absent agreement”。总库版译文相对统一，例句8译为“where there is no such an agreement in ...”，例句9—12译为“where/if there is no agreement”。

结合前文对几种短语的分析，此处可优先使用“in the absence of such (an) agreement”或“if there is no such (an) agreement”。首先，such的使用，直接指向该条文中前句所述的“约定”，简洁又明确，比之不加such，更具针对性。其次，由于“约定”对象的缺失，只能用if引导依赖语境条件句。

例句12的总库版译文补充了“没有约定”的对象，即the term of suretyship，但the term of suretyship作为法律术语，意思并不单一，既可以指担保或保证关系的具体条款，也可以指条件或有效期限，因此该译文的具体解释仍然无法脱离语境，同样应当使用if引导条件句。

15.3.2 “或者约定不明确”结构的翻译

法宝版译文较为多样，包括“or (if) such an agreement is ambiguous”，如例句1、例句5、例句9和例句10；“or such agreement is not clear”，如例句2；“or (if) the agreement is not clear”，如例句4和例句12；“or the agreement is undefined”，如例句6；“or is not clear”，如例句7和例句8；“or (in the absence) of an express agreement”，如例句11。总库版译文则统一为“or the relevant agreement is unclear”，如例句1—12。

通过观察可得，本结构的翻译主要存在两个问题：第一，翻译“不确定”，ambiguous、not clear、undefined、unclear哪个更合适？第二，such或relevant是否必要？

关于第一个问题，首先分析词义。ambiguous表示可以有多种解释或含义,强调了模糊性和可能的多重解读。unclear 和 not clear 意思没有差别,通常指某件事情不明朗或难以理解,强调的是信息传达或含义的不清楚。undefined 指缺乏定义或没有标准化的解释,通常更强调完全缺乏定义,而不是某种意义上的不明确。由此可以排除 undefined。

在法律文书(如合同、协议等)中,明确条款的可能多义性和潜在的理解差异非常重要。用 ambiguous 指代不明确的约定,可以更加准确地表达出其多重解释性和模糊性,以及可能引发的争议;如果使用 unclear,可能会给人一种只需简单澄清即可解决问题的印象,并不强调其潜在的法律复杂性。可见 ambiguous 更准确地捕捉了法律文件中条款可能存在的含糊性和不确定性。那么如果译为“unclear and ambiguous”呢?的确,两词同时使用可以充分表达条款的不确定性(unclear)和可能存在多重解释性(ambiguous),但也显得有些冗余,因为 ambiguous 在某种程度上已经包含了 unclear 的意思。而且简明法律英语要求使用更精确、简洁且专业的法律术语,译为 ambiguous 相对更可取。

原生英语法律语料库的检索结果(见表 15.3),也证实了我们的判断。我国香港、英国法律以及美国联邦法规中,鲜见“约定不确定”的表述,但美国法典中有一定词频,尤以 ambiguous 为多。

表 15.3 “约定不明确”的英文表达方式及检索频次

表达方式	国内	国外		
	香港法例库	英国立法库	美国联邦法规库	美国法典库
agreement is ambiguous	0	0	0	1888
agreement is unclear	0	0	1	190
agreement is not clear	0	0	0	125
agreement is unclear and ambiguous	0	0	0	2

关于第二个问题,从准确度考虑,“the agreement”的表述让人感觉可能会指代任何约定,而不一定明确指向特定的前文提到的约定,缺乏具体

性；使用 such 或 relevant 可以明确指向讨论的特定约定，提供了更强的上下文关联，尤其是 relevant 能清楚地传达该约定与当下讨论绝对关系密切，将可能的模糊性降到最低，增加了法律条款的清晰度与准确性。总库版译文因此更可取。

至于法宝版例句 11 使用的 an express agreement，是指当事方的意图和条款清晰明了的协议或约定。“in the absence of such an agreement or of an express agreement”的含义为：没有任何可依据的约定(无论是明示的或隐含的)。这种表述适用于法律文本中强调完全不具备任何约定的情况。但是原文“没有约定或者约定不明确”强调两种情况：完全缺乏约定和现有约定含糊不清。可见该译文并不合适。

小　结

在《民法典》中，“没有约定”结构一般与“的”字结构连用，表示条件；多数情况下，“没有约定”后缀“或者约定不明确”，用以描述在特定情境下，当事各方之间要么没有达成明确协议，要么已有的协议存在歧义或缺少清晰度。本章主要讨论了三种句式：“没有约定……或者约定不明确的”“对/就……没有约定或者约定不明确的”，以及“没有约定或者约定不明确的”。对于前两句，建议优先翻译为“in the absence of (an) agreement on ... or if the relevant agreement is ambiguous”或“where/if there is no agreement on ... or the relevant agreement is ambiguous”。如果使用第二种译文，需要判断“没有约定”所在的语段是否意思完整，是否无须依赖语境或上下文即可独立存在或实施的法律条文。如果是，则使用 where；如果否，则使用 if。第三种句式，即“没有约定或者约定不明确的”所在的语句通常都非法理充分、自圆其说的完整语段，可翻译为“in the absence of such (an) agreement or if the relevant agreement is ambiguous”或“if there is no such (an) agreement or the relevant agreement is ambiguous”。根据法律语言同一性原则，同一译本应使用统一表述。

16 “向……申请”结构的翻译

16.1 结构特点及其在《民法典》中的运用

16.1.1 结构特点

“向……申请”结构在法律条文中，体现了法律行为的程序性，主要指法律主体根据法律规定，向特定机构、组织或个人提出申请，以获得某种权利或许可。该结构前通常会阐明申请的背景、条件及申请主体；介词“向”后为具体的申请对象，如“向人民法院申请”“向登记机构申请”；“申请”一词后跟具体内容、理由、依据等。该结构通过明确指出申请对象和申请内容，使法律条文中的申请行为具有明确性和程序性。

16.1.2 在《民法典》中的运用

《民法典》中“向……申请”结构一共出现了 21 次，表明法律行为人需要向特定机关或机构提出申请，包括但不限于权利的设立、变更，许可申请，审批程序，以及纠纷的解决等。该结构有“主语＋向……申请”和“……的，应当向……申请”两种句式。例如，第 1146 条规定：“对遗产管理人的确定有争议的，利害关系人可以**向**人民法院**申请**指定遗产管理人。”又如第 368 条规定：“设立居住权的，应当**向**登记机构**申请**居住权登记。”

(1)"主语+向……申请"句式

该句式以主语为起点,直接指出申请行为的主体,突出了申请者的主动性和申请行为的直接性。其中,申请对象可分为具有明确审批或管理职能的机构,如人民法院、登记机构;还有个人或实体,如贷款人。如第40条规定:"自然人下落不明满二年的,利害关系人可以**向**人民法院**申请**宣告该自然人为失踪人。"该例句的申请对象是职能机构人民法院,利害关系人要按照法定程序向人民法院提出申请和提交相关证明材料,以便人民法院进行审查和宣告。再如,第678条规定:"借款人可以在还款期限届满前**向**贷款人**申请**展期;贷款人同意的,可以展期。"该例句中贷款人为申请行为的对象,不涉及第三方机构(如具备审批或管理职能的人民法院或登记机构),双方可就具体事宜达成一致。

(2)"……的,应当向……申请"句式

该句式客观性较强,通常用于描述某种法律或实际情况下的必要条件或要求,并在此基础上明确指出应当采取的申请行动,有更强的规范性和指导性。如第349条规定:"设立建设用地使用权的,应当**向**登记机构**申请**建设用地使用权登记。"该例句首先阐明"设立建设用地使用权"这一前提,随后指出应向申请对象申请某具体内容,使法律规范的实施有明确的指向性和可操作性。

16.2 译文对比

表 16.1 《民法典》中"向……申请"结构的翻译对比

序号	出处（条）	原文	北大法宝译文（法宝版译文）	国家法规总库译文（总库版译文）
1	24	不能辨认或者不能完全辨认自己行为的成年人，其利害关系人或者有关组织，可以向人民法院申请认定该成年人为无民事行为能力人或者限制民事行为能力。	For an adult incapable of discerning or fully discerning his or her conduct, an interested party or a relevant organization may apply to a people's court for determining the adult as a person without capacity for civil conduct or a person with limited capacity for civil conduct.	Where an adult is unable to comprehend or fully comprehend his conduct, any interested person of such an adult or a relevant organization may request the people's court to declare that the said adult be identified as a person with no or limited capacity for performing civil juristic acts.
2	31	对监护人的确定有争议的，由被监护人住所地的居民委员会、村民委员会或者民政部门指定监护人，有关当事人对指定不服的，可以向人民法院申请指定监护人；有关当事人也可以直接向人民法院申请指定监护人。	In case of any dispute over the determination of guardian, the urban residents' committee, villagers' committee, or civil affairs department of the place of the ward's domicile may designate the guardian, and against the aforesaid designation, the relevant parties may apply to the people's court for designating the guardian; and the relevant parties may, notwithstanding, directly apply to the people's court for designating the guardian.	Where a dispute arises over the determination of a guardian, the guardian shall be appointed by the residents' committee, the villagers' committee, or the civil affairs department in the place where the ward's domicile is located, and a party not satisfied with such an appointment may request the people's court to appoint a guardian; the relevant parties may also directly request the people's court to make such an appointment.

续表

序号	出处（条）	原文	北大法宝译文（法宝版译文）	国家法规总库译文（总库版译文）
3	40	自然人下落不明满二年的，利害关系人可以**向**人民法院**申请**宣告该自然人为失踪人。	Where a natural person has disappeared for two years, an interested party may **apply to** a people's court **for** a declaration of absence of the natural person.	If a natural person's whereabouts have been unknown for two years, an interested person may **request** the people's court to declare the natural person as a missing person.
4	1146	对遗产管理人的确定有争议的，利害关系人可以**向**人民法院**申请**指定遗产管理人。	Where there is any dispute over the determination of an estate administrator, an interested party may **apply to** the people's court **for** designating an estate administrator.	Where a dispute arises over the determination of an administrator of the estate, any interested person may **request** the people's court to appoint an administrator.
5	335	土地承包经营权互换、转让的，当事人可以**向**登记机构**申请**登记；未经登记，不得对抗善意第三人。	In case of the exchange or transfer of the conventional usufruct on rural land for agricultural operations, the party may **apply to** the registration authority **for** registration; and if it is not registered, it shall not be set up against a bona fide third party.	Where the rights to contractual management of land are exchanged or transferred, the parties may **apply to** the registration authority **for** registration; without registration, such exchange or transfer may not be asserted against a bona fide third person.

续表

序号	出处(条)	原文	北大法宝译文(法宝版译文)	国家法规总库译文(总库版译文)
6	341	当事人可以向登记机构申请土地经营权登记；未经登记，不得对抗善意第三人。	A party may apply to the registration authority for the registration of the land operating right; and if it is not registered, it shall not be set up against a bona fide third party.	The parties may apply to the registration authority for registration of the right to management of land; without registration, such a right may not be asserted against a bona fide third person.
7	678	借款人可以在还款期限届满前向贷款人申请展期；贷款人同意的，可以展期。	The borrower may apply to the lender for extension of the loan term before its maturity. Upon consent by the lender, the loan term may be extended.	A borrower may apply to the lender for an extension of the term of the loan before the loan becomes due. The term of the loan may be extended upon consent of the lender.
8	349	设立建设用地使用权的，应当向登记机构申请建设用地使用权登记。	For the creation of the right to use land for construction, an application for the registration of the right to use land for construction shall be filed with the registration authority.	To create a right to use a lot of land for construction purposes, application shall be filed with the registration authority for the registration of the right.
9	355	建设用地使用权转让、互换、出资或者赠与的，应当向登记机构申请变更登记。	Where the right to use land for construction is transferred, exchanged, contributed as capital, or gifted, an application for modification registration shall be filed with the registration authority.	Where a right to use a lot of land for construction purposes is transferred, exchanged, offered as capital contribution, or given away as a gift, an application for registration of the change shall be filed with the registration authority.

续表

序号	出处（条）	原文	北大法宝译文（法宝版译文）	国家法规总库译文（总库版译文）
10	368	设立居住权的，应当向登记机构申请居住权登记。	If the right of habitation is created, an application for the registration of the right of habitation shall be filed with the registration authority.	To create a right of habitation, an application for the registration of the right shall be filed with the registration authority.

16.3 译文分析

以下对比分析两个版本中“向……申请”结构的译文，探讨各种情况下较为可取的翻译方法。

16.3.1 “主语＋向……申请”句式的翻译

例句1—7同属该结构。法宝版的译文均为“apply to ... for”，总库版译文有“apply to ... for”和“request”两种译文。

从句式结构角度分析，中文句式“主语＋向……申请”是一个典型的主谓结构，其中“主语”是行为的发起者，“向……”是介词短语，指明申请的对象或方向，“申请”是动词，表示主语的行为。该结构强调了主语在申请行为中的主动性和目的性，在翻译时，译者应保留主动语态，突出主体的主动性。

从词汇角度分析，apply和request均有“申请、请求”之意。根据《布莱克法律词典》，apply的定义为：To make a formal request or petition, usually in writing, to a court, officer, board, or company, for the granting of some favor, or of some rule or order, which is within his or their power or discretion. For example, to apply for an Injunction, for a pardon, for a policy of insurance。request的定义为：An asking or petition;

the expression of a desire to some person for something to be granted or done; particularly for the payment of a debt or performance of a contract. The two words, "request" and "require," as used in notices to creditors to present claims against an estate, are of the same origin, and virtually synonymous. 由此可见,apply 的使用语境更加正式,强调申请者要以书面的形式向法院、官员、董事会或公司提出正式请求或请愿,请求相关机构在权力或裁量权范围内给予某种恩惠、规定或命令;而 request 表达请求或请愿,如向某人表达希望给予或完成某事的愿望,尤其是偿还债务或履行合同。因此,在翻译该结构句式时,申请的接受者和请求的内容不同,则所选择的动词也会发生改变。通常来说,当申请对象为具有一定权力和职责,或申请时需要官方流程的机构或组织时,"申请"一词可译为 apply to;当申请对象是个人,即双方可能更多地基于合同关系或私人关系进行协商,而非遵循某个正式的程序或规则时,"申请"一词可译为 request。

例句 1—6 中,申请对象均为"人民法院"和"登记机构",申请的内容涉及法律程序、官方事务或权益的确认,申请者需要遵循严格的法律程序和规定,并提交必要的材料和证明文件,以确保申请事项的合法性和有效性。使用"apply" 可以准确地表达申请过程的正式性和规范性,与原文的语境和含义保持一致。例句 7 描述了借款人向贷款人表达自己的愿望,并希望双方能够就展期事宜做进一步沟通的过程。虽然贷款行为本身受到法律或合同条款的约束,但在具体执行过程中,如借款人希望展期还款,往往涉及双方之间的协商。在该情况下,"request" 一词更能体现出申请过程的灵活性和协商性,突出借款人希望贷款人能够理解其困境并给予一定宽限的愿望。

16.3.2 "……的,应当向……申请" 句式的翻译

例句 8—10 同属该结构。法宝版和总库版的译文均为 "an application for...shall be filed with"。

从句式结构角度分析,中文句式"……的,应当向……申请"是一个

条件性建议的句式。“的”字用于描述需要执行后续行动的前提或条件，“应当向……申请”是句子的核心部分，明确指出了在满足前面条件时应采取的具体行动。其中，“应当”是一个情态动词，表示一种义务或责任，强调执行后续行动的必要性；“向……申请”是一个动宾短语，指明了行动的方向和对象。该句式采用无主语的形式，突出申请行动的过程，而非申请的主体。这种表达方式在法律、规章、政策等正式文本中尤为常见，能够更加客观地传达出一种普遍适用的规定或建议，因此，在翻译时，译者可将其译为被动语态，突出申请的过程，保留法律语言的严谨性和客观性。

从词汇角度分析，“shall” 作为情态动词，具有强制性或建议性的语气，与“应当”在语义上高度对应，都表示了一种必须遵守的规定或建议。通过查阅《柯林斯英语词典》可知，application 的定义为：An application for something such as a job or membership of an organization is a formal written request for it。该词强调书面且正式的请求，例句 8—10 中，申请对象均为“登记机构”此类官方组织，要求申请者按照规定的格式和内容提交申请材料，因此“申请”一词可译为 application。在中文中，“向”字常用来表示方向或对象，引导出行为的目标或接收者。在翻译时，英文通常会使用介词来对应这种指向关系。此处“with”作为介词，与“file”这一动词搭配使用，形成了“be filed with”的被动语态结构，不仅传达了申请的行为本身，还清晰地指明了申请的目标对象，即“登记机构”等官方组织，是为可取译文。

小　结

“向……申请”结构可分为“主语＋向……申请”和“……的，应当向……申请”两种句式。针对该结构的翻译，我们可以从词汇和句式结构角度进行分析和总结，提出如下翻译建议：

“主语＋向……申请”：①当申请对象为需要正式流程的官方机构或组

织时,可译为“sb. apply to... for”;②当申请对象为可进行协商的个人或实体时,可译为“sb. request”。

“……的,应当向……申请”可译为“an application for...shall be filed with”。

17 “向……追偿”结构的翻译

17.1 结构特点及其在《民法典》中的运用

17.1.1 结构特点

“向……追偿”结构在法律条文中，主要是指某一主体在承担了超过其应分担的责任、债务或其他费用后，有权依法向其他相关责任主体要求偿还超出的部分。该结构为动宾结构，介词“向”前通常为执行追偿行为的主体、条件背景；“向”字明确了追偿行为是针对某个特定主体进行的，动词“追偿”为短语的核心部分，表明行为的性质，即要求偿还或追回超出自身应承担的费用等。该结构的运用可以确保各方之间的利益关系得到平衡，体现了法律的公平性。

17.1.2 在《民法典》中的运用

《民法典》中“向……追偿”结构一共出现了 27 次。其中，“可以向……追偿”句式结构共出现 9 次；“有权向……追偿”句式结构共出现 18 次。该结构主要涵盖了连带责任、担保责任、合伙债务、侵权责任等多种情形，为相关主体在遭受损失时提供了法律保障和救济途径。例如，第 520 条规定：“部分连带债务人履行、抵销债务或者提存标的物的，其他债务人对债权人的债务在相应范围内消灭；该债务人可以依据前条规定<u>向</u>其他债务人追偿。”第 1215 条规定:“保险人在机动车强制保险责任限额范围内垫付抢救费用的,有权向交通事故责任人追偿。”

(1)“可以向……追偿”句式

该句式通常用于表明追偿的可能性或条件,并未直接强调这种追偿权利的确定性和强制性。即在一定条件下,一方有权要求另一方进行赔偿或补偿。然而,这种追偿权利的具体行使可能还需要满足特定的法律条件、合同条款或事实情况。该句式体现了法律的灵活性和适应性,有助于适应不同的法律情境和实际需求。如第 719 条规定:“次承租人代为支付的租金和违约金,可以充抵次承租人应当向承租人支付的租金;超出其应付的租金数额的,**可以向**承租人**追偿**。”这体现了租赁关系中次承租人和承租人之间的财务结算和责任分担机制。追偿的具体金额和条件还需要根据租赁合同的具体条款和实际情况来确定。

(2)“有权向……追偿”句式

该句式直接表明追偿权利已经得到法律的明确认可和保护,受损方有权在特定条件下要求责任方进行赔偿,通常不需要进一步的法律解释或证据支持,强调了追偿行为的正当性和强制性。该句式体现了追偿权利的权威性,以保证受损方依法行使追偿权,维护自己的合法权益。如第 973 条规定:“合伙人对合伙债务承连带责任。清偿合伙债务超过自己应当承担份额的合伙人,有权向其他合伙人追偿。”该条表明追偿权利的行使是基于合伙债务的连带责任原则,且这一权利得到了法律的明确认可和保护,受损方可以依法进行债务追偿。

17.2 译文对比

表 17.1 《民法典》中“向……追偿”结构的翻译对比

序号	出处（条）	原文	北大法宝译文（法宝版译文）	国家法规总库译文（总库版译文）
1	62	法人承担民事责任后，依照法律或者法人章程的规定，可以向有过错的法定代表人追偿。	The legal person may, after assuming such civil liability, claim reimbursement from the legal representative at fault in accordance with the laws or its by laws.	After assuming the aforementioned civil liability, the legal person has the right to indemnification, in accordance with law or its articles of association, against its legal representative who is at fault.
2	520	部分连带债务人履行、抵销债务或者提存标的物的，其他债务人对债权人的债务在相应范围内消灭；该债务人可以依据前条规定向其他债务人追偿。	Where a joint and several debtor performs or sets off the obligation, or tenders and deposits the subject matter, the obligation owed by the other debtors to the creditor shall be extinguished to the corresponding extent; and the debtor may exercise recovery against the other debtors in accordance with the provisions of the preceding article.	Where one of the debtors subjected to joint and several liabilities has performed his obligation, offset his obligation, or placed the subject matter of the obligation in escrow, the obligation of the other debtors owed to the creditor is extinguished to the corresponding extent, and such a debtor has the right to contribution against the other debtors in accordance with the provisions of the preceding Article.

续表

序号	出处(条)	原文	北大法宝译文(法宝版译文)	国家法规总库译文(总库版译文)
3	719	次承租人代为支付的租金和违约金,可以充抵次承租人应当向承租人支付的租金;超出其应付的租金数额的,可以向承租人追偿。	The rent and liquidated damages so paid may be set off against the rent payable by the sublessee to the lessee; and the excess over the rent payable by the sublessee may be recovered from the lessee.	The rent and liquidated damages paid by the sublessee for the lessee may be used to offset the rent payable by the sublessee to the lessee. If the amount of rent and liquidated damages thus paid by the sublessee exceeds the rent, the sublessee has the right to indemnification against the lessee.
4	1192	提供劳务期间,因第三人的行为造成提供劳务一方损害的,提供劳务一方有权请求第三人承担侵权责任,也有权请求接受劳务一方给予补偿。接受劳务一方补偿后,可以向第三人追偿。	During the period of providing labor services, if a third party causes harm to the party providing labor services, the party providing labor services shall have the right to require the third party to assume the tort liability or to require the party receiving labor services to pay compensation. After payment of compensation, the party receiving labor services may claim reimbursement from the third party.	Where an act of a third person causes damage to the service-providing party when such services are provided, the service-providing party has the right to request the third person to bear tort liability, or to request the service-receiving party to make compensation. The service-receiving party may, after making the compensation, claim indemnification against the third person.

续表

序号	出处(条)	原文	北大法宝译文(法宝版译文)	国家法规总库译文(总库版译文)
5	178	实际承担责任超过自己责任份额的连带责任人,**有权向**其他连带责任人**追偿**。	If the liability actually assumed by a person jointly and severally liable exceeds the person's share of liability, the person **shall be entitled to claim indemnities from** other persons jointly and severally liable.	A person who has assumed the liability more than his share of fault **has the right to contribution against** the other person(s) subjected to the joint and several liability.
6	973	合伙人对合伙债务承连带责任。清偿合伙债务超过自己应当承担份额的合伙人,**有权向**其他合伙人**追偿**。	Partners shall be jointly and severally liable for partnership obligations. A partner who performs a partnership obligation in excess of its share **shall be entitled to reimbursement** from the other partners.	The partners shall bear joint and several liabilities for the partnership obligations. A partner who has performed the partnership obligations in excess of his share **has the right to contribution against** the other partners.
7	392	提供担保的第三人承担担保责任后,**有权向**债务人**追偿**。	The third party providing security shall **have the right of recovery against** the debtor after fulfilling its liability.	After the third person who provides security has assumed such liability, he **has the right to indemnification against** the debtor.
8	1204	因运输者、仓储者等第三人的过错使产品存在缺陷,造成他人损害的,产品的生产者、销售者赔偿后,**有权向**第三人**追偿**。	Where any harm is caused to another person by a defective product and the defect is caused by the fault of a third party such as carrier or warehouseman, the manufacturer or seller of the product that has paid the compensation **shall be entitled to be reimbursed by** the third party.	Where the damage is caused by a defect of a product due to the fault of a third person, such as a transporter or a warehouser, the manufacturer or seller of the product who has paid compensation **has the right to indemnification against** the third person.

续表

序号	出处（条）	原文	北大法宝译文（法宝版译文）	国家法规总库译文（总库版译文）
9	1215	保险人在机动车强制保险责任限额范围内垫付抢救费用的，**有权向**交通事故责任人**追偿**。	The insurer that makes advances for rescue expenses within the liability limit of the mandatory motor vehicle insurance **shall be entitled to be reimbursed by** the person liable for the traffic accident.	Where an insurer pays the expenses for rescue within the limits of the compulsory insurance liability for motor vehicles, it **has the right to indemnification against** the person who is liable for the traffic accident.
10	1216	道路交通事故社会救助基金垫付后，其管理机构**有权向**交通事故责任人**追偿**。	After advances are made out of the Social Assistance Fund for Road Traffic Accidents, the governing body of the fund **shall be entitled to be reimbursed by** the person liable for the traffic accident.	After the Social Assistance Fund for Road Traffic Accidents makes the payment, its administrative agency **has the right to indemnification against** the person who is liable for the traffic accident.
11	700	保证人承担保证责任后，除当事人另有约定外，**有权**在其承担保证责任的范围内**向**债务人**追偿**，享有债权人对债务人的权利，但是不得损害债权人的利益。	Unless otherwise agreed by the parties, a surety who has assumed the suretyship liability **shall have the right to reimbursement from** the debtor to the extent of the suretyship liability it has assumed and be subrogated to the rights of the creditor against the debtor, without prejudice to the interests of the creditor.	After a surety has assumed the suretyship liability, unless otherwise agreed by the parties, the surety **has the right to indemnification against** the debtor within the scope of his suretyship liability, and may enjoy the right of a creditor against the debtor, provided that the creditor's interests may not be harmed.

17.3 译文分析

以下对比分析两个版本中"向……追偿"结构的译文，结合词汇和句式结构角度，探讨各种情况下较为可取的翻译方法。

17.3.1 从词汇角度分析

在"向……追偿"结构中，法宝版给出了"claim reimbursement from"（例句 1、例句 4）、"be reimbursed by"（例句 8—10）、"exercise recovery against"（例句 2）、"be recovered from"（例句 3）、"claim indemnities from"（例句 5）几种译文；总库版译文主要给出了"(claim) indemnification against"（例句 1、例句 3、例句 4、例句 7—11）、"contribution against"（例句 2、例句 5、例句 6）两种译文。以上几个译文均围绕"reimbursement""indemnification""contribution"和"recovery"四个词汇及其变体展开，可以从这四个词汇的内涵、用法及变体的使用频率角度展开分析。

(1)词汇内涵及用法

通过查阅《柯林斯英语词典》和《布莱克法律词典》可知，reimbursement 的释义为：If you receive reimbursement for money that you have spent, you get your money back, for example because the money should have been paid by someone else。该词主要指一方要求另一方对已经支付或产生的费用、损失等进行补偿或退还。在《民法典》的语境中，它常用于描述一方为另一方垫付了费用后，要求对方进行偿还的情况。reimbursement for 表示因某事而进行的偿还或报销。例如，reimbursement for expense 表示因费用而进行的报销。reimbursement to 表示向某人进行的偿还或支付。例如，reimbursement to the creditor 表示向债权人进行偿还。

indemnify（indemnification 的动词形式）的释义为：To save harmless; to secure against loss or damage; to give security for the reimbursement of a person in case of an anticipated loss falling upon him. Also to make good; to compensate; to make reimbursement to one of a loss already incurred by him。该词主要指一方(赔偿方)承诺在另一方(受偿方)因第三方索赔而遭受损失时,对受偿方进行赔偿,同时向第三方进行追偿,以免受损失或伤害,更多地用于描述一种保护机制或保险责任。indemnification against sth.,表示对某事的赔偿。例如,indemnification against losses 表示对损失的赔偿。

contribution 的释义为:The sharing of a loss or payment among several. The act of any one or several of a number of co-debtors, co-sureties, etc., in reimbursing one of their number who has paid the whole debt or suffered the whole liability, each to the extent of his proportionate share。该词涉及共同责任或费用的分担。在《民法典》中,当多方对同一债务承担连带责任时,若一方偿还了超出自己份额的债务,则有权向其他连带责任人追偿其应分担的部分,这种追偿可以视为一种"分担"追偿。在法律文本中,该词常见的搭配短语有 joint contribution、capital contribution。

recover (recovery 的动词形式)的释义为:to gain (something) by the judgement of a court of law。该词突出通过法律程序(如诉讼)收回损失、费用或债权。在法律文本中,该词常见的搭配有 recover damages(获得损害赔偿)、recover judgment against sb.(获得不利于某人的判决,即胜诉)。

(2)使用频率

在法宝版和总库版译文中,contribution 的短语搭配只有"contribution against"一种表述。而 reimbursement 及其变体有"claim reimbursement from""be reimbursed by"两种表述;indemnification 及其变体有"claim indemnities from""indemnification against"两种表述;recovery 及其变体有"be recovered from""exercise recovery against"两种表述。在同样的法律语境下,同一个词汇有多种短语搭配可供选择,译者应在同一文本下统一表述,以彰显法律语言的严谨性。根据四大数据库中检索上述六个短语的使用频次(见表 17.2)和情境,可为译者提供 reimbursement、indemnification 和

recovery 搭配短语的普适性翻译。对于"向……追偿"结构，reimbursement 的短语搭配可使用 be reimbursed by；indemnification 的短语搭配可使用 indemnification against；recovery 的短语搭配可使用 be recovered from；contribution 的短语搭配可使用 contribution against。

表 17.2 "向……追偿"的英文表达方式及检索频次

表达方式	国内	国外		
	香港法例库	英国立法库	美国联邦法规库	美国法典库
claim reimbursement from	0	4	998	553
be reimbursed by	5	178	2668	1365
claim indemnities from	0	0	343	96
indemnification against	0	137	203	89
be recovered from	46	＞200	2693	509
exercise recovery against	0	＞200	167	185
contribution against	1	5	5	3723

17.3.2 从句式结构角度分析

(1)"可以向……追偿"句式

例句 1—4 同属该结构。该中文句式使用"主语＋情态动词(可以)＋介词(向)＋宾语＋动词(追偿)"的结构，用于表达一种可能性或允许性，并明确指出动作的对象和目标。在翻译该句式时，译者应最大限度保持原文结构的特点，根据英文表达习惯，可采用"主语＋情态动词＋动词短语＋宾语"的结构。对于情态动词的选择，"可以"在英文中通常翻译为"can"或"may"，但是"can"更侧重于能力，而"may"更常用于表达一种法律上的权利、允许或建议，是更为正式、礼貌的语气，符合法律文件的用语规范。

例句 1 中的"追偿"是指法人在承担了因法定代表人过错而产生的民事责任后，有权依法要求该法定代表人赔偿法人因此遭受的损失。此处强调依照法律规定和法律手段进行追偿，与 recover 的释义和侧重点相照应，因此该句式可译为“may be recovered from”。

例句2是指当其中一个债务人向债权人履行了全部或部分债务后，有权根据法律规定或约定，要求其他债务人按照一定比例分担他所支付的债务。此处强调债务主体应共同分担债务，因此该句式可译为“may request for contribution against”。

例句3描述的是一个基于次承租人实际支付的费用（租金和违约金）而产生的追偿权。此处使用reimbursement最符合原文情境，因为次承租人实际支付了费用（租金和违约金），并有权要求承租人偿还超出其应付租金的部分。这是一个基于先前支付的直接补偿。因此该句式可译为“may be reimbursed by”。

例句4是指当提供劳务一方因第三人的行为受到损害时，接受劳务一方可能会基于与提供劳务一方的合同关系或法律规定而先对其进行补偿。在接受劳务一方履行了补偿义务后，他们就有权向真正的责任方（即第三人）追偿，以弥补自己支付的补偿金额，同时也是对提供劳务一方的一种保护机制。该语境与indemnification使用场景相契合，因此该句式应译为“may claim indemnification against”。

（2）“有权向……追偿”句式

例句5—11同属该结构。中文句式为“主语+‘有权’+‘向’+宾语+‘追偿’”，该句式强调权利的客观存在性和强制性，因此在翻译时要格外注意“有权”一词。在“享有……权利”一节中可以知道，“have the right”强调权利存在和归属；“be entitled to”是指权利主体做出某种贡献、符合某一标准或资格，从而被某权力机构赋予一定权利。本句式中权利为主体享有的平等权利，因此可译为“have the right to”。此外，shall虽体现法律语言中的义务性和强制性，但“有权……”句式结构属于简单的陈述句，根据简明英语的要求，此处最好省去shall，以避免冗余。

例句5、例句6都涉及某一主体在承担了超出其应分担的责任或损失后，要求其他责任主体分摊这部分额外的责任或损失的行为，因此该两例句中的结构应译为“have the right to contribution against”。

例句 7、例句 8 中的“追偿”均涉及赔偿方因第三方损失而进行担保性赔偿，并向第三方追偿，同时突出了对受偿方的预防保护机制，因此此处该结构可译为“have the right to indemnification against”。

例句 9、例句 10 都涉及一方为另一方支付了费用或承担了损失后，要求对方进行偿还的行为，因此该结构应译为“have the right to be reimbursed by”。

例句 11 表明行为主体要在承担保证责任的范围内，即依据法律规定和程序进行追偿，因此该结构应译为“have the right to be recovered from”。

小　结

“向……追偿”结构可分为“可以向……追偿”和“有权向……追偿”两种句式。针对该结构的翻译，从词汇和句式结构角度进行分析总结，可提出如下翻译建议：

“可以向……追偿”：①当强调对已支付的费用进行追偿时，可译为“may be reimbursed by”；②当强调赔偿方因第三方损失而对受偿方进行担保性赔偿，并同时向第三方追偿时，可译为“may claim indemnification against”；③当强调多方共同承担责任或费用时，可译为“may request for contribution against”；④当强调通过法律程序追偿利益时，可译为“may be recovered from”。

“有权向……追偿”：①当强调对已支付的费用进行追偿时，可译为“have the right to be reimbursed by”；②当赔偿方因第三方损失而对受偿方进行担保性赔偿，并同时向第三方追偿时，可译为“have the right to indemnification against”；③当强调多方共同承担责任或费用时，可译为“have the right to contribution against”；④当强调通过法律程序追偿利益时，可译为“have the right to be recovered from”。

18 “有……约束力”结构的翻译

18.1 结构特点及其在《民法典》中的运用

18.1.1 结构特点

“有……约束力”结构在法律条文中，主要指某一法律规范、合同条款等对特定对象（如个人、组织、国家机关等）的行为具有强制性的限定和要求。该结构为动宾结构，其中，“有”是动词，表示存在或具备某种性质或能力；“……约束力”是宾语部分，指必须遵守或执行的法律约束。该结构前通常涉及法律文件和条款制定的背景条件、目的、适用范围等；其后可能进一步说明该法律文件和条款的执行、监督与解释。该结构的运用体现了法律的权威性和强制性。

18.1.2 在《民法典》中的运用

《民法典》中“有……约束力”结构一共出现了 13 次。其中，“对……有……约束力”句式结构共出现 7 次；“对……不具有……约束力”句式结构共出现 2 次；“自始没有……约束力”句式结构共出现 4 次。

当“有……约束力”结构作为法律条款的表述时，通常直接规定了某一法律规范或合同条款对特定对象具有法律约束力。如第 119 条规定：“依法成立的合同，对当事人具<u>有</u>法律<u>约束力</u>。”该条款直接规定依法成立的合同对当事人的法律约束力。这种约束力是由法律赋予，具有不可抗拒性。当“有……约束力”作为法律解释或说明时，通常用于对某一法律规范或合同条款的法律效果或法律地位进行解释。如第465条规定：“依法成立的合同，仅对当事人具有法律约束力，但是法律另有规定的除外。”其中的“仅对当事人具有法律约束力”是对前面依法成立合同的进一步解释和说明，强调了合同的约束力具有相对性。

(1)“对……有……约束力”句式

该句式通常用于表述某个法律文件、协议或合同条款对特定主体产生的法律约束效果。在具有约束力的情况下，当事人必须按照法律文件、协议或合同条款的约定履行义务，否则将承担相应的法律责任。如第1065条规定：“夫妻对婚姻关系存续期间所得的财产以及婚前财产的约定，对双方具有法律约束力。”这体现了夫妻双方对财产作出的约定，一旦符合法律规定，即对双方产生法律约束，不得擅自变更或解除约定。

(2)“对……不具有……约束力”句式

该句式用于表述某个法律文件、协议或合同条款对特定主体不产生法律约束效果，通常出现在合同无效、被撤销或特定条款被排除适用的情况下。如第717条规定：“承租人经出租人同意将租赁物转租给第三人，转租期限超过承租人剩余租赁期限的，超过部分的约定对出租人不具有法律约束力，但是出租人与承租人另有约定的除外。”该句式明确了出租人在转租合同中的权利范围，即约定以外的内容不受法律约束，起到了明确法律界限、维护双方利益的作用。

(3)“自始没有……约束力”句式

该句式用于表述某个法律行为或合同从一开始就不具备法律约束力，在时间上更具追溯力。在自始就没有约束力的法律情况下，法律行为或合同无法产生约束效果，因此行为主体也无须履行相应的义务。如第1113条规定：“无效的收养行为自始没有法律约束力。”该规定明确了无效收养行为的法律后果，无效的收养行为可能意味着收养关系并未合法建立，因此被收养人和收养人的权益都可能受到损害。该规定有助于保护双方的合法权益，避免因无效收养行为而产生的法律纠纷。

18.2 译文对比

表 18.1 《民法典》中“有……约束力”结构的翻译对比

序号	出处（条）	原文	北大法宝译文（法宝版译文）	国家法规总库译文（总库版译文）
1	119	依法成立的合同，对当事人具有法律约束力。	A contract entered into in accordance with the law shall be legally binding upon the parties to the contract.	A contract formed in accordance with law is legally binding on the parties to the contract.
2	383	供役地以及供役地上的土地承包经营权、建设用地使用权等部分转让时，转让部分涉及地役权的，地役权对受让人具有法律约束力。	When the servient land and the conventional usufruct on rural land for agricultural operations or the right to use land for construction thereon, among others, is partially transferred, if servitude is involved in the transferred part, the servitude shall be legally binding upon the transferee.	Where a right to easement is involved when the servient land and a right to contractual management of land, a right to use a lot of land for construction purposes, and the like rights thereon are partially transferred, the easement is legally binding on the transferee.
3	1016	民事主体变更姓名、名称的，变更前实施的民事法律行为对其具有法律约束力。	Where a party to civil legal relations changes his name, the civil legal acts conducted before the change shall be legally binding upon him or it.	For a person of the civil law who changes the name or entity name, the civil juristic acts performed by the person before the name change is legally binding on the person.

续表

序号	出处（条）	原文	北大法宝译文（法宝版译文）	国家法规总库译文（总库版译文）
4	465	依法成立的合同，仅**对**当事人具**有**法律**约束力**，但是法律另有规定的除外。	A contract legally formed **shall be legally binding** only **on** the parties, except as otherwise provided by the law.	A contract formed in accordance with law **is legally binding** only **on** the parties to the contract, unless otherwise provided by law.
5	1065	夫妻对婚姻关系存续期间所得的财产以及婚前财产的约定，**对**双方具**有**法律**约束力**。	The agreement reached between husband and wife on the property acquired during the marriage and on their prenuptial property **shall be legally binding on** both parties.	The agreement on their premarital property and the property acquired during the marriage **is legally binding on** both parties to the marriage.
6	717	承租人经出租人同意将租赁物转租给第三人，转租期限超过承租人剩余租赁期限的，超过部分的约定**对**出租人**不具有**法律**约束力**，但是出租人与承租人另有约定的除外。	Where a lessee subleases the leased property to a third party with the consent of the lessor under a sublease term in excess of the remaining lease term in favor of the lessee, the agreement in connection with the excess **shall be without legal binding force on** the lessor, unless otherwise agreed by the lessor and the lessee.	Where a lessee, upon consent of the lessor, subleases the leased object to a third person, if the term of the sublease exceeds the remaining term of the original lease, the sublease beyond the term of the original lease **is not legally binding on** the lessor unless otherwise agreed by the lessor and the lessee.

续表

序号	出处(条)	原文	北大法宝译文(法宝版译文)	国家法规总库译文(总库版译文)
7	719	承租人拖欠租金的,次承租人可以代承租人支付其欠付的租金和违约金,但是转租合同**对**出租人**不具有**法律**约束力**的除外。	Where a lessee is in default on rent, the sublessee may pay the rent and liquidated damages owed on behalf of the lessee, unless the sublease contract **is without legal binding force on** the lessor.	Where a lessee defaults on payment of the rent, the sublessee may pay the rent in arrears and the liquidated damages for the lessee, unless the sublease contract **is not legally binding on** the lessor.
8	155	无效的或者被撤销的民事法律行为**自始没有**法律**约束力**。	A void or revoked juridical act **is not legally binding from the outset.**	A void or revoked civil juristic act **does not have any legal force *ab initio*.**
9	1054	无效的或者被撤销的婚姻**自始没有**法律**约束力**,当事人不具有夫妻的权利和义务。	An invalid or annulled marriage **is not legally binding from the outset**, and the parties concerned are devoid of any rights or duties of a husband and a wife.	A void or annulled marriage **has no legal effect *ab initio*,** and neither party to such a marriage shall have any rights or duties arising from the marital relationship.
10	1113	无效的收养行为**自始没有**法律**约束力**。	A void adoption **is not legally binding from the outset.**	A void adoption **has no legal effect *ab initio*** .

18.3 译文分析

以下对比分析两个版本中"有……约束力"结构的译文,从不同角度探讨各种情况下较为可取的翻译方法。

18.3.1 "对……有……约束力"句式

例句1—5同属该句式。法宝版译文为"shall be legally binding upon"(例句1—3)和"shall be legally binding on"(例句4、例句5),总库版译文为"is legally binding on"(例句1—5)。基于该两版译文的不同,我们可以就shall和binding的运用情况进行分析。

(1)是否使用shall

在法律语境中,"shall"与第二、第三人称一起使用时通常表达一种义务、责任或必须性(李克兴,2007),突出了法律条款或合同所规定的行为必须被严格遵守和执行,从而体现了法律的强制性。从句式结构角度来看,该句为陈述句,"对"作为介词,清晰地指明了约束力的施加对象,"有"是谓语动词,表示存在或具有某种性质或状态,而"约束力"则是这种性质或状态的具体内容。从语义角度来看,这一句式通常用于表达法律条款或合同对特定对象所产生的限制,句式本身更多的是在描述一种约束力存在的客观状态,而非行为的强制性或必须性。因此,直接使用一般现在时可以更加简洁地表达某法条或合同对特定对象存在约束力的客观事实。

(2)binding的运用情况

通过查阅《布莱克法律词典》可知,bind的释义为:To obligate; to affect one in a constraining or compulsory manner with a contract or a judgment. So long as a contract, an adjudication, or a legal relation remains in force and virtue, and continues to impose duties or obligations, it is said to be "binding"。legally binding的释义是:Lawful action, such as an agreement consciously agreed to by two or more entities, establishing lawful accountability。通过以上释义可知,"bind"在法律语境中通常表示使承担义务或责任;"binding"强调某种行为、合同或法律关系仍然有效并具有法律约束力;而"legally binding"则进一步明确了这种约束力是合法的,由两个或多个实体自觉达成的协议所确立的。bind一词有多种搭配,例如,bind over(具结、保释)、binding authority(具有法律约

束力的裁定)、binding agreement(具有约束力的协议)、binding instructions(对陪审团做的有约束力的指示,等同于 binding jury instruction)等。

be legally binding on 和 be legally binding upon 虽都表示某个协议、合同或规定具有法律约束力,但其使用场景仍有细微差别。be legally binding on 通常用于描述某个法律文件、合同、协议或规定对某个体、组织或实体产生的法律约束力,更侧重于描述约束力本身。该结构用于较为直接、简洁的表述中,强调法律约束力的客观性和直接性。be legally binding upon 在某些情况下更侧重于强调被约束对象的义务和责任,即特定对象必须遵守或履行某事物或协议的规定。该结构在语体上更加正式和书面化,带有一定的庄重和强调意味。通过上文对"对……有……约束力"句式结构和语义分析可知,该句式强调某法条或合同对特定对象存在客观上的约束力,而非约束对象行为的强制性。因此,be legally binding on 可视为该句式结构的最佳译文。例句 4 中的约束力指的是合同所设定的权利和义务对合同当事人的约束,是客观存在的,但并不直接等同于强制执行。同样,例句 3 强调尽管主体的身份标识发生了变化,但其在变更前所做出的法律行为仍然有效,并对其产生约束力。这种约束力是客观的,来源于法律对民事法律行为效力的认可和保护。此外,简明法律英语的趋势也要求使用 binding on 这样更简洁、直接的表述,在四大数据库中对两短语使用频次的检索结果(见表 18.2),也验证了我们的结论。

表 18.2 "对……有……约束力"的英文表达方式及检索频次

表达方式	国内	国外		
	香港法例库	英国立法库	美国联邦法规库	美国法典库
(be legally) binding on	153	>200	2374	1159
(be legally) binding upon	11	>200	1182	589

18.3.2 "对……不具有……约束力"句式

例句 6、例句 7 同属该结构。法宝版的译文为"shall be without legal

binding force on" 和 "is without legal binding force on"。总库版译文为 "is not legally binding on"。

该句式源自"对……有……约束力"的否定形式,它同样着重强调了一种状态,即某事物或规定对特定对象不产生法律上的约束效力。例句 6 明确指出了转租期限超出部分对出租人没有法律上的约束效力,即出租人不受这部分约定的限制。例句 7 指出转租合同中的条款对出租人没有法律上的强制要求,即出租人不受转租合同的约束。这两个案例清晰地界定了出租人、承租人和次承租人之间的法律关系,通过客观、明确的表述方式避免潜在的法律纠纷。

因此,在翻译此类句式时,我们无须保留 "shall",仅通过添加否定词来构建否定关系,即可简洁明了地传达出相应的法律含义。"be not legally binding on" 句式与"对……有……约束力"的译文 "be legally binding on" 相对应,通过添加否定词直接否定了法律约束力的存在,明确指出某事物或规定对某对象并无法律上的限制。这种表达更加直接,是法律文本中常见的表述方式。

"be without legal binding force" 中 force 一词在法律语境下特指 "binding power", "binding",即法律上的约束力或强制力。与介词 of 搭配时,它表示:In force; extant; not obsolete; existing as a binding or obligatory power,即作为具有约束力或义务性的权力而存在。然而,鉴于 binding 一词已经充分表达了法律约束力的含义,为了避免重复,保持法律语言的严谨性和简洁性,我们在翻译时无须额外翻译 "force" 一词。

18.3.3 "自始没有……约束力" 句式

例句 8—10 同属该结构。法宝版译文为 "be not legally binding from the outset",总库版译文为 "does not have any legal force *ab initio*"(例句 8)和 "have no legal effect *ab initio*"(例句 9、例句 10)。

中文句式"自始没有……约束力"表达了一个明确的时间起点(自始)和一个否定的状态(没有约束力),指某种规定、条款或协议从一开始就不具备法律上的约束力。例句 8 表明从一开始各方当事人就不受这些无效或被撤销行为的约束，任何基于这些无效或被撤销行为的交易、合同或协议都将被视为无效，各方无须承担由此产生的法律责任。例句 9 指明该条件下的夫妻，从开始就不具有夫妻的权利和义务，包括夫妻共同财产、继承权、抚养义务等。例句 10 同样表明，无效的收养行为下，收养人无须承担抚养、教育等责任，被收养人也无法享受收养关系带来的权益。这也有助于解决因无效收养行为而产生的身份确认、财产分配等一系列法律问题。因此，在翻译该句式时，译者要注意清晰传达时间的起点和法律术语“约束力”一词。

法宝版译文将“自始”译为“from the outset”，将“没有……约束力”这一法律状态译为“be not legally binding”，通过采用“对……不具有……约束力”的译文句式结构，不仅强调了某规定从开始就不具备约束力的客观事实，还使得整个译文句式紧凑、流畅，与中文原句在语义和逻辑上保持了高度的一致性。但是“from the outset”与“*ab initio*”相比，正式性较弱，在法律文件中显得不够专业。

总库版译文将“自始”译为“*ab initio*”，其英文释义为：Latin, for from the first act or meaning from the start。该词为拉丁词汇，强调从最开始就不具备某种法律状态或效力。例如，an agreement declared void *ab initio* 指的是一个自始无效的协议。对于“约束力”一词，总库版给出了“legal effect”和“legal force”两种译文。“legal effect”通常指的是法律上的效果或影响，虽然也涵盖“约束力”的含义，但相对于“legally binding”来说，它更侧重于描述法律条文、规定或行为所产生的效力，而不仅仅是约束力。而“legal force”则更多强调法律上的强制力，指法律条文、规定或协议等所具备能够强制要求人们遵守的某种力量，而这种力量确保了法律的权威性和执行力，与原文中强调“约束力”是否存在的客观状态不相符。

因此，考虑到明晰中文句式的时间点和法律术语，结合原生英语法律语料库中的检索结果（见表 18.3），建议将“自始没有……约束力”译为“be not legally binding *ab initio*”。

表 18.3 “自始没有……约束力”的英文表达方式及检索频次

表达方式	国内	国外		
	香港法例库	英国立法库	美国联邦法规库	美国法典库
from the outset	0	142	9	0
ab initio	6	25	55	13860

小　结

“有……约束力”结构可分为“对……有……约束力”“对……不具有……约束力”和“自始没有……约束力”三种句式。针对该结构的翻译，从各个角度进行分析，可提出如下一般性翻译建议：

“对……有……约束力”可译为“be legally binding on”；“对……不具有……约束力”可译为“be not legally binding on”；“自始没有……约束力”可译为“be not legally binding *ab initio*”。

19 “在……期限内”结构的翻译

19.1 结构特点及其在《民法典》中的运用

19.1.1 结构特点

“在……期限内”结构在法律条文中，主要指在法律明确规定的特定时间段内，相关的法律主体需要完成特定的法律行为或遵守特定的法律要求。该结构前通常会明确法律行为的主体，该期限设定的背景及期限内要完成的行为。“在”字引出时间范围，并用“期限内”进行限定，使得时间范围变得明确且具体。该结构后可能会明确列出如果未能在规定期限内完成行为或满足条件将面临的法律后果或需要采取的后续行动。该结构的运用体现了法律中时间因素的重要性，确保了法律行为的规范。

19.1.2 在《民法典》中的运用

《民法典》中“在……期限内”结构一共出现了60次。其中，“在(……)合理期限内”句式结构共出现37次；“在(其他有明确约定的)期限内”句式结构共出现了23次。该结构在《民法典》中运用广泛，涉及合同履行、权利行使等期限要求。如第306条规定：“其他共有人应当**在**合理**期限内**行使优先购买权。”此处“合理期限”虽是模糊的时间概念，其具体的时间长度仍需根据具体的情况进行分析，但该结构在保障其他共有人的优先购买权及维护市场秩序上有重要意义。又如第495条规定：“当事人约定**在**将来一定**期限内**订立合同的认购书、订购书、预订书等，构成预约合同。”“将来一定期限内”通常指的是在未来的某个具体时间范围内，尽管这个时间段在当下是未知或模糊的，但“一定期限”意味着该期限是基于双方约定或法律规定而存在的，对双方依法履行合同有约束力。

(1)“在(……)合理期限内”句式

该句式通常用于表述某个行为或事件应当在一个公认为合理或适当的时间范围内进行。这里的“合理期限”是一个相对模糊但具有重要意义的时间概念，其具体的时间长度因情况而异，包括但不限于当事人的合理预期、交易习惯、市场情况、法律规定以及行业标准等因素。如第916条规定：“储存期限届满，存货人或者仓单持有人不提取仓储物的，保管人可以催告其**在合理期限内**提取。”该条中的“合理期限”应根据具体情况进行判定。例如，如果仓储物是易腐食品，为防止食品变质，那么合理期限可能会相对较短；而如果仓储物是耐用品，那么合理期限可能会相对较长。

(2)“在(其他有明确约定的)期限内”句式

该句式通常用于表述某个行为或义务等应当在双方明确约定的具体时间范围内进行。此处的“期限”除是法律法规或一般交易习惯所规定外，还可以是当事人根据双方意愿和协商达成的具体期限。如第531条规定：“执行政府定价或者政府指导价的，**在合同约定的交付期限内**政府价格调整时，按照交付时的价格计价。”该条中“合同约定的交付期限”是双方当事人在签订合同时，根据交易的具体情况和双方的需求，通过协商达成的具体期限。这一期限具有明确的起止时间，是双方共同认可的。通过明确期限，双方可以顺利进行交易，保护自身的合法权益。

19.2 译文对比

表 19.1 《民法典》中"在……期限内"结构的翻译对比

序号	出处(条)	原文	北大法宝译文(法宝版译文)	国家法规总库译文(总库版译文)
1	306	其他共有人应当在合理期限内行使优先购买权。	Other co-owners shall exercise the preemptive right within a reasonable period.	The other co-owners shall exercise their right of pre-emption within a reasonable period of time.
2	807	发包人未按照约定支付价款的，承包人可以催告发包人在合理期限内支付价款。	If the employer failed to pay the price in accordance with the contract, the contractor may demand payment from the employer within a reasonable period.	Where a contract-offering party fails to pay the price in accordance with the agreement, the contractor may demand the contract-offering party to make the payment within a reasonable period of time.
3	916	储存期限届满，存货人或者仓单持有人不提取仓储物的，保管人可以催告其在合理期限内提取。	At the expiry of the warehousing period, if the depositor or holder of the warehouse receipt fails to take delivery of the warehoused property, the depositary may demand delivery taken within a reasonable period.	Where a depositor or a holder of the warehouse receipt fails to collect the stored goods upon expiration of the warehousing period, the warehouser may demand the depositor or the holder of the warehouse receipt to collect the goods within a reasonable period of time.
4	481	要约以非对话方式作出的，承诺应当在合理期限内到达。	If the offer is made in forms other than a dialog, the acceptance shall reach the offeror within a reasonable time limit.	where an offer is not made through real-time communication, the acceptance shall reach the offeror within a reasonable period of time.

续表

序号	出处（条）	原文	北大法宝译文（法宝版译文）	国家法规总库译文（总库版译文）
5	944	业主违反约定逾期不支付物业费的，物业服务人可以催告其**在合理期限内**支付。	If the owner fails to pay the management fee overdue in breach of the agreement, the property management service provider may demand its payment **within a reasonable time limit**.	Where an owner fails to pay the property management fees within the agreed period in breach of the agreement, the property management service provider may demand the payment be made **within a reasonable period of time.**
6	486	受要约人超过承诺期限发出承诺，或者**在承诺期限内**发出承诺，按照通常情形不能及时到达要约人的，为新要约。	Where an offeree makes an acceptance beyond the time limit for acceptance, or makes an acceptance **within the time limit** for acceptance which is unable to reach the offeror in a timely manner under normal circumstances, the acceptance shall be a new offer.	Where an offeree makes an acceptance beyond the time limit for acceptance, or an acceptance is made **within the time limit** for acceptance but it cannot reach the offeror in time under normal circumstances, such an acceptance constitutes a new offer.
7	495	当事人约定**在将来一定期限内**订立合同的认购书、订购书、预订书等，构成预约合同。	A subscription order, purchase order, pre-order, etc., under which the parties agree to enter into a contract **within a certain time limit** in the future shall constitute a preliminary agreement.	A letter of subscription, letter of order, letter of reservation, or the like, in which the parties agree to conclude a contract **within a certain period of time** in the future, constitutes a preliminary contract.

续表

序号	出处(条)	原文	北大法宝译文(法宝版译文)	国家法规总库译文(总库版译文)
8	513	执行政府定价或者政府指导价的,**在合同约定的交付期限内**政府价格调整时,按照交付时的价格计价。	Where a price set by the government or based on government issued pricing guidelines is adopted, if the price is adjusted **within the time limit** for delivery as stipulated in the contract, the payment shall be calculated according to the price at the time of delivery.	Where a government-set or government-guided price is adopted in a contract, if the said price is adjusted **within the** delivery **period** agreed in the contract, the contract price shall be the price as adjusted at the time of delivery.
9	621	当事人约定检验期限的,买受人应当**在检验期限内**将标的物的数量或者质量不符合约定的情形通知出卖人。	Where the parties have agreed upon an inspection period, the buyer shall notify the seller of any non-compliance in quantity or quality of the subject matter **within** such inspection **period**.	Where the parties have not agreed on a period of inspection, the buyer shall notify the seller of any inconformity of the subject matter with the agreed quantity or quality **within a** reasonable **period of time** after he discovers or should have discovered the inconformity.
10	816	旅客因自己的原因不能按照客票记载的时间乘坐的,应当**在约定的期限内**办理退票或者变更手续。	Where the passenger is unable to board the means of transportation at the time stated on the passenger ticket due to any reason attributable to himself, he or she shall undergo the formalities for ticket cancellation and refund or for ticket modification **within the** agreed **period**.	A passenger who is unable to get on board at the time indicated on the ticket due to his own reason shall, **within the period of time** agreed by the parties, undergo the procedures for refund or change of the ticket.

19.3 译文分析

以下对比分析两个版本中"在……期限内"结构的译文，从词汇和句式角度探讨各种情况下较为可取的翻译方法。

19.3.1 从词汇角度分析

在"在……期限内"结构中，法宝版给出了"within the/a period"（例句1—3、例句9、例句10）和"within the/a time limit"（例句4—8）两种译文；总库版给出了"within the/a period"（例句8）、"within the/ a time limit"（例句6）和"within the/a period of time"（例句1—5、例句7、例句9、例句10）三种译文。我们可从period、period of time、time limit的释义、用法等方面进行对比分析。

①period：Any point，space，or division of time. "The word 'period' has its etymo-logical meaning，but it also has a distinctive signification，according to the subject with which it may be used in connection. It may mean any portion of complete time，from a thousand years or less to the period of a day；and when used to designate an act to be done or to be begun，though its completion may take an uncertain time，as，for instance，the act of exportation，it must mean the day on which the exportation commences，or it would be an unmeaning and useless word in its connection in the statute." 根据《布莱克法律词典》的解释，period通常指的是一个具体的、有明确起始和结束点的时间段，可以长至一千年，也可以短至一天。在法律语境中，该词用于描述某个事件、合同或法律程序的有效期或持续时间，可能包括合同的有效期、法律的适用期、权利的行使期等。例如，在香港法规中，中期报告期（interim reporting period）就认可机构而言，指该机构的财政年度的首6个月（2016年第195号法律公告）。半年度报告期（semi-annual reporting period）就认可机构而言，指该机构的

财政年度的第一或第二个 6 个月期间(2016 年第 195 号法律公告)。季度报告期(quarterly reporting period)就认可机构而言,指该机构的财政年度的第一、第二、第三或第四个 3 个月期间(2016 年第 195 号法律公告)。上述例子中,“中期报告期”“半年度报告期”和“季度报告期”都是对认可机构财政年度内不同时间段的具体划分。这些时间段都有明确的起始和结束点,即它们都是具体的“period”。

此外,当 period 用于指定一个行动时,它通常指的是该行动开始的时间点,而非行动完成的时间,因为法律往往关注行动的开始,以确定其是否符合特定的法律要求或期限。period 还可以与其他词汇结合,形成更具体的法律概念,如 contract period(合同期限),probation period(特指雇佣关系中的试用期),period of employment(雇佣期间),period of adjournment(休会期)等。

②period of time:相比于 period 着重强调时间的起止以避免某种歧义,该短语则是一个更宽泛的时间概念,通常用于描述那些不需要精确到具体日期,而是根据法律要求、合同条款或实际情况来灵活确定的时间范围。例如,在合同中,当双方需要规定某个事件或行为必须发生或持续的时间范围时,可能会使用“period of time”这一表述。这个时间段可能是一个月、一年或者更长的时间,通常会在合同中用“合理时间”“适当”等表述来进行限定。这样的表达具有一定的灵活性,能够适应不同情况下的实际需求。如香港法规中《内地和香港特别行政区关于对所得避免双重征税和防止偷漏税的安排》第一至二十七条中提到的:The competent authorities of the both Sides shall notify each other of significant changes that have been made in their respective taxation laws within a reasonable period of time after such changes.。(双语对照:双方主管当局应将各自税法所作出的实质变动,在其变动后的适当时间内通知对方)

③time limit:A time limit is a date before which a particular task must be completed. 该词可译为“时限”,通常指的是一个明确的、严格的截止日期或时间。在法律语境中,time limit 通常被解释为“期限”或“限期”,指的

是法律文件、合同、诉讼程序等所规定的必须完成某项任务的时间限制。这个时间限制具有法律约束力，超过该期限会产生不利的法律后果，如丧失权利、承担法律责任等。除非法律另有规定或当事人另有约定，time limit 还具有不可更改性。通常来说，该短语会与具体的时期或时间共同使用，以明确任务必须完成的截止日期。例如，美国联邦法规"7.33 What time limits apply to DOT with respect to administrative appeals (final determinations)?"中提到，"DOT issues a determination with respect to any appeal made pursuant to §7.32(d) within twenty Federal working days after receipt of such appeal, except that in unusual circumstances DOT may extend this time limit by up to ten Federal working days in accordance with §7.34(a) or for more than ten Federal working days in accordance with §7.34(b)."。此处 time limit 后跟具体的时间，确保在收到上诉后有足够的时间做出决定，同时也为当事人提供了明确的预期。

19.3.2 从句式角度分析

(1)"在(……)合理期限内"句式

例句 1—5 同属该句式。该句式主要由介词"在"以及"合理期限内"这个表达时间范围的短语组成。"在"作为时间状语的引导词，用于指出某个动作或状态发生的时间背景或条件。"(……)合理期限内"为句式的核心部分，其中"合理期限"前为某些具体范围或依据，"合理期限内"则强调了时间的合理性和限定性，表示某个行为或事件需要在一个被认为是合适的时间段内完成或发生。该结构在语义上更加灵活，强调根据实际情况和特定目的确定一个既公平又合理的时间范围，在实际应用中具有一定的可协商性。这一句式与 period of time 的释义及用法相对应。

例句 1 指其他共有人需要在一定时间内表明其行使优先购买权的意愿，并可能需要在更短的时间内完成购买行为。此处的"合理期限"取决于具体情况，如共有财产的性质、市场情况、转让通知的方式等。例句 2 中的"合理期限"取决于合同的约定、双方的关系、工程的进度等，旨在保护承包人的合法权益,同时给予发包人一定的宽限期以履行其支付义务。例句3中"合理期限"是保管人给予存货人或仓单持有人提取仓储物的最后通知期限,这个期限的合理性取决于仓储合同的约定、货物的性质、存储条件等,目的为确保仓库资源的有效利用,避免因长时间占用而产生额外费用。例句4指接收方需要在"合理期限内"作出承诺,即表示同意要约的条款并愿意与其订立合同,这个期限的合理性取决于要约的具体内容、双方的关系、交易的性质等,但期限时间通常不应过长,以免丧失交易机会或造成不必要的延误。例句5中的"合理期限"取决于物业服务合同的约定、业主的支付能力、物业服务的性质等,目的是保护物业服务企业的合法权益,防止其因业主的违约行为而遭受损失。通过上述分析可以看到,"合理期限内"在不同情境下的具体长度应根据具体情况进行确定,受到法律或合同条款的约束,这与 period of time 对于时间范围的灵活性把控相呼应。

此外,译者还需关注 period of time 短语前的冠词选择。当"合理期限内"前标明具体范围时,即中文句式强调的是一个特定的、已知的合理期限,则应使用定冠词 the。例如,"在合同约定的合理期限内",这里的"合同约定的"是一个定语,修饰"合理期限",表明这个期限是特定的,该句式则需翻译成"within the reasonable period of time stipulated in the contract"。当"合理期限内"前无范围所指,即中文句式强调的是一个泛指的、不特定的合理期限,则使用不定冠词 a。如"在合理期限内",这里的期限是没有特定指向的,因此应译为"within a reasonable period of time"。在《民法典》中,"合理期限"前表达具体范围的表述较少,通常情况下译者可将该结构译为"within a reasonable period of time"。

(2)"在(其他有明确约定的)期限内"句式

例句6—10同属该句式。"期限内"这一表述前为某类"有明确约定"的修饰语,强调了时间限制的明确性。这意味着双方对于时间期限有共同的理解和认可,不存在模糊或歧义。此外,该句式通常出现在有具体截止日期或时间范围的合同中,在语义上更加明确,具有不可更改性。这与 time limit 这一表述的释义与用法相呼应。

例句 6 中的"承诺期限内"指的是要约人设定的、受要约人应当作出承诺的时间范围。这个期限是双方明确约定的、具有法律约束力的时间范围。例句 7 中"将来一定期限内"指的是双方明确约定的、未来某个时间点或时间段内将订立正式合同的时间范围。这个期限是预约合同的核心要素之一。如果双方未能在这一期限内订立正式合同,那么预约合同可能会失效或产生其他法律后果。例句 8 中"合同约定的交付期限内"指的是双方明确约定的货物或服务的交付时间范围。在这个期限内,如果政府价格发生调整,那么合同价格将按照交付时的价格来确定。这一规定确保了合同价格的稳定性和可预测性,避免了因价格变动而引发的纠纷。例句 9 中的"检验期限内"指的是双方明确约定的对标的物进行检验的时间范围。如果买受人未能在这一期限内提出异议,则会被视为对标的物数量或质量的认可。例句 10 中"约定的期限内"指的是旅客与运输企业明确约定的办理退票或变更手续的时间范围。旅客必须在这个期限内完成相关手续,否则可能会面临额外的费用或失去退票或变更的权利。这些例句中的"期限内"都是双方明确化且需要各方履行的严格的时间限制,因此均可译为 time limit。此外,考虑到该句式强调双方对时间限制的共识,最好选择定冠词 the 来突出时间限制的特定性。

小　结

"在……期限内"结构可分为"在……合理期限内""在合理期限内"和"在(其他有明确约定的)期限内"三种情况。当该结构为"在……合理期限内"时,可译为 "within the reasonable period of time..."。当该结构为"在合理期限内"时,可译为 "within a reasonable period of time"。当该结构为"在(其他有明确约定的)期限内"可译为 "within the time limit..."。

20 “按照……约定”结构的翻译

20.1 结构特点及其在《民法典》中的运用

20.1.1 结构特点

“按照……约定”在法律条文中强调行为主体应按照合同约定或法律规定进行行动，体现了法律约束力，保障当事人的合法权利。通常情况下，“按照”作为介词，引出某一行为所依据的标准或准则，“约定”指双方或多方达成的协议或共识，其后跟行为主体的具体行动。在少数情况下，“按照”作为动词，与“约定”连用，出现在句末，表明要依照约定行事。在逻辑上，“按照……约定”用于表达因果关系或条件关系，即如果双方之间有约定，那么行为主体应按照约定行动。

20.1.2 在《民法典》中的运用

《民法典》中“按照……约定”结构一共出现了103次。其中，“按照约定”结构出现了94次，“按照……的约定”结构出现了9次。

(1)“按照约定”结构

该结构通常用于双方或多方在某一事项上达成共识或协议，并依据该共识或协议进行具体行动。该结构分为“主体＋按照约定＋行动”和“……的，按照约定”两种句式。

①“主体＋按照约定＋行动”句式结构在《民法典》中尤其常见。该短语结构将主体置于句首，强调主体依据约定采取行动的主动性。“按照”一词为介词，用于明确行动所依据的标准，即“约定”。“约定”后为动词或动词短语，表示主体依照约定所采取的具体行动。如第509条规定：“当事人应当**按照约定**全面履行自己的义务。”其中，“当事人”作为法律关系的主体，其行为应遵循“按照约定”这一介词短语所界定的准则。而“全面履行自己的义务”则具体描述了当事人根据该约定，应直接采取“履行义务”这一行动。

②“……的，按照约定”句式结构较为少有。“……的”为条件状语，用于描述行动的前提条件，“按照约定”为动宾短语，出现在句子末尾，带有强调的语气，表明在双方有争议的情况下，应该采取“按照约定”这一行为来解决争议。如第283条规定：“建筑物及其附属设施的费用分摊、收益分配等事项，有约定**的**，**按照约定**。”其中，“有约定的”是前提条件，意味着在涉及与物业管理、共有财产的管理和使用等问题时，应该严格按照双方之前达成的约定来执行。

(2)“按照……的约定”结构

该结构为完整的介词短语结构。“……的约定”是介词“按照”的宾语，由定语“……”和中心语“约定”组成，表示具体的约定内容。该结构在语义上更加明确，突出“约定”本身的内容、性质或重要性，进一步明确双方的权利和义务。如第1213条规定：“不足部分，由承保机动车商业保险的保险人**按照**保险合同**的约定**予以赔偿。”其中，“保险合同”为定语，明确约定的具体范围，即双方就机动车商业保险事宜所达成的共识。动词短语“予以赔偿”是保险人按照约定的行为结果，明确保险人在保险赔偿金额不足以覆盖损失时应采取的赔偿行为，有助于维护双方的合法权益。

20.2 译文对比

表 20.1 《民法典》中"按照……约定"结构的翻译对比

序号	出处(条)	原文	北大法宝译文(法宝版译文)	国家法规总库译文(总库版译文)
1	300	共有人**按照约定**管理共有的不动产或者动产;没有约定或者约定不明确的,各共有人都有管理的权利和义务。	Co-owners shall manage the co-owned immovable or movable **as agreed upon**; in the absence of such an agreement or if such an agreement is ambiguous, all co-owners have the management rights and obligations.	The co-owners shall manage the co-owned immovable or movable property **in accordance with** their agreement. Where there is no agreement or the relevant agreement is unclear, each co-owner is entitled and obligated to manage it.
2	509	当事人应当**按照约定**全面履行自己的义务。	Each party shall fully perform its own obligations **as agreed**.	The parties shall fully perform their respective obligations **as agreed** in the contract.
3	868	技术秘密转让合同的让与人和技术秘密使用许可合同的许可人应当**按照约定**提供技术资料,进行技术指导,保证技术的实用性、可靠性,承担保密义务。	A transferor under a contract for transfer of know-how or a licensor under a know-how licensing contract shall, **in accordance with** the contract, supply the technical materials, provide technical guidance, and warrant the practical applicability and reliability of the technology, and shall abide by its confidentiality obligations.	A transferor under a technological know-how transfer contract or a licensor under a technological know-how licensing contract shall, **in accordance with** the agreement, provide technological materials, give technological guidance, guarantee the practical applicability and reliability of the technology, and perform confidentiality obligations.

续表

序号	出处(条)	原文	北大法宝译文(法宝版译文)	国家法规总库译文(总库版译文)
4	944	业主应当**按照约定**向物业服务人支付物业费。物业服务人已经**按照约定**和有关规定提供服务的,业主不得以未接受或者无需接受相关物业服务为由拒绝支付物业费。	An owner shall pay a management fee to the property management service provider as agreed. If the property management service provider has provided services in accordance with the agreement and relevant provisions, the owner shall not refuse to pay the management fee on the grounds that it has not accepted or need not accept relevant property management services.	An owner shall pay property management fees to the property management service provider in accordance with the agreement. Where a property management service provider has provided services in accordance with the agreement and the relevant regulations, an owner may not refuse to pay the property management fees on the ground that he has not accepted or need not accept the relevant property management service.
5	283	建筑物及其附属设施的费用分摊、收益分配等事项,有约定**的**,**按照约定**。	Where there is an agreement on such matters as the apportioning of expenses for a building and its ancillary facilities and the distribution of proceeds therefrom, such an agreement shall prevail.	Where there is an agreement on matters such as allocation of expenses on and distribution of income gained from a building and its auxiliary facilities, such matters shall be determined in accordance with the agreement.

续表

序号	出处（条）	原文	北大法宝译文（法宝版译文）	国家法规总库译文（总库版译文）
6	303	共有人约定不得分割共有的不动产或者动产，以维持共有关系的，应当按照约定，但是共有人有重大理由需要分割的，可以请求分割。	Where the co-owners have agreed not to partition the co-owned immovable or movable in order to maintain the co-ownership, such an agreement shall prevail; however, a co-owner that has any material reason for partition may request partition.	Where the co-owners have agreed not to partition the co-owned immovable or movable property in order to maintain the co-ownership, the agreement shall be followed, except that a co-owner may request partition if there is a compelling reason for partition.
7	359	该土地上的房屋以及其他不动产的归属，有约定的，按照约定。	If there is an agreement on the attribution of buildings and other immovables on the aforesaid land, such an agreement shall prevail.	The ownership of the buildings and other immovable property on such lot of land shall be determined in accordance with the agreement.
8	582	履行不符合约定的，应当按照当事人的约定承担违约责任。	Where performance fails to satisfy the agreement, the liability for breach of contract shall be borne as agreed upon by the parties.	Where a party's performance does not conform to the agreement, the party shall bear default liability as agreed in the contract.
9	970	按照合伙合同的约定或者全体合伙人的决定，可以委托一个或者数个合伙人执行合伙事务。	As agreed in the contract of partnership or decided by all partners, one or more partners may be mandated to manage partnership business.	One or more partners may be authorized to manage the partnership business in accordance with the partnership contract or the decision made by all partners.

续表

序号	出处(条)	原文	北大法宝译文(法宝版译文)	国家法规总库译文(总库版译文)
10	1213	不足部分,由承保机动车商业保险的保险人**按照**保险合同**的约定**予以赔偿。	For any shortfall, the insurer underwriting the commercial motor vehicle insurance shall make compensation **in accordance with** the insurance contract.	The deficiencies shall be paid by the insurer that underwrites the commercial motor vehicle insurance **in accordance with** the stipulations of the insurance contract.

20.3 译文分析

以下对比分析两个版本中"按照……约定"及类似结构的相应译文,探讨各种情况下较为可取的翻译方法。

20.3.1 "按照约定"结构的翻译

(1)"主体+按照约定+行动"句式

例句1—4同属该句式。法宝版译文为"as agreed upon""as agreed""in accordance with";总库版译文为"as agreed""in accordance with"。

从词汇角度来看,根据《柯林斯英语词典》,in accordance with 定义为:If something is done in accordance with a particular rule or system, it is done in the way that the rule or system says that it should be done.。该短语用于描述某行为或决策是基于某种法律、规定、原则或先前达成的协议进行的,其后常接法律、规定、原则或协议的具体名称,作为行动的依据或标准。如:..., and under other circumstances, shall be dealt with **in accordance with** Item 1.(来源:全国人民代表大会常务委员会关于根据《中华人民共和国香港特别行政区基本法》第一百六十条处理香港原有法律的决定);..., provided that the credit so allowed does not exceed the amount of Hong Kong Special Administrative Region tax computed in respect of that income **in accordance with the tax laws of the Hong Kong Special Administrative Region.**(来源:《中华人民共和国香港特别行政区与罗马尼亚关于对收入税项避免双重课税和防止逃税的协定》);..., who shall be elected by the voters of the District of Columbia **in accordance with the District of Columbia Election Act.**(来源:*2 USC 25a*:*Delegate to House of Representatives from District of Columbia*)。因此,当强调某行为是基于某具体规定或原则时,应使用 in accordance with。

根据《柯林斯英语词典》,agreed 定义为:If people are agreed on something, they have reached a joint decision on it or have the same opinion about it.。该词用于描述双方或多方之间已经存在的共识或协议。as agreed 通常用于简洁明了地表达行为是基于已达成的协议进行的;as agreed upon 的使用场景则更加正式,通常用于强调协议内容已经过充分讨论、协商和确认。如:...any other manner **as agreed by the competent authorities of both Sides.**(来源:《内地和香港特别行政区关于对所得避免双重征税和防止偷漏税的安排》第四议定书第一至六条)。此处 as agreed 用于描述双方已经达成的协议,符合法律文件简明的特点。Services and assistance made available to the Office by the Government Accountability Office in accordance with this section may be provided with or without reimbursement from funds of the Office, **as agreed upon by the Board and the Comptroller General.**(来源:*2 USC 478*:*Utilization of the Government Accountability Office*),此处 as agreed upon 用于强调协议的内容已经经过了董事会和总审计长的充分讨论、协商和确认,该表达方式更加体现了对协议过程的重视。但从四大数据库中两短语的使用频次(见表 20.2),可以看出 as agreed 的使用频率更高,这种情况可能与多数法律文本不强调协商的过程,而重在表述行动与先前达成共识的一致性有关。

表 20.2 “按照约定”的英文表达方式及检索频次

表达方式	国内	国外		
	香港法例库	英国立法库	美国联邦法规库	美国法典库
as agreed	2	3	9592	1585
as agreed upon	0	0	4742	1049

从语义角度结合词汇内涵分析，“主体＋按照约定＋行动”句式中的“按照约定”是一个概括性的表述，是主体行动的总指导原则，并未详细说明所依据的某具体条款或原则。此外，该句式通过表述主体应根据约定行动，突出主体行为的主动性，强调双方已经达成的约定结果，而非协商的过程。因此，该句式中的“按照约定”应当翻译为 as agreed。例句 1 中的“按照约定”是共有人管理共有财产的总指导原则，约定内容可能涉及共有财产的使用方式、管理责任、收益分配等方面。例句 2 中的约定是双方自愿达成的协议，规定了双方的权利和义务。例句 3 中的约定是行动指导的依据，涉及技术秘密转让和使用相关的协议。例句 4 中的“按照约定”分别指业主支付物业费和物业服务人提供服务的依据，强调了双方之间基于协议的权利和义务关系。

从句式结构角度来看，“主体＋按照约定＋行动”这一句式是“主语＋状语＋谓语”结构。在翻译时，译者既应传达中文原句内涵，最大限度地避免歧义，又要顺应英文表达方式，有效传递原文信息。因此，该句式结构可以处理为“主语＋谓语＋状语”，将主要行为放在句首，把“按照约定”处理成方式状语，将其转化为从句或分词短语以贴近英文表达习惯。译为 as agreed 既能保留原句的结构和语义重点，又保证了英文法律语言的简洁性。

(2)“……的，按照约定”句式

例句 5—7 同属该句式。法宝版译文为“such an agreement shall prevail”，总库版译文为“in accordance with the agreement”“the agreement shall be followed”。

从词汇角度分析，根据《柯林斯英语词典》，prevail 的释义为：to prove

superior; gain mastery。follow 的释义为：If you follow advice, an instruction, or a receipt, you act or do something in the way that it indicates。prevail 是指优先、占主导地位，表示当存在冲突时，该约定具有更高的法律效力或优先级。follow 则侧重于表达一种行为上的义务或责任，即必须遵守约定。从中文句式内涵分析，可知"……的"表述了限定的情况、条件，"按照约定"，指出行动的依据是此前达成的约定或协议，即在某些特定情况下，"约定"具有优先性，应当按照约定行事。此外，该句式中的"约定"并不强调某具体的规定或原则，而是表明行动具有依据性。如例句 5 和例句 7 均指如果有预先的协议或约定，则优先按照约定解决相应问题；例句 6 强调了共有人之间关于不得分割共有财产的协议，除非有重大理由需要改变，否则应首先依照约定行事，强调了约定的优先性。

从句式结构角度分析，"……的，按照约定"句式前面部分为条件状语，"按照约定"是动宾结构，为句子的主要成分，代表主体采取的最终行动。在翻译时，译者要理清逻辑结构，确保主次分明。为突出行动主体的主动性和行为的优先性，"按照约定"也应翻译成动宾结构。在英文句子中，in accordance with 通常作状语，shall prevail 和 shall be followed 虽为动词结构，作谓语成分，但 prevail 更能突出约定的主导性。综上，such an agreement shall prevail 更适合作为该句式的普适性翻译。

20.3.2 "按照……的约定"结构的翻译

例句 8—10 同属该句式。法宝版译文为"as agreed""as agreed upon""in accordance with"，总库版译文为"as agreed""in accordance with"。

从词汇和语义角度看，根据上文分析可知，in accordance with 后加具体的法律、法规、合同条款、约定协议等，强调约定的范围和内容；agree 本身并不直接指出协议的具体内容，只表示双方或多方已经达成约定，主体按照约定行事即可。"按照……的约定"结构由定语"……"和中心语"约定"组成，"……"可能是形容词性或名词性短语或从句，用于修饰和限定"约定"的具体内容或范围。例如，例句 8—10 中的"按照当事人的约定"

"按照合伙合同的约定""按照保险合同的约定"。相比于"按照约定"结构强调行为主体的主动性,该结构将语义中心放在约定本身,突出约定的具体性和明确性,因此,采用 in accordance with 翻译该句式更为合适。

从句式结构看,"按照……的约定"中"按照"是介词,用于引导行为所依据的标准或规则。"……的约定"是介词"按照"的宾语。整个结构作状语,用于修饰动词或整个句子,表明行动的依据。in accordance with 表示某行为符合一定的规则或协议,该短语是一个介词短语,其后接名词或名词性短语,整个结构在英文句子中作状语。这种对应性能够极大程度地保证原文的语义和句式结构,提高译文的准确性和流畅性。

20.3.3 区分"按照"与"根据"

"按照"和"根据"两词都常用于引导法律规则、合同条款、协议及约定等,二者在法律语境中的应用场景极为相似,但并非可以始终互换。因此译者在翻译时仍要注意区分。

根据《现代汉语词典》,"按照"意为依据、根据;"根据"作介词时,意为以某种事务作为结论的前提或语言行动的基础。"按照"在法律语境中常用于引导合同条款或约定,表示遵循或依照某个规则或约定,侧重于强调执行的程序性和规范性。例如,"当事人应当按照合同约定履行义务"。此处"按照"引导的是具体的合同条款,强调的是双方必须严格遵循合同条款来履行各自义务。而"根据"在法律语境中更侧重于引出某个结论或判断的前提,这个前提可能是一个法律条文、原则、广泛的事实或数据等,强调的是以这些前提为基础来做出决策或判断。例如,"根据法律规定,被告应当承担侵权责任"。此处"根据"引出法律规定作为判定责任的前提,强调要以法律为依据判定被告的责任,体现了法律对于行动或决策的指导和约束作用。因此,只有当"根据"一词后引导具体的法律规定、约定或条款,且后续的行为或决定是通过规范性地遵循这些规定、约定或条款而进行的,该词才可以与"按照"互换,译者可根据具体语境将其译为"in accordance with""as agreed"或"as agreed upon"。

小 结

“按照……约定”可分为“按照约定”和“按照……的约定”两种结构。针对该类结构的翻译，可以从词汇、语义和句式结构角度进行分析总结，给出一般性的翻译参考。译者在翻译时，仍需具体情况具体分析。

“按照约定”结构有“主体＋按照约定＋行动”和“……的，按照约定”两类句式。①“主体＋按照约定＋行动”句式，可译为“主语＋谓语＋as agreed”。②“……的，按照约定”句式，可译为“…, such an agreement shall prevail”。

“按照……的约定”结构可译为 in accordance with。

21 “依照……规定”结构的翻译

21.1 结构特点及其在《民法典》中的运用

21.1.1 结构特点

“依照……规定”在法律条文中通常作为引导性结构，用于引出具体的法律、行政法规或规定，作为行为、决定或裁决的处理依据，体现了法律的准确性和权威性。通常情况下，该结构在句中作状语，“依照”作为介词，“……规定”将规定的内容或范围具体化。在少数情况下，该结构前会明确法律、规章的内容，该结构在句中作谓语成分，其中“依照”作为动词，与“规定”连用，出现在句末，表明要依照规定行事。在某些情况下，“依照……规定”后可能有补充或限制性的内容，如“但是……除外”等，用以进一步说明或限定法律适用的范围或条件。

21.1.2 在《民法典》中的运用

在《民法典》中“依照……规定”结构一共出现了111次。其中，“依照其规定”共出现了39次。

(1)“依照……的规定”结构

“依照……的规定”是“依照……规定”结构中运用最广泛的句式，该句式通常出现在句子的开头或中间部分，作方式状语。“依照”有时作介词，有时作动词，后跟具体的法律、行政法规或法人章程等作为行为的依据。该句式结构简洁明了，无需特别补充其他情况，强调规定的明确性和权威性。如第537条规定："债务人对相对人的债权或者与该债权有关的从权利被采取保全、执行措施，或者债务人破产的，**依照**相关法律**的规定**处理。"其中"依照"作介词，"相关法律的规定"作为"依照"的宾语，涵盖了所有与民事诉讼、破产相关的具体法律及司法解释。又如第645条规定："拍卖的当事人的权利和义务以及拍卖程序等，**依照**有关法律、行政法规**的规定**。"其中的"依照"用作动词。该句式结构体现了法律的明确性、权威性和简洁性。

(2)"依照其规定"结构

该结构在《民法典》中通常用于处理指示性条件、特殊例外的情况，或对一般性规定进行补充。该结构分为"……规定……的，依照其规定"和"另有规定的，依照其规定"两种句式。

①"……规定……的，依照其规定"句式结构相对复杂，体现了法律文本的灵活性和适应性。"……规定……的"在句中作前提条件，明确某一特定情况，"依照其规定"则阐明相应情况下应当遵循的规定。如第68条规定："法人终止，法律、行政法规**规定**须经有关机关批准**的，依照其规定**。"该条中"法律、行政法规规定须经有关机关批准的"为句子的前提条件，明确法人终止需要经有关机关批准这一特殊情况。"依照"在句中作谓语，强调在遇到上述情况时，应当根据规定采取行动或进行裁决等，体现了法律文本的具体性、灵活性和适用性。

②"另有规定的，依照其规定"是一个条件句结构，通常出现在句末，用于对一般规定进行补充或特别说明，以应对特殊或例外的情况，强调规定的优先性和排他性。如第12条规定："中华人民共和国领域内的民事活动，适用中华人民共和国法律。法律**另有规定的，依照其规定**。"此处，"中华人民共和国领域内的民事活动，适用中华人民共和国法律"是一般规定，适用于大多数情况。然而，当存在特殊规定时，如国际条约、双边协议或特别法规定等，这些特殊规定将优于一般规定被适用。

21.2 译文对比

表 21.1 《民法典》中“依照……规定”结构的翻译对比

序号	出处(条)	原文	北大法宝译文(法宝版译文)	国家法规总库译文(总库版译文)
1	61	依照法律或者法人章程的规定,代表法人从事民事活动的负责人,为法人的法定代表人。	In accordance with the provisions of laws or the bylaws of a legal person, the person in charge who conducts civil activities on behalf of the legal person shall be the legal representative of the legal person.	The person with the responsibility of representing a legal person in conducting civil activities in accordance with law or the legal person's articles of association is the legal representative of the legal person.
2	1186	受害人和行为人对损害的发生都没有过错的,依照法律的规定由双方分担损失。	Where neither the victim nor the actor is at fault for the occurrence of a damage, both of them may share the damage according to the provisions of the law.	Where neither the victim nor the actor is at fault for the occurrence of the damage, the losses shall be shared by both parties in accordance with the provisions of law.
3	58	法人成立的具体条件和程序,依照法律、行政法规的规定。	The specific conditions and procedures for formation of a legal person shall be governed by laws and administrative regulations.	The specific conditions and procedures for the establishment of a legal person shall be in accordance with laws and administrative regulations.
4	645	拍卖的当事人的权利和义务以及拍卖程序等,依照有关法律、行政法规的规定。	In a sale by auction, matters such as the rights and obligations of the parties and the auctioning procedure, etc. are governed by the relevant laws and administrative regulations.	The rights and obligations of the parties to an auction, as well as the procedures of the auction, are governed by the provisions of the relevant laws and administrative regulations.

续表

序号	出处（条）	原文	北大法宝译文（法宝版译文）	国家法规总库译文（总库版译文）
5	68	法人终止，法律、行政法规**规定**须经有关机关批准**的**，**依照其规定**。	Where the termination of a legal person is subject to the approval of the relevant authority in accordance with any law or administrative regulation, such a law or administrative regulation shall apply.	Where there are laws or administrative regulations providing that the termination of a legal person shall be subject to approval of the relevant authority, such provisions shall be followed.
6	103	设立非法人组织，法律、行政法规**规定**须经有关机关批准**的**，**依照其规定**。	Where the formation of an unincorporated organization shall be subject to the approval of the relevant authority in accordance with any law or administrative regulation, such law or administrative regulation shall apply.	Where laws or administrative regulations provide that establishment of an unincorporated organization shall be subject to approval by the relevant authority, such provisions shall be followed.
7	1244	承担高度危险责任，法律**规定**赔偿限额**的**，**依照其规定**，但是行为人有故意或者重大过失的除外。	Where any legal provision prescribes a limit of compensation for liability for an ultrahazardous activity, such a provision shall apply, unless the actor is with intent or grossly negligent.	Where there are provisions of law providing for a limit of compensation for liability incurred as a result of an ultra-hazardous activity, such provisions shall be followed unless the damage is caused by the actor intentionally or with gross negligence.

续表

序号	出处(条)	原文	北大法宝译文(法宝版译文)	国家法规总库译文(总库版译文)
8	12	中华人民共和国领域内的民事活动,适用中华人民共和国法律。法律**另有规定的,依照其规定**。	The law of the People's Republic of China shall apply to civil activities within the territory of the People's Republic of China, **except as otherwise provided for by** any law.	The laws of the People's Republic of China shall apply to the civil activities taking place within the territory of the People's Republic of China, **except as otherwise provided by** law.
9	70	法人的董事、理事等执行机构或者决策机构的成员为清算义务人。法律、行政法规**另有规定的,依照其规定**。	The members of a legal person's executive organ or decision-making organ, such as directors or council members, are liquidation obligors, **except as otherwise provided for by** any law or administrative regulation.	**Unless otherwise provided by** laws or administrative regulations, members of the legal person's executive or decision-making body, such as the directors or councilors, are the persons with the duty to liquidate the legal person.
10	1194	网络用户、网络服务提供者利用网络侵害他人民事权益的,应当承担侵权责任。法律**另有规定的,依照其规定**。	A network user or network service provider who infringes upon the civil right or interest of another person through network shall assume the tort liability, **unless otherwise provided by** law.	Network users and network service providers who, through the network, infringes upon the civil-law rights and interests of another person shall bear tort liability, **unless otherwise provided by** law.

21.3 译文分析

以下对比分析两个版本中“依照……规定”及类似结构的相应译文，探讨各种情况下较为可取的翻译方法。

21.3.1 “依照……的规定”结构的翻译

例句1—4同属该句式。其中，例句1和例句2中“依照”作介词，法宝版译文为“according to”和“in accordance with”；总库版译文为“in accordance with”。例句3和例句4中“依照”作动词，法宝版译文为“be governed by”；总库版译文为“be in accordance with”和“be governed by”。

首先是“依照”作介词的情况。在“按照……约定”一节中，我们已对in accordance with的内涵以及适用场景进行了分析，该短语表示某事物与某个规则或法律是一致的，后常接法律、规定、原则或协议的具体名称，作为行动的依据或标准。查阅《柯林斯英语词典》可知，according to的定义为：If something is done according to a particular set of principles, these principles are used as a basis for the way it is done.。该短语强调原则是行动的基础，“基础”在一定意义上表明，只要行为主体在规定下行动，就可以有一定的自主权和决策空间，能够发挥主观能动性，这与规定和行为的一致性原则并不完全契合。“依照……的规定”短语本身强调行为与规定的一致性，要求行为或决策必须基于特定的法律文件、规章制度或合同条款来进行，以确保其合法性。此外，该短语通常用于明确具体的法律文件或规章制度，即使有时引用的是某一类法律文件（如“法人规章”），但总体上仍指向具体的、可查找的法律条文或规定。例句1表明，在某些情况下，法人章程可以替代或补充法律规定，成为确定法定代表人的依据，突出了法律的具体性和明确性。例句2中的“法律规定”前已经给出限定，故此处特指那些能够应对双方对损害的发生均无过错情形的法律规定。

其次是“依照”作动词的情况。在“适用……规定”一节中，已分析了be

governed by 的内涵以及适用场景，该短语意为"受……管辖"或"由……控制"，表示某行为是由某个规定或法律所支配或管理的。该短语更多地用于描述一种宏观的、普遍性的管理关系，而不特指某具体的法律条文或规定，也不强调行为和规定的一致性。但是，例句 3 强调了行为与规定之间的一致性，即任何关于法人成立的相关内容都不能偏离这些法律文件的要求。例句 4"依照有关法律、行政法规的规定"涵盖了拍卖活动的多个方面，包括当事人的权利和义务、拍卖程序等，明确了法律框架，确保了拍卖活动的规范性。可见，例句 3 的总库版译文更可取。

从句式结构角度来看，当"依照"作介词时，"依照……的规定"是一个介词短语结构，在句子中作方式状语，说明动作或状态的依据。在翻译时，译者可以将该结构同样处理成介词短语结构，其后翻译出具体的宾语内容，即"……的规定"所指的具体法律、规定或政策等。当"依照"作动词时，"依照……的规定"是一个动宾短语结构，在句子中作谓语，译文中同样应当译为谓语。英文中的(be)in accordance with 可以兼顾英文法律语言的完整性和简洁性。该词对应"依照"一词，且该短语后常跟随名词短语、从句，作为介词的宾语，用以明确"依照"的具体规定。翻译法律文本时，译者应在保持语义一致的基础上，尽量保持中英文句式的相似性，准确简洁地传达原文内容。

21.3.2 "依照其规定"结构的翻译

(1)"……规定……的，依照其规定"句式

例句 5—7 同属该句式。对于"法律、行政法规规定……的，依照其规定"句式，法宝版译文为"... in accordance with any law or administrative regulation, such (a) law or administrative regulation shall apply"，总库版译文为"Where there are laws or administrative regulations providing that..., such provisions shall be followed" "Where laws or administrative regulations provide that..., such provisions shall be followed"。对于"法律规定……的，依照其规定"句式，法宝版译为"Where any legal provision prescribes...，such a provision shall apply”，总库版译文为“Where there are provisions of law providing for...，such provisions shall be followed”。对此，笔者将从词汇翻译和句式翻译两方面进行分析。

①词汇翻译

对于“法律、行政法规”，两版译文都翻译为“(a/any) law(s) or administrative regulation(s)”，没有疑义。但是例句 7 中“法律规定”的“法律”，法宝版译文译为“any legal provision”，总库版译文译为“provisions of law”。查阅《柯林斯英语词典》可知，provision 的定义是：A provision in a law or an agreement is an arrangement which is included in it，用以指法律、合同或协议中的具体条款或规定。“legal provisions”和“provisions of law”在语义侧重点上略有不同：前者通常指的是具体的条款或规定，这些条款出现在法律、法规、合同或其他法律文件中，多为单个或特定的条款或条文；后者则更为宽泛，指的是整个法律体系中关于某个特定主题的规定，可以包括多个个别法律条款或条文的集合，涵盖了更广泛的法律背景。例句 7 中的“法律”并非指特定的法律条款，而是法律原则和法规的整体内容，可见，“legal provisions”不是合适的译文。

对于动词“规定”，法宝版译文有时将它与“法律、行政法规”融为一体，译为“in accordance with any law or administrative regulation”(如例句 5、例句 6)，意思为“依照法律、行政法规的规定”，有时译为动词“prescribe”(如例句 7)。总库版译文则译为 provide(如例句 5、例句 6)或 provide for (如例句 7)。根据《柯林斯英语词典》的释义，“If a person or set of laws or rules prescribes an action or duty，they state that it must be carried out”。也就是说，prescribe 注重强制性的法律规定，常带有强制性和明确的指示性，强调一套特定的规定或程序。“If a law or agreement provides that something will happen，it states that it will happen”。可见，provide 反映了法律的赋予和条款的设定，侧重于描述规定的存在状态。“If a law or agreement provides for something，it makes it possible”。provide for 侧重于为特定情况或需求设置条款或安排，较多用于描述某种支持或保障的设

定，而不是简单地赋予条款或规定的状态。例句 5 和例句 6 中“……规定须经有关机关批准”，“批准”是一个需要遵循的具体法律程序，将“规定”译为“prescribe”可以体现法律和行政法规对批准程序的强制性要求，说明必须按照法律的具体规定进行。例句 7 中“法律规定赔偿限额的”，描述的是存在规定的状态。此处法律的作用在于设定（即规定）赔偿限额，而不单是为这一行为提供条件或安排，因此译为“provide”似乎更合适。

②句式翻译

例句 5 和例句 6 中，法宝版译文将“的”字结构中的“……规定”译为“in accordance with any law or administrative regulation”，在句中作方式状语，后接主句 “such law or administrative regulation shall apply”；例句 7 则将“的”字结构中的“……规定”译为 where 条件句的主语和谓语，后接主句“such a provision shall apply”。总库版译文则统一将“的”字结构中“……规定”译为 where 条件句的主语和谓语，后接主句“such provisions shall be followed”。

这几种译文句式都符合英语语法规则，都能有效传达原文的语义和逻辑，但是考虑到与中文句式的呼应程度，将“的”字结构中的“……规定”译为 where-条件句中的主、谓语，与中文句式更相近。总库版例句 5 和例句 7 在 where-条件句中使用了“there be”句式，以强调规定的存在状态，但给人冗长的感觉，不如例句 6 更加直接和简洁，语言更流畅，更符合法律英语简明要求。

在“适用……规定”一节中，已分析了 apply 的词汇用法，该词表示“适用”“实施”，即某规定适用于某对象，通常强调主体主动地去执行或应用某项规定。follow 的词汇用法在“按照……约定”一节中已进行了探讨，该词侧重于表达客观行为上遵循规定，履行义务或责任。

中文句式“……规定……的，依照其规定”是一个条件句，其中“依照”在句中为动词作谓语，“其规定”为“依照”的宾语，构成了句子的核心结构。因此，在翻译时，该结构也应对应翻译成动词作谓语。此外，从语义角度分析，该句式表示如果法律或行政法规规定某事，那么就要按照该规定来执行，即强调对既定规定的遵循和执行，而非某个行动主体主动地执行某规定。因此，翻译成 such provisions shall be followed 这一被动语态，可以更好地强调规定执行和遵守的事实。这不仅符合中文原句的语义特点，也能保证英文法律语言的客观性要求。需要注意的是，provision 最好使用复数，法宝版例句 7 译文使用单数形式“a provision”可能会给人一种误导，似乎只是在指代某一个特定的条款，而在原文情况下通常涉及多个条款，使用复数形式更为自然和准确。

(2)“另有规定的，依照其规定”句式

例句 8—10 同属该结构。法宝版译文为“except as otherwise provided for by”“unless otherwise provided by”，总库版译文为“unless otherwise provided by”“except as otherwise provided by”。

关于该句式，本书在“另有规定”一节有详细讨论，此处不再赘述。例句 8—10 均符合该节中“另有规定/约定”句式紧密依附于主条款语句的情况，因此，建议统一译为“except as otherwise provided by”，即总库版例句 8 的译文更可取。

小 结

“依照……规定”可分为“依照……的规定”和“依照其规定”两种结构。针对该类结构的翻译，笔者从词汇、语义和句式结构等角度进行分析总结，给出一般性的翻译参考。译者在翻译时，仍需具体情况具体分析。

“依照……的规定”结构：①当“依照”作介词时，可译为 in accordance with；②当“依照”作动词时，可译为 be in accordance with。

“依照其规定”结构有“……规定……的，依照其规定”和“另有规定的，依照其规定”两类句式。①“……规定……的，依照其规定”句式中，如果规定侧重强制性，该句式可译为 Where ... prescribe..., such provisions shall be followed。如果只是描述规定存在的状态，该句式可译为 Where ... provide..., such provisions shall be followed。②“另有规定的，依照其规定”句式的翻译，可参照“另有规定”一节的讨论，可译为 expect as otherwise provided by。

22 “采用……形式”结构的翻译

22.1 结构特点及其在《民法典》中的运用

22.1.1 结构特点

“采用……形式”结构在法律文本中通常指某法律行为或法律文件应当采取的具体形式或方式，具有明确规定性和指导性。“采用”前是对法律行为、法律事件或法律关系的描述，为后文的形式要求提供了背景铺垫。同时，该词前通常会标注出行为主体，如“当事人”“双方”等。“采用”一词后则是对具体形式的明确限定，如“采用书面形式”“采用公证形式”等，通过形式的具体化来确保法律行为的规范性、准确性。此外，“采用……形式”结构在法律文本中还可能隐含着对未遵守该规定的法律后果的暗示，对增强法律的权威性和约束力有重要意义。

22.1.2 在《民法典》中的运用

“采用……形式”在《民法典》中共出现了 32 次，该结构形式单一，在法律条文中用来指定某项法律行为、合同或协议应当遵循的具体形式或程序。这种表达强调了进行某项活动或达成某项协议时必须采用的标准或方式，比如“书面形式”“口头形式”“公证形式”等，以确保法律行为的有效性和可执行性。该结构的具体运用场景包括合同订立、民事法律行为、具体约定等。“采用……形式”这一结构为当事人提供了明确的指导，以确保相关活动或协议符合法律要求。如第 354 条规定:“建设用地使用权转让、互换、出资、赠与或者抵押的,当事人应当采用书面形式订立相应的合同。”“采用书面形式”是法律对合同形式的具体要求,这意味着当涉及建设用地使用权的转让、互换、出资、赠与或抵押等关键法律行为时,当事人必须以书面形式明确双方的权利和义务,保证合同的有效性。此外,书面形式具有明确性、稳定性和可证明性,能够确保合同内容的清晰、准确和不易篡改,当双方出现法律纠纷时,书面合同可以提供有力的证据支持,有助于维护交易秩序和社会公共利益。

22.2 译文对比

表 22.1 《民法典》中“采用……形式”结构的翻译对比

序号	出处(条)	原文	北大法宝译文(法宝版译文)	国家法规总库译文(总库版译文)
1	135	民事法律行为可以采用书面形式、口头形式或者其他形式;法律、行政法规规定或者当事人约定采用特定形式的,应当采用特定形式。	Juridical acts may be made in written, verbal, or other forms; but if any law or administrative regulation requires or the parties agree upon a particular form, such a particular form shall be adopted.	A civil juristic act may be done in writing, orally, or in any other form; where a specific form is required by laws or administrative regulations, or agreed by the parties, it shall be done in such a form.
2	354	建设用地使用权转让、互换、出资、赠与或者抵押的,当事人应当采用书面形式订立相应的合同。	Where the right to use land for construction is transferred, exchanged, contributed as capital, gifted, or mortgaged, the parties shall enter into a corresponding contract in a written form.	Where a right to use a lot of land for construction purposes is transferred, exchanged, offered as capital contribution, given away as a gift, or mortgaged, the parties shall enter into a contract thereon in writing.

续表

序号	出处（条）	原文	北大法宝译文（法宝版译文）	国家法规总库译文（总库版译文）
3	373	设立地役权，当事人应当采用书面形式订立地役权合同。	To create servitude, the parties shall enter into a servitude contract in a written form.	To create an easement, the parties shall enter into an easement contract in writing.
4	427	设立质权，当事人应当采用书面形式订立质押合同。	To create pledge, the parties shall enter into a pledge contract in a written form.	To create a pledge, the parties shall enter into a pledge contract in writing.
5	490	当事人采用合同书形式订立合同的，自当事人均签名、盖章或者按指印时合同成立。	Where the parties enter into a contract in the form of a written contract, the contract is formed when each party affixes its signature, seal, or fingerprint.	Where the parties conclude a contract in the form of a written agreement, the contract is formed at the time when the parties all sign, stamp, or put their fingerprints on the written agreement.
6	668	借款合同应当采用书面形式，但是自然人之间借款另有约定的除外。	A contract for loan of money shall be in written form, except where the loan is between natural persons who have agreed otherwise.	A loan contract shall be made in writing, unless the loan is between natural persons who agree otherwise.
7	707	租赁期限六个月以上的，应当采用书面形式。当事人未采用书面形式，无法确定租赁期限的，视为不定期租赁。	Where the lease term is six months or longer, the lease shall be in writing. If the parties fail to adopt a writing form, rendering the determination of a lease term impossible, the lease is deemed an indeterminate-term lease.	A lease contract with a term exceeding six months shall be made in writing. Where the lease contract between the parties is not in writing, if the term cannot be determined, the lease shall be deemed as a lease with an indefinite term.

续表

序号	出处(条)	原文	北大法宝译文(法宝版译文)	国家法规总库译文(总库版译文)
8	736	融资租赁合同应当采用书面形式。	A financial leasing contract shall be in written form.	A contract for financing lease shall be made in writing.
9	938	物业服务合同应当采用书面形式。	A property management service contract shall be in written form.	A property management service contract shall be in writing.
10	1065	约定应当采用书面形式。	The agreement shall be made in writing.	The agreement shall be in writing.

22.3 译文分析

以下对比分析两个版本中"采用……形式"结构相应的译文，探讨各种情况下较为可取的翻译方法。

例句1—10同属该结构，法宝版和总库版译文均给出了"in...form""in the form of"" adopt...form"和"in (doing)"四种形式。下面针对这四类表述分别进行分析和探讨。

22.3.1 in...form

①结构特点：这是一个介词短语，其中in是介词，表示处于某种状态中，form为名词，表示形式或状态。form前通常为形容词，以进一步明确形式特征。以"采用书面形式"为例，该短语可翻译成in written form。其中，"written"作为形容词，能够更明确地表达"以书面文字呈现的、已经被写下来的"的静态的形式特征。此外，从词序角度来看，该短语遵循英语中一般的介词短语结构顺序，即介词在前，修饰语及名词在后，这种简单的结构符合法律语言简洁性的要求，方便法律从业者解读和应用。

②强调重点：该短语用来描述某物或某事以某种形式存在或进行，侧重于对事物现有形式的客观描述，强调形式在法律文本中的客观存在状态，而非形式确立的主体或确立的过程。这种描述方式有助于明确法律所涉及的对象（如文件、证据、通知等）的具体形式，从而确保法律条款的准确性和可执行性。

③在法律文本中的优劣：该短语结构清晰，形式简洁，易于理解和应用；具有广泛的适用性，可用于描述各种类型的形式要求；强调形式的客观存在状态，有助于确保法律条款的准确性和可执行性。但该短语更多的是描述一种客观的状态，未能涉及形式存在的其他相关信息，如基于的法律原则、确立形式的主体和过程等。在某些情况下，可能因缺乏动态性而难以表达主体主动采用形式的过程。

基于上述分析，在 10 个例句中找出了适合使用 in...form 的情形。例句 1 中的“民事法律行为可以采用书面形式、口头形式或者其他形式”，适合使用 in...form，因为该句只是客观陈述民事法律行为能够以哪些具体的形式存在，符合对这些形式的一般性描述。例句 6 应将“采用书面形式”译为 in written form，可以简洁表达借款合同在一般情况下应具备的书面形式要求。例句 7 中的“租赁期限六个月以上的，应当采用书面形式”，可将“采用书面形式”译为 in written form，表明租赁期限超过六个月时租赁行为应具备的书面形式要求，突出了形式的客观状态。例句 8—10 结构相似，均为“……应当采用书面形式”，阐明在不同情况下应当呈现的客观形式状态，使用 in...form 结构能够准确快速传达关键信息，符合法律语言中对一般情况下约定形式的简洁性要求。

22.3.2 in the form of

①结构特点：该结构是一个介词短语，其中介词 in 表示某物或某事是以这种形式存在的，定冠词 the 特指某种特定的形式。form 是名词，表示“形式”，介词 of 后通常跟名词或名词短语，用以具体说明“形式”的内容或类型。例如，in the form of a written contract（采用合同书的形式）。在句

子中，in the form of 通常充当状语，用于描述动作或事物所呈现的具体形式，也可充当表语，说明主语的存在形式。

②强调重点：与 in...form 只强调一般的形式的状态相比，in the form of 更加强调形式的具体细节和特定类型，这是因为 of 后面能够对形式进行更加详细的描述和限定，包括形式的结构、特征、内容等。因此，在法律文本中，in the form of 常用于需要明确形式的具体细节和类型的场合。

③在法律文本中的优劣：该短语的表达更加具体和详细，规范“形式”的相关内容，有利于确保法律条款的精确性和正确实施，避免因形式表述的笼统或模糊而导致法律漏洞或解释上的争议。但在描述一般性形式时，该短语显得过于烦琐。例如，当只需说明某文件应以书面形式呈现时，in written form 就已足够，而 in the form of a written document 则会使语言表达冗长，不够简洁明快，不符合英文的表达习惯。

基于上述分析，在 10 个例句中，只有例句 5 可以将“采用……形式”译为 in the form of。因为在例句 5 中，读者需要明确具体的形式是“合同书形式”，即一种具有特定格式和内容要求的书面合同形式，这不仅能体现形式的内容，还暗含一些合同书应该注意的具体细节。译为 in the form of 能够更准确、详细地描述所采用的形式，突出形式的具体性和规范性，与法律条文中对合同订立形式的详细规定相照应。

22.3.3 adopt...form

①结构特点：该结构是一个动词短语结构，在句子中通常作谓语。adopt 前为实施“采用”这一行为的主体，如当事人、组织或机构等法律主体。adopt 作为及物动词，有“采用、采纳、接受”等含义，其后接 form 作为 adopt 的宾语，形成动宾结构，表示主体所采用的具体形式。该结构简单直接，符合英语中动词短语的基本构成方式。例如，the parties should adopt written form。这里行动的主体是 the parties（当事人），written 直接限定了所采用的形式为书面形式，整个结构清晰地表明了当事人应当主动采用书面形式。

②强调重点：该结构着重强调行为主体的主观意愿和主动选择去采用某种形式。从词汇角度分析，查阅《柯林斯英语词典》可知，adopt 的定义为：to accept or act in accordance with (a plan, principle, etc.)，即主动地接纳。这意味着当一个主体 adopt 某种形式时，该主体是经过思考、判断或根据一定的规则、目的而主动地选择该种形式。此外，该短语的主谓宾结构也清晰地表明了是主体发起“采用”这一动作，直接作用于 form 所指的具体形式。

③在法律文本中的优劣：该短语能够帮助明确责任主体，便于对主体的行为进行规范和监督，符合法律实践中对主体行为规范的要求。但同样，该结构在运用上存在很大局限性。例如，该短语的运用会使读者过度关注行为主体，而忽视掉“形式”本身。此外，相比于介词短语的表达，该表述需要注意时态语态，缺乏一定的简洁性。

基于上述分析，以下例句适合使用 adopt...form 结构。例句 1 中“法律、行政法规规定或者当事人约定采用特定形式的，应当采用特定形式”。该句的前半句可使用主动语态，突出主体是主动去采用特定形式的行为；后半句可译为“such a particular form shall be adopted”，强调特定形式是必须被采用的，整体准确地表明当事人在采用相应形式后应当承担的责任。例句 2—4 和例句 7 中的“当事人未采用书面形式，无法确定租赁期限的，视为不定期租赁”，也适合使用 adopt...form 结构，因为上述例句均以当事人为主语，突出当事人的行为选择，也能够明确当事人作为行为主体的责任和行为规范。

22.3.4 in (doing)

①结构特点：该短语中，介词 in 表示“在……过程里”，doing 为动名词，表示一种行为动作。在语法上，该结构可以在句中充当状语、表语等成分。例如，总库版例句 8 译文中“A contract for financing lease shall be made in writing”(融资租赁合同应当采用书面形式)，其中 in writing 作状语，修饰 be made 这个动作。

②强调重点：与 in...form 不同，该短语结构虽也表示状态，但更强调动作性，表示动作与形式之间存在某种关联，如总库版例句 8 译文使用“in writing”表明合同的有效性与“书写”这个行为紧密相连。该短语适用于涉及法律程序、行为步骤以及所产生的形式结果等，能够准确地表达行为的实施方式如何影响法律形式的产生和认定，有助于分析法律行为的有效性与形式之间的内在逻辑。

③在法律文本中的优劣：该结构体现了行为与形式的因果关系以及法律程序的严谨性。例如，遗嘱的设立形式需要 in writing，这能清楚地表明遗嘱这种法律形式是通过书写这个行为来实现的，强调了书写行为是遗嘱成立的必要条件。但是当描述多个行为与形式互相关联时，这种表述会显得冗长和复杂，影响文本的可读性。考虑到法律英语简洁性的文体要求，该结构在形式上比 in...form 结构更简洁明了，易于理解，因此如果不涉及多个行为与形式互相关联的情况，in writing 可以替代 in written form，前者的使用频率更高，原生英语法律语料库中的检索结果也证实这一点（见表 22.2）。

表 22.2 “采用书面形式”的英文表达方式及检索频次

表达方式	国内	国外		
	香港法例库	英国立法库	美国联邦法规库	美国法典库
be/is/are in writing	344	＞200	2500	52759
be/is/are in written form	3	14	19	580

基于上述分析，例句 6—10 均适合使用 in writing 结构。

小　结

针对“采用……形式”结构的翻译，从“in...form”“in the form of”“adopt...form”和“in (doing)”这四种常用的表达方式进行分析，可提出如下一般性翻译建议：

当对某形式进行一般性描述或强调其客观的存在方式时，可译为 in...form；当需要阐述具体的形式内容和规范性时，可译为 in the form of；当强调主体的主动性，明确主体的责任和义务时，可译为 adopt...form；当需要突出动作与形式的关系，强调通过特定动作来体现某形式时，可译为 in (doing)。此外，如果不涉及多个行为与形式互相关联的情况，可译为 in...form 的情况均可译为 in (doing)结构，且后者是更好的选择。译者在翻译时，仍需具体情况具体分析。

23 “承担……责任”结构的翻译

23.1 结构特点及其在《民法典》中的运用

23.1.1 结构特点

“承担……责任”结构在法律条文中，指主体因违法或违约行为而应当对他人或社会承担的法律义务和后果，包括赔偿损失、承担惩罚性赔偿等。“承担”一词前通常为责任主体，如“当事人应当承担”“所有人承担”等；“承担”一词后通常与具体的责任类型连用，如“赔偿责任”“民事责任”“违约责任”等。该结构有助于明确当事人的法律责任，以维护法律的公正性和权威性。

23.1.2 在《民法典》中的运用

《民法典》中“承担……责任”结构一共出现了 292 次。其中“承担+具体责任类型”结构出现了 265 次。此类结构有助于增强法律适用的准确性，使法律主体清晰了解其权利和义务。如第 43 条规定：“财产代管人因故意或者重大过失造成失踪人财产损失的，应当**承担赔偿责任**。”句中“财产代管人”为责任主体，“承担”是主要动词，“赔偿责任”是责任类型。此外，“承担责任”也可连用，此类结构在《民法典》中出现了 27 次。如第 1174 条规定：“损害是因受害人故意造成的，行为人不**承担责任**。”此类结构更为灵活，有助于应对复杂多变的法律实践，也更具概括性，可为后续责任追究或处理留下一定余地。“承担……责任”结构可分为两种情况：

(1)“承担＋具体责任类型”

该结构通常为“责任主体＋应当承担……责任”或“由＋责任主体承担……责任”。其中，具体的责任类型主要分为赔偿责任、民事责任、连带责任、违约责任、侵权责任。

赔偿责任共出现58次，主要是指当特定主体因自身行为(故意、重大过失、提供虚假材料、保管不善等)导致他人或他人财产遭受损失时，需要承担的法律责任。如第714条规定：“**承租人**应当妥善保管租赁物，因保管不善造成租赁物毁损、灭失的，**应当承担赔偿责任**。”

民事责任共出现36次，主要指民事主体不履行或者不完全履行民事义务应当依法承担的不利后果。如第70条规定：“**清算义务人**未及时履行清算义务，造成损害的，**应当承担民事责任**。”

连带责任共出现22次，主要用于保护受害人或债权人的权益，确保在特定情况下，多个当事人能够共同承担责任。如第164条规定：“代理人和相对人恶意串通，损害被代理人合法权益的，**代理人和相对人应当承担连带责任**。”

违约责任共出现25次，主要用于处理当事人一方不履行合同义务或者履行合同义务不符合约定的情况，其承担方式包括继续履行、采取补救措施、赔偿损失和支付违约金等。如第856条规定：“**合作开发合同的当事人**违反约定造成研究开发工作停滞、延误或者失败的，**应当承担违约责任**。”

侵权责任共出现55次，主要用于处理因侵害他人民事权益而产生的各种法律关系和责任承担问题。如第1241条规定：“遗失、抛弃高度危险物造成他人损害的，**由所有人承担侵权责任**。”

(2)“承担责任”连用

该结构通常为“行为人＋(不)承担责任”，适用于行为人的具体责任类型模糊，或所需承担的责任范围较广，抑或方便法官根据具体情况进行裁量等情况。如第1174条规定：“损害是因受害人故意造成的，**行为人不承担责任**。”在该法条中，由于已经明确了免责事由(受害人故意造成损害)，因此无须再进一步讨论行为人的具体责任类型或责任分担比例。

23.2 译文对比

表 23.1 《民法典》中"承担……责任"结构的翻译对比

序号	出处(条)	原文	北大法宝译文(法宝版译文)	国家法规总库译文(总库版译文)
1	43	财产代管人因故意或者重大过失造成失踪人财产损失的,应当承担赔偿责任。	Where the property custodian causes damage to the absentee's property intentionally or with gross negligence, the custodian shall assume compensatory liability.	A custodian who, intentionally or due to gross negligence, causes damage to the property of the missing person shall be liable for compensation.
2	222	当事人提供虚假材料申请登记,造成他人损害的,应当承担赔偿责任。	Any party that provides false application materials for registration, thus causing any damage to another person, shall assume compensatory liability.	A party who provides false materials upon application for registration and thus causes damage to another person shall be liable for compensation.
3	1210	当事人之间已经以买卖或者其他方式转让并交付机动车但是未办理登记,发生交通事故造成损害,属于该机动车一方责任的,由受让人承担赔偿责任。	Where a motor vehicle has been transferred and delivered from one party to another through sale or in any other method but the registration has not been conducted, if the liability for any harm caused in a traffic accident is attributed to the motor vehicle, the transferee shall assume the compensatory liability.	Where a party has transferred and delivered a motor vehicle by way of sale or other means but fails to file for registration, the transferee of the motor vehicle shall bear the liability for compensation if damage is caused as a result of a traffic accident and the liability is attributed to the motor vehicle driver.

续表

序号	出处(条)	原文	北大法宝译文(法宝版译文)	国家法规总库译文(总库版译文)
4	70	清算义务人未及时履行清算义务,造成损害的,应当承担民事责任……	Where the liquidation obligors fail to fulfill their liquidation obligation in a timely manner, causing any damage, they shall assume civil liability;...	The persons with the duty to liquidate the legal person who fail to perform their duties in time and thus cause damage to others shall bear civil liability;...
5	182	因紧急避险造成损害的,由引起险情发生的人承担民事责任。	Where any damage is caused by necessity to avoid a danger in emergency, the person causing the danger shall assume civil liability.	Where a person when seeking to avoid a peril in response to an emergency causes harm to others, the person who creates the peril shall bear civil liability.
6	164	代理人和相对人恶意串通,损害被代理人合法权益的,代理人和相对人应当承担连带责任。	Where an agent and the opposite party in malicious collusion damages the principal's lawful rights and interests, the agent and the opposite party shall be jointly and severally liable.	Where an agent maliciously colludes with a third person, thus harming the lawful rights and interests of the principal, the agent and the third person shall bear joint and several liability.
7	1214	以买卖或者其他方式转让拼装或者已经达到报废标准的机动车,发生交通事故造成损害的,由转让人和受让人承担连带责任。	Where an illegally assembled motor vehicle or a motor vehicle having reached the standard of retirement, which has been transferred through sale or in any other method, causes a traffic accident and a harm, the transferor and the transferee shall be liable jointly and severally.	Where damage is caused as a result of a traffic accident involving a motor vehicle that has been illegally assembled or has reached the end-of-life standard which is transferred by way of sale or by other means, the transferor and the transferee shall assume joint and several liability.

续表

序号	出处（条）	原文	北大法宝译文（法宝版译文）	国家法规总库译文（总库版译文）
8	522	当事人约定由债务人向第三人履行债务，债务人未向第三人履行债务或者履行债务不符合约定的，应当向债权人<u>承担</u>违约<u>责任</u>。	Where the parties agree that the debtor shall perform the obligation to a third party, and the debtor fails to perform its obligations to such third party or the performance of the obligations is not in conformity with the agreement, the debtor <u>shall be liable</u> to the creditor for breach of contract.	Where the parties agree that the debtor shall perform the obligation to a third person, if the debtor fails to perform the obligation to the third person or the performance does not conform to the agreement, the debtor <u>shall bear</u> default <u>liability</u> to the creditor.
9	856	合作开发合同的当事人违反约定造成研究开发工作停滞、延误或者失败的，应当<u>承担</u>违约<u>责任</u>。	Where a party to a cooperative development contract breaches the contract, thereby causing stoppage, delay or failure of the development, it <u>shall be liable for</u> the breach of contract.	Where a party to a cooperative development contract defaults, thus causing the stoppage, delay, or failure of the research and development work, the party <u>shall bear</u> default <u>liability.</u>
10	1175	损害是因第三人造成的，第三人应当<u>承担</u>侵权<u>责任</u>。	Where any harm is caused by a third party, the third party <u>shall assume</u> the tort <u>liability</u>.	Where a damage is caused by a third person, the third person <u>shall bear</u> tort <u>liability</u>.
11	1241	遗失、抛弃高度危险物造成他人损害的，由所有人<u>承担</u>侵权<u>责任</u>。	Where any harm is caused to another person by the loss or abandonment of ultrahazardous materials, the owner <u>shall assume</u> the tort <u>liability</u>.	Where damage is caused to another person by an ultra-hazardous thing that is lost or abandoned, the owner of the ultra-hazardous thing <u>shall bear</u> tort <u>liability</u>.

续表

序号	出处（条）	原文	北大法宝译文（法宝版译文）	国家法规总库译文（总库版译文）
12	749	承租人占有租赁物期间，租赁物造成第三人人身损害或者财产损失的，出租人不承担责任。	If in the possession of the lessee, the leased property causes personal injury or property damage to a third party, the lessor is not liable.	Where a leased object causes any personal injury or property damage to a third person during the period it is under the lessee's possession, the lessor does not bear any liability.
13	1174	损害是因受害人故意造成的，行为人不承担责任。	The actor shall not be liable for any harm that is caused intentionally by the victim.	An actor does not assume liability for any damage intentionally caused by the victim.

23.3 译文分析

以下对比分析两个版本中"承担……责任"结构的相应译文，探讨各种情况下较为可取的翻译方法。

23.3.1 "承担+具体责任类型"结构翻译

该结构可分为"责任主体+应当承担……责任"和"由+责任主体承担……责任"两种句式。其中，"应当承担……责任"这一表述强调了责任的必要性和法律强制性，表明责任主体在法律上负有承担某种责任的义务。根据《布莱克法律词典》中 shall 的定义：the word is generally imperative or mandatory，可以得出 shall 一词在法律中有强制性的意味。对此，李克兴(2007)指出，专门从事法律翻译的资深专家似乎在重要法律的翻译实践中逐渐达成共识，并正在约定俗成一条规矩："shall" 与"须""应""应当"对等。因此，该结构句式可译为 "sb. shall..."。

而“由＋责任主体承担……责任”这一结构更侧重于从外部视角来阐述责任的承担者，强调责任要由某个特定主体来承担。该表述在中文中是一种典型的被动意义表达，强调责任主体是责任的接受者或执行者，而非主动发起者，与英文的被动语态相一致。此外，被动语态可以使句子更加客观、中立，减少歧义，确保信息的准确传达。考虑到该结构在语义上仍强调责任主体应尽责任或义务，该结构句式可译为“sth. shall be done by sb.”。

(1)“承担赔偿责任”结构翻译

例句 1—3 同属该结构，法宝版的译文均为“assume compensatory liability”；总库版译文为“be liable for compensation”或“bear the liability for compensation”。

涉及“赔偿”相关的法律含义，《牛津学习词典》中 liable 的定义为：legally responsible for paying the cost of something，如：You will be liable for any damage caused。而“liability”通常与其他词语合用，如“individual liability”“products liability”“joint liability”等，其定义为 the state of being legally responsible for something; the amount of money that a person or company owes，如：The company is reported to have liabilities of nearly $ 90 000。由此可见，“liability”除所划定的法律责任范围更大，在涉及金钱相关的含义上，只强调负债的钱数；而“liable”侧重于依法承担偿还的责任。因此，在翻译“承担赔偿责任”时，“be liable for compensation”为最佳译文。

(2)“承担民事责任”结构翻译

例句 4、例句 5 同属该结构。法宝版译文为“assume legal/ civil liability”，总库版译文均为“bear civil liability”。

通过查阅《布莱克法律词典》可知，assume 表示接受、承担或担任某种责任、义务或地位，强调个人或实体主动承担因某种行为或关系而产生的责任。bear 更多地表示“承受、负担”之意，突出承受责任或义务的结果或状态，即某人或某实体由于法律、合同或侵权行为而不得不承担某种责任。

因此，在翻译“承担民事责任”时，译者需要根据具体情况进行分析。

此外，根据上文可知，民事责任是指个人或组织因违反法律规定或合同义务，而需要向受损方承担的法律上的不利后果或责任。legal liability是一个广泛的概念，它可以涵盖因违反法律、合同或其他法律义务而产生的各种责任。相比之下，civil liability 则是一个更为具体的术语，通常指因民事侵权行为或违反民事合同而产生的责任。因此，civil liability 更适用于作为“民事责任”的普适性翻译。

例句 4 结构为“责任主体＋应当承担民事责任”，结合语义，这里的“承担民事责任”更侧重于清算义务人需要接受因自己的过失行为而导致的损害结果，因此该句中的结构可译为“shall bear civil liability”。

例句 5 结构为“由＋责任主体承担民事责任”，结合语义，此处“承担民事责任”同样是在描述一种责任的归属，但也可以理解为某人的行为（引起险情发生）导致了损害，从而主动地“承担”相应民事责任。在该语境下，assume 和 bear 皆可，因此可译为“civil liability shall be born/assumed by”。

(3)“承担连带责任”结构翻译

例句 6、例句 7 同属该结构。法宝版译文为“be jointly and severally liable”或“be liable jointly and severally”；总库版译文为“bear joint and several liability”或“assume joint and several liability”。

法宝版将“连带”一词译为副词，而总库版将其译为形容词。虽从语法上二者皆可，但从句式结构角度，中文里“连带责任”作为动词“承担”的宾语，说明了责任主体应当承担的具体责任。因此，在英文翻译中，为保持句式结构的一致性，将“连带”翻译为形容词“joint and several”修饰“liability”，可以更加明确地描述多个责任主体之间的一种特定责任关系。相比之下，如将“连带”翻译为副词形式，则更多地强调了行为的方式（责任主体行为的共同性或可分别性），而非责任本身的性质（责任主体之间的法律责任关系）。因此，“joint and several liability”为“连带责任”的最佳译文。此外，在法律文本中，与 joint and several 组合为短语的还有 joint and several bond（连带保函；连带债券）、joint and several contract（连带合同）、

joint and several judgment(连带判决)等,可见,joint and several 作为修饰语在法律语境中非常常见。

(4)"承担违约责任"结构翻译

例句 8、例句 9 同属该结构。法宝版译文为"be liable for breach of contract",总库版译文为"bear default liability"。

根据《布莱克法律词典》,default 的定义为:the omission or failure to perform a legal or contractual duty; esp., the failure to pay a debt when due。breach 的定义为:a violation or infraction of a law, obligation, or agreement, esp., of an official duty or a legal obligation, whether by neglect, refusal, resistance, or inaction。default 指应做未做、不履行,更偏向于指财务上的违约,如贷款违约等;而 breach 涵盖范围更广泛,包括疏于履行、拒绝履行和未履行等。

此外,be liable for 强调的是一种法律上的"可归责性"或"责任性",通常与具体的法律责任、后果或债务搭配使用,如 be liable for damages, be liable for breach of contract 等;bear 有不得不承担之意,通常需要与其他词汇搭配使用以明确责任的具体内容,如:bear the cost、bear the loss。be liable for breach of contract 指出了责任的原因(合同违约)和性质(法律责任),但"bear default liability",更多地指向一种未能履行财务义务(如偿还债务)的责任,而不是广义上的合同违约责任。因此,"be liable for breach of contract"更适用于"承担违约责任"的普适性翻译。

(5)"承担侵权责任"结构翻译

例句 10、例句 11 同属该结构。法宝版译文为"assume the tort liability",总库版译文为"bear tort liability"。对于 assume liability 和 bear liability 的区别,上文已进行说明,译者应根据具体法条进行分析。此外,"assume the tort liability"一般指承担某项特定的侵权责任,liability 后面有限定成分。下面附上三种表述在四大数据库的使用频次(见表 23.2),以供参考。

表 23.2 “承担侵权责任”的英文表达方式及检索频次

表达方式	国内	国外		
	香港法例库	英国立法库	美国联邦法规库	美国法典库
assume the tort liability	0	0	0	166
assume tort liability	0	0	0	23
bear tort liability	0	0	0	2

23.3.2 “承担责任”连用结构翻译

该结构通常为“行为人+(不)承担责任”。该表述会伴随一定的条件或前提,这些条件或前提限定了责任承担的具体情境。相比于“责任主体+应当承担……责任”和“由+责任主体承担……责任”两种句式,该结构不强调责任主体是否“应该”承担某责任,而是陈述事实或情况。在翻译该类结构时,需要注意保持原文的直接性和条件性,使用一般现在时即可。

例句 12、例句 13 同属该结构。法宝版的译文为“be liable”,总库版译文为“assume/bear liability”。根据上文分析可知,“be liable”更侧重于描述一种法律上的责任状态,而“assume/bear liability”则可能引入额外的积极或被动承担责任的意味。在翻译“承担责任”结构时,“be liable”可以保持原文的直接性,同时清晰地传达出责任主体在特定条件下是否需要承担责任的事实。

小　结

“承担……责任”结构在《民法典》中有“承担+具体责任类型”和“承担责任”连用两种情况。

“承担+具体责任类型”通常分为“责任主体+应当承担……责任”和“由+责任主体承担……责任”两种句式。“应当承担……责任”这一表述强调了责任的必要性和法律强制性,可译为“sb. shall...”。“由+责任主体承担……责任"这一结构更侧重于从外部视角来阐述责任要由某个特定主体来承担,可译为"sth. shall be done by sb."。

此外,将出现频次较高的具体责任类型进行归纳,可得出结论如下:①"承担赔偿责任"可译为"be liable for compensation";②"承担民事责任"可译为"bear/assume civil liability";③"承担连带责任"可译为"bear/assume joint and several liability";④"承担违约责任"可译为"be liable for breach of contract";⑤"承担侵权责任"可译为"bear/assume tort liability"。bear 有不得不承担某种责任之意,assume 更突出责任主体主动承担,在翻译时,译者应根据语境进行选择。

当"承担责任"连用时,该结构通常为"行为人+(不)承担责任",即陈述是否需要承担责任这一事实,因此对于这一句式建议不加情态动词。此外,在翻译"承担责任"这一短语时,"be liable"可以保持原文的直接性。

24 “具备……条件”结构的翻译

24.1 结构特点及其在《民法典》中的运用

24.1.1 结构特点

“具备……条件”和“具有……资格”在法律条文中结构相似，均强调某种条件或资格的必要性，即只有满足这些条件或具备相应资格，才能进行一定的行为或享有特定的权利。通常情况下，“具备”或“具有”前无直接限定词，但会出现在句子的开头或中间，作为对后续条件或资格的引导。“条件”或“资格”前为该结构的核心部分，其后可能包括一系列的具体要求、标准或可以行使的权利等。

24.1.2 在《民法典》中的运用

《民法典》中“具备……条件”结构一共出现了 9 次。其类似结构“具有……资格”共出现 19 次，包括“具有……资格”11 次，“取得……资格”8 次。

(1)“具备……条件”结构

该结构通常用于描述实施行为或行使权利之前必须满足的一系列具体条件或要求。分为“具备……条件的……”和“具备……条件”两种句式。如第 92 条规定：“**具备**法人**条件**，为公益目的以捐助财产设立**的**基金会、社会服务机构等，经依法登记成立，取得捐助法人资格。”其中“具备法人条件"作为前提条件之一，与"为公益目的以捐助财产设立"和"经依法登记成立"共同构成了取得捐助法人资格的必要条件。又如第1098条规定："收养人应当同时具备下列条件。"该结构用于引出下文一系列具体、明确的要求或标准，旨在确保法律行为的合法性和公正性。

(2)"具有……资格"结构

该结构与"具备……条件"类似，但更侧重于描述某一主体在法律上被赋予的某种身份或能力。可细分为"具有……资格"和"取得……资格"两类。

①"具有……资格"结构通常指某人或某组织拥有某种特定的能力、条件或身份，从而被认可或赋予某种权利、地位，或可以从事某项活动。该结构有"具有……资格的……"和"具有……资格"两种句式。如第32条规定："没有依法**具有**监护**资格的**人的，监护人由民政部门担任，也可以由具备履行监护职责条件的被监护人住所地的居民委员会、村民委员会担任。"该结构明确了"监护人"所需具备的特定资格，即"依法具有监护资格"，且以此为条件引出下文，当不存在符合法律规定的自然监护人时，进一步明确了承担监护职责的主体。再如，第90条规定："依法不需要办理法人登记的，从成立之日起，**具有**社会团体法人**资格**。"此处"具有……资格"结构在内容上明确了社会团体的法律地位，在逻辑上与前置条件紧密相连，为后续的法律效力延伸提供了基础。

②"取得……资格"结构通常指某一主体在满足特定条件后，通过法定程序获得某种法律上的资格或地位。该结构只有"取得……资格"一种句式。如第92条规定："依法设立的宗教活动场所，具备法人条件的，可以申请法人登记，**取得**捐助法人**资格**。"该结构从主体"宗教活动场所"到条件"依法设立""具备法人条件"，再到行为"申请法人登记"和结果"取得捐助法人资格"，形成了完整的逻辑关系，为宗教活动场所提供了明确的法律指引和保障。

24.2 译文对比

表 24.1 《民法典》中“具备……条件”结构的翻译对比

序号	出处（条）	原文	北大法宝译文（法宝版译文）	国家法规总库译文（总库版译文）
1	88	具备法人条件，为适应经济社会发展需要，提供公益服务设立的事业单位，经依法登记成立，取得事业单位法人资格。	A public institution satisfying the conditions for a legal person and to be formed for meeting the needs of economic and social development and providing public welfare services obtains the status of a public institution legal person upon formation through registration in accordance with the law.	A public institution established for the purpose of providing public services to meet the needs for economic and social development attains the status of a public-institution legal person if it satisfies the requirements for being a legal person and is legally registered as such.
2	92	具备法人条件，为公益目的以捐助财产设立的基金会、社会服务机构等，经依法登记成立，取得捐助法人资格。	A foundation or a social service organization, among others, satisfying the conditions for a legal person and to be formed with donated property for public welfare purposes obtains the status of a donation-based legal person upon formation through registration in accordance with the law.	A foundation, social service institution, or any other institution established with donated property for the purpose of public welfare attains the status of a donation-funded legal person if it meets the requirements for being a legal person and is legally registered as such.
3	143	具备下列条件的民事法律行为有效。	A juridical act satisfying all of the following conditions shall be valid.	A civil juristic act is valid if the following conditions are satisfied.

续表

序号	出处（条）	原文	北大法宝译文（法宝版译文）	国家法规总库译文（总库版译文）
4	1098	收养人应当同时**具备**下列**条件**。	An adopter shall **satisfy** all of **the** following **requirements**.	A prospective adopter shall **meet** all **the** following **conditions**.
5	32	没有依法**具有**监护**资格的**人的，监护人由民政部门担任，也可以由具备履行监护职责条件的被监护人住所地的居民委员会、村民委员会担任。	Where there is no person legally **qualified for** guardianship, the civil affairs department may or the urban residents' committee or villagers' committee of the place of the ward's domicile satisfying the conditions for performing the duty of guardianship may act as the guardian.	Where there is no person legally **qualified to be** a guardian, the civil affairs department shall act as the guardian, and the residents' committee or villagers' committee in the place where the ward's domicile is located may also act as the guardian if they are competent in performing the duties of guardian.
6	36	本条规定的有关个人、组织包括：其他依法**具有**监护**资格的**人，居民委员会、村民委员会、学校、医疗机构、妇女联合会、残疾人联合会、未成年人保护组织、依法设立的老年人组织、民政部门等。	For the purposes of this article, the relevant individuals and organizations include but are not limited to: any other person legally **qualified for** guardianship, an urban residents' committee, a villagers' committee, a school, a medical institution, a women's federation, a disabled persons' federation, an organization for the protection of minors, an organization legally formed for seniors, and a civil affairs department.	The relevant individual and organization referred to in this Article include any other person legally **qualified to be** a guardian, the residents' committee, the villagers' committee, a school, a medical institution, the women's federation, the disabled persons' federation, a child protection organization, a legally established organization for senior people, the civil affairs department, and the like.

续表

序号	出处（条）	原文	北大法宝译文（法宝版译文）	国家法规总库译文（总库版译文）
7	90	依法不需要办理法人登记的，从成立之日起，**具有**社会团体法人**资格**。	or if the law does not require it to undergo legal person registration, **obtains the status** of a social group legal person from the date of formation.	Where the law does not require such a social organization to be registered, it **attains the status** of a social-organization legal person from the date of its establishment.
8	101	居民委员会、村民委员会**具有**基层群众性自治组织法人**资格**，可以从事为履行职能所需要的民事活动。	An urban residents' committee or a villagers' committee **has the status** of a basic self-governing mass organization legal person, and may conduct civil activities necessary for performing its functions.	An urban residents' committee or a villagers' committee, as a primary-level self-governing organization, **attains the status** of a legal person, and may engage in civil activities necessary for the performance of their responsibilities.
9	92	依法设立的宗教活动场所，具备法人条件的，可以申请法人登记，**取得**捐助法人**资格**。	A venue for holding religious activities formed in accordance with the law and satisfying the conditions for a legal person may apply for legal person registration and **obtain the status** of a donation-based legal person.	A site legally established to hold religious activities may be registered as a legal person and **attains the status** of a donation-funded legal person if it meets the requirements for being a legal person.
10	100	城镇农村的合作经济组织依法**取得**法人**资格**。	An urban or rural cooperative economic organization shall **obtain the status** of a legal person in accordance with the law.	An urban or rural economic cooperative **attains the status** of a legal person in accordance with law.

24.3 译文分析

以下对比分析两个版本中“具备……条件”及类似结构的相应译文，探讨各种情况下较为可取的翻译方法。

24.3.1 “具备……条件”结构的翻译

(1)“具备……条件的……”句式

例句1—3同属该句式。法宝版译文为“satisfy the conditions”；总库版译文为“satisfy the requirements”“meet the requirements”和“conditions are satisfied”。

从词汇角度来看，“具备”一词可译为“satisfy”和“meet”。根据《柯林斯英语词典》，satisfy定义为：If you satisfy the requirements for something, you are good enough or have the right qualities to fulfill these requirements; meet的定义为：If something meets a need, requirement, or condition, it is good enough to do what is required. 由此可见，satisfy强调主体具有足够的资质、能力或品质来“满足”或“达到”某个要求或条件，常常带有一种主观的满足感或达到期望的意味；meet则更侧重于某物或某事“符合”或“达到”某个要求或条件，更多的是一种客观上的匹配。此外，satisfy后面常跟需求(need)、期望(expectation)、条件(condition)等主观性较强的词语；而meet后面则常跟要求(requirement)、标准(standard)、条件(terms)等，强调符合客观上的规定或条件。对于“条件”一词，condition的定义为：A condition is something which must happen or be done in order for something else to be possible, especially when this is written into a contract or law; anything called for as a requirement before the performance or completion of something else; provision; stipulation。requirement的定义为：A requirement is something that you must have in order to be allowed to do something or to be suitable for something。由此可见，condition侧重的是

在某一事件、行为或合同之前必须满足的先决条件，这些基础条件通常是双方协商一致或是法律规定的，具有一定的灵活性或可协商性；而 requirement 则更强调必要性，即为了进行某项活动或满足某个标准而必须拥有的条件，在法律或政策层面上往往被视为强制性的、不可协商的规定。

由上述分析可知，"satisfy the conditions"适用于强调主体需要满足一系列先决条件，且这些条件是合同、法律、协议规定的或双方可协商的；"satisfy the requirements"和"meet the requirements"都强调主体需要达到某种强制性的标准、条件或要求，但"satisfy"强调达到要求时主观上的满足感，而"meet"一词更侧重于客观上的条件匹配。例句 1 中"具备法人条件"是事业单位取得法人资格的必要条件，该条件具有强制性意味，且满足该条件是一种客观要求，并未表达事业单位的主观期望，因此应译为 "meet the requirements"。同上，在《民法典》中，该句式结构中的"具备"一词通常不带有额外的情感色彩，"条件"也是法律规定且无可协商的。因此，在正式的法律语境中，为凸显法律客观规范的标准，"meet the requirements" 更适合作为该句式的普适性翻译。

从句式结构角度来看，原句里，该结构作为前置定语修饰主语，使句子结构紧凑，信息表达更为直接。法宝版将该结构处理为现在分词短语作后置定语，通过直接修饰主语，读者能够迅速理解主语应具备的一系列条件。总库版将该结构处理为条件状语从句，通过改变中文原句的句式结构，使主句结构相对简单明了，凸出句式之间的逻辑关系。但从保持原文句式结构和信息表达直接性的角度来看，法宝版译文还原度更高，让英文文本能够更加准确和高效地传递信息。

因此，结合词汇角度和句式结构角度，"具备……条件的……"句式的最佳译文为 "meeting the requirements"。

(2)"具备……条件"句式

法宝版译文为 satisfy the requirements，总库版译文为 meet the conditions。

从词汇角度分析，根据上文可知，"satisfy the requirements"表达主体在达到某些强制性要求时表现出一种积极、主动的态度。“meet the conditions”表达主体需要符合一些先决条件，这些条件可能是合同、法律、政策或其他任何形式的规则所规定的。在例句 4 中“收养人应当同时具备下列条件”的语境下，收养人需要达到的条件不仅限于先决条件，还包括一些具体的要求或标准。此外，该句子的重点也并非收养人为具备条件而表现的积极态度。因此，“meet the requirements”能够更好地表达主体需要“客观”符合一系列明确的条件。

从句式结构角度分析，“具备……条件”是一个动宾结构，其中“具备”是动词，表示收养人的行为或状态，“……条件”是该动词的宾语，具体说明了收养人需要具备的某种条件。因此，在翻译该句式时，将其译为动宾结构“meet the requirements”即可。

24.3.2 “具有……资格”结构的翻译

(1)“具有……资格的……”句式

例句 5、例句 6 同属该句式。法宝版译文为 qualified for，总库版译文为 qualified to be。

从词汇搭配的角度来看，“qualified for＋某种资格、职责或工作”，通常用于描述某人目前符合特定的标准或条件，能够胜任某项工作、任务或角色，可以被考虑或选择。例如，“He is qualified for the job”。强调他满足这份工作的具体要求和条件，有资格胜任这份工作。“qualified to be ＋表明身份、角色或职位的名词”，着重于强调个人知识技能和一种潜在的、未来的或理论上的资格，例如，“She is qualified to be a doctor”。强调她具备成为医生所需的知识、技能和经验。例句 5 和例句 6 都强调组织在法律上或实际上已经具备了担任监护人的资格或条件，而非监护人所需的知识、技能和经验等。同上述例句，《民法典》中，该句式结构通常表达主体符合一定标准而具有某种资格，因此“qualified for”为最佳翻译。

从句式结构看，“具有……资格的……”在句中作前置定语修饰主语，法宝版和总库版译文均使用过去分词短语作后置定语，相比于定语从句，这种处理方式能确保法律语言的简明性，避免过多的从句结构而引起的歧义，突出被修饰主语的重要性。

综上，结合词汇角度和句式结构角度，“具有……资格的……”句式的最佳译文为作后置定语的“qualified for”。

(2)“具有……资格”句式

例句7、例句8同属该句式。法宝版译文为“obtain the status”“have the status”，总库版译文为“attain the status”。

从词汇角度来看，“具有”一词通常用于描述某人已经拥有、具备或处于某种状态、特性、能力或资格。这种表述强调的是一种静态的、已经存在的状态，而不是一个动态的获取过程。在法律文本中，“obtain the status”通常用于描述个人、组织或实体通过满足特定法律要求、完成必要程序或达到法定条件而获得某种法律地位或身份，突出从无到有的过程。“attain the status”同样描述获得某种法律地位或身份，但更侧重于强调通过不懈的努力而达到某种更高的标准。“have the status”用于简单地陈述某人、组织或实体已经具有某种法律地位或身份，不强调获得的过程或手段，而是侧重于当前存在的状态。结合“具有”暗含之意，“have the status”更适合作为该句式的普适性翻译。例句7强调社会团体在成立之日起就获得法人资格；例句8中，居民委员会和村民委员会自设立或依法成立后即具备法人资格。这两个例句都描述一种已经存在且不需要通过额外努力或程序即可确认的法律地位或身份，因此可译为“have the status”。

从句式结构角度来看，该结构在句中为动宾结构，在英译过程中，译者应在保持句式基本含义的基础上，最大限度地再现句式结构，减少译文与原文的信息偏差。综上，“have the status”为“具有……资格”句式的最佳译文。

24.3.3 “取得……资格”结构的翻译

例句9、例句10同属该结构。法宝版译文为“obtain the status”，总库版译文为“attain the status”。

该结构只有“取得……资格”一种句式，同“具有……资格”一样，该句式结构译为动宾结构短语，能够最大限度地保留原文风格，增强译文的可读性和准确性。

根据上文分析可知两短语的异同。“取得”一词强调的是一种动态的、从“无”到“有”的获取过程，与“具有”所表达的静态的状态有所不同。如果原句中明显突出是“坚持不懈”获得的资格，该结构应译为“obtain the status”。例句9中“取得捐助法人资格”是通过“申请法人登记”这一具体行动来实现的。这里只强调了从“无”到“有”的获取过程，因此译为“obtain the status”更合适。例句10虽然没有明确说明是通过何种方式获得的法人资格，但“依法取得”暗示了相应的法律程序，因此也应译为“obtain the status”。同时，通过检索四大数据库中两短语的使用频次（见表24.2），也可以证实，“obtain the status”的使用频率更高，更适合作为法律文本的普适性翻译。

表24.2 “取得……资格”的英文表达方式及检索频次

表达方式	国内	国外		
	香港法例库	英国立法库	美国联邦法规库	美国法典库
obtain the status	0	37	3201	994
attain the status	0	0	376	263

小 结

“具备……条件”和“具有……资格”为相似结构。其中，“具有……资格”可分为“具有……资格”和“取得……资格”两种结构。译者在翻译时，需具体情况具体分析。针对该类结构的翻译，从词汇和句式结构角度进行分析总结，可提出如下一般性翻译建议：

“具备……条件”有“具备……条件的……”和“具备……条件”两类句

式。①“具备……条件的……”句式，可译为 meeting the requirements。②“具备……条件”句式，可译为 meet the requirements。

“具有……资格”有“具有……资格的……”和“具有……资格”两类句式。①“具有……资格的……”句式，可译为 qualified for。②“具备……资格”句式，可译为 have the status。

“取得……资格”仅有一种句式，可译为 obtain the status。

25 “履行……义务”结构的翻译

25.1 结构特点及其在《民法典》中的运用

25.1.1 结构特点

“履行……义务”和“尽到……义务”“负有……义务”在法律条文中结构相似，都明确界定了主体在特定法律关系或情境下所要承担的某种义务。该结构前通常包括法律主体的身份属性、权利义务关系等，也可能进一步阐述义务的具体履行方式、时间限制等。“义务”一词前为主体需要承担的具体义务，“义务”一词后也会阐明违反义务的法律后果等，或者与其他法律条款进行关联和补充。该结构与“行使……权”相对应，两者在保障法律关系的平衡稳定，维护法律制度的公正性上发挥重要作用。

25.1.2 在《民法典》中的运用

《民法典》中“履行……义务”共出现了 66 次。该结构强调按照法律规定，实际地、完整地执行或完成某项义务。如第 317 条规定：“权利人悬赏寻找遗失物的，领取遗失物时应当按照承诺**履行义务**。”该条明确了权利人作为主体，要完整地履行之前做出的悬赏承诺，以维护民事交易秩序。“尽到……义务”共出现了 15 次。该结构强调主体在履行其法律义务时所应达到的某种标准或程度。如第 1026 条规定：“认定行为人是否**尽到**前条第二项规定的合理核实义务，应当考虑下列因素。”该条明确了行为人应尽的“合理核实义务”，并列举了多项评判因素。“负有……义务”共出现了11次。该结构表示主体在法律上承担或拥有某项义务，强调的是一种责任的状态，即主体在法律上被要求必须做某事或不做某事。如第451条规定：“留置权人负有妥善保管留置财产的义务。”该条突出了留置权人作为义务主体的责任状态，即必须对留置财产进行妥善保管。

(1)“履行……义务”结构

该结构不仅体现了法律对义务履行的强制性，还强调了义务履行的全面性和完整性。该结构有“履行义务”和“履行+具体义务”两种句式，涉及到合同、侵权责任、婚姻家庭及其他各个领域的责任义务。如第778条规定：“定作人不履行协助义务致使承揽工作不能完成的，承揽人可以催告定作人在合理期限内履行义务，并可以顺延履行期限。”此处“履行义务”是在一个更广泛的法律语境下，针对承揽合同中定作人可能存在的违约行为而作出的一般性规定，也意味着定作人必须按照约定或法律规定的方式来履行义务，否则将承担相应的法律责任。如第495条规定：“当事人一方不履行预约合同约定的订立合同义务的，对方可以请求其承担预约合同的违约责任。”该条文旨在明确和具体化当事人在预约合同中“订立合同”这一特定义务，此处将义务具体化，可以避免歧义。

(2)“尽到……义务”结构

该结构强调行为人在履行其法律或合同规定的义务时，要确保自己的行为达到或超过规定的标准。该结构只有一种句式。如第1219条规定：“医务人员未尽到前款义务，造成患者损害的，医疗机构应当承担赔偿责任。”这里的“尽到”不仅仅是一个简单的行为要求，更强调了医务人员必须达到或超越法律规定的、行业认可的甚至是更高的道德和专业标准。

(3)“负有……义务”结构

该结构侧重于义务的存在性和责任的归属，关注个体或实体是否承担了某项义务，以及这项义务的具体内容是什么，而非强调主体是如何履行这一义务的。该结构有“A对B负有……义务”和“A(本身)负有……义务”

两种句式。如第26条规定:“父母对未成年子女负有抚养、教育和保护的义务。”该句强调了义务双方的关系,“抚养、教育和保护”三个并列词语,共同构成了父母所负有的义务内容。又如第432条规定:“质权人负有妥善保管质押财产的义务。”该句重在强调义务承担者(质权人)自身的责任,无论是否涉及受益者,质权人都有保管质押财务的义务。

25.2 译文对比

表25.1 《民法典》中“履行……义务”结构的翻译对比

序号	出处(条)	原文	北大法宝译文(法宝版译文)	国家法规总库译文(总库版译文)
1	317	权利人悬赏寻找遗失物的,领取遗失物时应当按照承诺履行义务。	The right holder that offers a reward to find the lost property shall fulfill his or her obligation as promised when taking the property back.	Where a right holder has offered a reward for finding the lost thing, he shall, at the time of collecting the lost thing, perform his obligations as promised.
2	778	定作人不履行协助义务致使承揽工作不能完成的,承揽人可以催告定作人在合理期限内履行义务,并可以顺延履行期限。	Where the contracted work is unable to be completed due to the ordering party's failure in fulfilling its obligation of assistance, the contractor may urge the ordering party to perform its obligation within a reasonable time limit and may extend the term of its performance.	Where the client fails to perform such obligation, thus making the completion of the contracted work impossible, the contractor may demand him to perform his obligation within a reasonable period of time, and may also extend the period of performance accordingly.

续表

序号	出处(条)	原文	北大法宝译文(法宝版译文)	国家法规总库译文(总库版译文)
3	70	清算义务人未及时履行清算义务,造成损害的,应当承担民事责任;主管机关或者利害关系人可以申请人民法院指定有关人员组成清算组进行清算。	Where the liquidation obligors fail to fulfill their liquidation obligation in a timely manner, causing any damage, they shall assume civil liability; and the competent authority or an interested party may apply to a people's court for designating relevant persons to form a liquidation group to conduct liquidation.	The persons with the duty to liquidate the legal person who fail to perform their duties in time and thus cause damage to others shall bear civil liability; the competent authority or an interested person may request the people's court to appoint the relevant persons to form a liquidation committee to liquidate the legal person.
4	176	民事主体依照法律规定或者按照当事人约定,履行民事义务,承担民事责任。	The parties to civil legal relations shall perform their civil obligations and assume civil liabilities in accordance with the provisions of laws or the agreements of the parties.	A person of the civil law shall perform civil-law obligations and bear civil liability in accordance with law or the agreement of the parties.
5	495	当事人一方不履行预约合同约定的订立合同义务的,对方可以请求其承担预约合同的违约责任。	If one party fails to perform the obligation to contract as agreed in the preliminary agreement, the other party may claim liability of the party for breach of the preliminary agreement.	Where one of the parties fails to perform the obligation to conclude a contract agreed in the preliminary contract, the other party may request such party to bear the liability for breach of the preliminary contract.

续表

序号	出处（条）	原文	北大法宝译文（法宝版译文）	国家法规总库译文（总库版译文）
6	509	当事人应当遵循诚信原则，根据合同的性质、目的和交易习惯履行通知、协助、保密等义务。	The parties shall abide by the principle of good faith, and perform obligations of notification, assistance, confidentiality, etc. in accordance with the nature and purpose of the contract and the usage of trade.	The parties shall comply with the principle of good faith, and perform such obligations as sending notification, rendering assistance, and keeping confidentiality in accordance with the nature and purpose of the contract and the course of dealing.
7	1219	医务人员未尽到前款义务，造成患者损害的，医疗机构应当承担赔偿责任。	Where any medical staff member fails to fulfill the duties in the preceding paragraph and causes any harm to a patient, the medical institution shall assume the compensatory liability.	Where the medical staff fail to fulfill the obligations as provided in the preceding paragraph and thus cause damage to the patient, the medical institution shall assume the liability for compensation.
8	1026	认定行为人是否尽到前条第二项规定的合理核实义务，应当考虑下列因素。	To determine whether an actor has fulfilled the obligation of rational verification prescribed in item (2) of the preceding article, the following factors shall be considered.	To determine whether an actor has fulfilled the obligation to reasonably verify the information as provided in Subparagraph 2 of the preceding Article, the following factors shall be considered.
9	26	父母对未成年子女负有抚养、教育和保护的义务。	Parents have the obligations of maintenance, education, and protection of their minor children.	Parents have the duty to raise, educate, and protect their minor children.

续表

序号	出处（条）	原文	北大法宝译文（法宝版译文）	国家法规总库译文（总库版译文）
10	1066	一方负有法定扶养义务的人患重大疾病需要医治，另一方不同意支付相关医疗费用。	A person towards whom a spouse has a statutory duty of support suffers from a serious illness and needs medical treatment, while the other spouse refuses to pay the relevant medical expenses.	a person, whom one of the spouses has a statutory obligation to support, is suffering from a serious disease and needs medical treatment, but the other spouse does not agree to pay the relevant medical expenses.
11	432	质权人负有妥善保管质押财产的义务。	The pledgee is obliged to properly keep the pledged property.	A pledgee is obligated to well keep the pledged property.
12	451	留置权人负有妥善保管留置财产的义务。	The lienor is obliged to properly keep the property under lien.	A lienholder is obligated to well keep the retained property.

25.3 译文分析

以下对比分析两个版本中“履行……义务”和“尽到……义务”“负有……义务”的相应译文，探讨各种情况下较为可取的翻译方法。

25.3.1 “履行……义务”结构的翻译

例句1—6同属该句式。法宝版和总库版的译文都给出了“fulfill obligations”“perform obligations”“perform duties”几种表达方式。

从词汇角度分析，通过查阅《布莱克法律词典》可知，perform定义为：to do what one party is obliged to do by a contract；fulfill定义为：to do everything which is promised in a contract。因此，perform通常泛指合同

双方或多方根据合同条款履行各自的责任和义务，fulfill 更侧重于强调合同一方对合同中具体承诺或义务的完全实现。此外，fulfill 在英文中常用来表示“完全地、彻底地实现或完成（承诺、义务、责任等）”，而 perform 并不强调履行义务时的尽责程度。因此，在翻译“履行”一词时，译者需要结合具体的语境进行判断。对于“义务”一词，obligation 指的是强制性的、具有法律约束力的义务，这种义务源于法律规定、合同约定或其他形式的法律承诺，往往具有明确的法律后果。duty 通常指的是根据法律规定或道德要求应当履行的义务，更多的是基于道德和法律标准的自觉行为，而非仅仅因为外部强制力。duty 常常与 responsibility 一词相关联，强调对他人或社会的责任。在《民法典》中，“义务”一词更强调法律的强制性，如非原文刻意突出道德上的标准，“obligation” 更能代表法律中“义务”一词。

综上，对于使用 “perform obligations”或 “fulfill obligations”，我们需要根据合同的具体内容、义务的性质以及涉及的主体数量来进行判断。在大多数情况下，如果义务是由合同双方共同承担的，或者义务涉及多个方面和多个主体，那么使用 “perform obligations” 更为全面；如果义务是由一方单独承担的，并且强调对具体承诺的完全实现，那么使用 “fulfill obligations” 更为贴切。例句 1 中“履行义务”指的是权利人根据之前的悬赏承诺来履行义务。这是一个单向的承诺，由权利人给出，并强调了对具体承诺的完全实现，因此，这里更侧重于 “fulfill obligations”。例句 2—6 都是涉及合同双方或多方按照规定各自履行义务，且涵盖了合同中规定的所有相关责任和义务，因此应译为 “perform obligations”。

从句式结构分析，该句式分为“履行义务”和“履行……义务”两种。例句 1、例句 2 同属“履行义务”，此句型结构可直接翻译为 “perform/fulfill one's obligations”。“履行……义务”中“义务”一词前的定语可长、可短、可简单、可复杂，因此在翻译过程中，译者还要根据句子结构进行一定调整。如果“义务”前的定语较短，较简单，则可直接在其前加上形容词或者名词进行修饰限定，如例句 3 和例句 4，可译为 “perform their liquidation obligation” 和 “perform their civil obligations”；如果“义务”的修饰语较长、较复杂，在“义务”前加定语，会使译文内容冗长或出现歧义，则需在该词后加相应的内容予以修饰，如例句 5 和例句 6 使用不定式、介词短语等方式做进一步说明。

25.3.2 “尽到……义务”结构的翻译

例句 7、例句 8 同属该结构。法宝版为“fulfill the duties”“fulfill the obligations”，总库版译文为“fulfill the obligations”。

根据上文词义分析可以得出，“fulfill”更能凸显对义务的重视和尽责的态度，这与“尽到”一词所传达的“竭尽全力、尽心尽力”的意味相契合。“fulfill the duties”，强调的是按照某种角色、职位或工作描述中的要求，尽职尽责地完成各项任务。“duties”通常与个人的职责、岗位责任或工作任务紧密相连，要求个体在工作中展现出高度的责任感和敬业精神。而“fulfill the obligations”更侧重于法律、契约等方面所规定的必须履行的义务，强调对外部规定和约束的遵守，以及对自身行为所可能产生的后果的负责态度。例句 7 中的“义务”更多的是指医务人员在医疗过程中应当遵循的职业标准、操作规范以及为患者提供必要医疗服务的责任。这些义务通常与医务人员的专业职责、岗位责任或工作任务紧密相关，因此应译为“fulfill the duties”。例句 8 中的“义务”更侧重于法律规定中所明确要求的核实行为，强调行为人对外部规定的遵守，因此应译为“fulfill the obligations”。

25.3.3 “负有……义务”结构的翻译

(1) “A 对 B 负有……义务”

例句 9、例句 10 同属该结构。法宝版和总库版译文都给出了“have the(a) duty”“have the(a) obligation(s)”两种译文。

该结构强调的是 A 与 B 之间因法律原因而形成的特定关系，即 A 对 B 承担某种义务。这里的“对”字明确指出了义务关系的双方，体现了义务的指向性和特定性。在英文中，“have”除了表示“拥有”之外，还可以用来表达“具有、持有、负有”等含义。在“A对B负有……义务”的结构中，“have”能够很好地传达出A对B所持有的义务或责任的状态。这种状态是静态的、持续存在的，准确地反映了A对B的义务关系。

根据上文对duty和obligation两词词义的分析可知，“have the duty”侧重于表达一种内在的、自觉的义务感，这种义务感可能来自个人的道德观念、职业操守或社会期望，不因外部的监督或强制而履行。而“have the obligations”则更侧重于表达一种外在的、由外部因素所规定的责任和义务。这种义务来源于合同、法律、承诺等，具有明确的条款和规定，且需要主体人认真履行。例句9中“负有……义务”描述了一种基于家庭关系而履行的义务，这种义务与父母的身份和角色紧密相关，更是一种长期的、持续的义务，因此更建议翻译为“have the duty”。例句10中“负有法定扶养义务”明确指出了这种义务是由法律所规定的，具有强制性和明确性。因此，翻译成“have the obligations”更为贴切。

(2)“A(本身)负有……义务”

例句11、例句12同属该结构。法宝版译文为“be obliged to”，总库版译文为“be obligated to”。

该结构更侧重于A自身的义务，表示因为某种外部因素，如法律规定，而不得不承担某项责任。通过查阅《柯林斯英语词典》可知，oblige定义为：If you are obliged to do something, a situation, rule, or law makes it necessary for you to do that thing。obligate定义为：If you feel obligated to do something, you feel that it is your duty to do it. If you are obligated to someone, you feel that it is your duty to look after them。由此可见，oblige是外部法律、规则或情况对个体行为的强制性要求；而obligated更多地与个人的道德观念、责任感或内心驱动相关，突出个人履行义务时的自觉性。在《民法典》中，该结构通常表达一种法律所规定的强制性要求，如例句11和例句12，都强调义务主体必须承担的义务，而非基于义务主体的道德观念等，因此该类句式结构应当译为“be obliged to”。

小　结

“履行……义务”和“负有……义务”“尽到……义务”为相似结构，表达特定主体在某种情况下需要承担的义务。

“履行……义务”结构分为“履行义务”和“履行……义务”两种句式。如非原文刻意强调主体受道德影响而履行义务，一般情况下两种句式可译为“perform obligations”或“fulfill obligations”。当强调合同双方或多方各自承担义务时，通常译为“perform obligations”；而在强调义务由一方单独承担时，则应译为“fulfill obligations”。此外，当句式“履行……义务”中“义务”的修饰语较长时，译文可在 obligation 后加不定式、介词短语等进一步解释说明。

“尽到……义务”结构可译为“fulfill the duties”和“fulfill the obligations”。当强调主体因某种角色、职位或工作描述等要求而主动尽到义务时，应译为“fulfill the duties”；当强调因法律、契约等方面规定而不得不尽到义务时，则译为“fulfill the obligations”。

“负有……义务”结构分为“A 对 B 负有……义务”和“A(本身)负有……义务”两种句式。①“A 对 B 负有……义务”句式可译为“have the duty”和“have the obligations”。当强调义务感源于个人的道德观念、职业操守或社会期望，并且这种义务是长期且需要持续的，可以译为“have the duty”；当强调义务责任来自有明确规定的合同、法律、承诺等，突出其强制性时，则可译为“have the obligations”。②“A(本身)负有……义务”句式，可译为“be obliged to”。

26 “实施……行为”结构的翻译

26.1 结构特点及其在《民法典》中的运用

26.1.1 结构特点

“实施……行为”结构在法律文本中通常用于描述行为主体的主动作为、完成的某种法律行为、实施法律规定的责任或义务，以及执行法律规定的程序或措施等。

26.1.2 在《民法典》中的运用

《民法典》中该结构一共出现了 57 次，多数情况下用于描述相关主体完成的某种法律行为或主动作为，如第 18 条中的“成年人为完全民事行为能力人，可以独立实施民事法律行为”和第 1168 条中的“二人以上共同实施侵权行为，造成他人损害的，应当承担连带责任”。少数情况下，该结构用于描述实施法律规定的义务或责任等。如第 36 条中“实施严重损害被监护人身心健康的行为”，此处的行为是指监护人违反应尽的法定义务——保护被监护人的身心健康。

根据“实施……行为”在《民法典》中的使用频率，该结构主要分为两种情况：

(1)“实施民事法律行为”

本结构在《民法典》中出现了 24 次。这种情况下,“实施”用于描述某种已完成的法律行为,突出行为的结果。同类型结构还包括“实施代理行为”(《民法典》中出现 4 次)。该结构前文通常会交代民事主体的身份地位,后文则可能进一步说明法律行为的效力、后果等。本结构于前文内容起到补充作用,于后文形成递进关系。如第 34 条规定:“监护人的职责是代理被监护人实施民事法律行为,保护被监护人的人身权利、财产权利以及其他合法权益等。”实施该行为的主体是监护人,效力则是保护被监护人的合法权益,“实施民事法律行为”则是对监护人职责的具体内容的补充说明。

(2)“实施侵权行为”

本结构在《民法典》中共出现 6 次,主要用于描述行为主体的主动作为,强调了行为人的主观能动性。类似的结构还包括“实施欺诈行为”。此外,该结构将主体与其应承担相应法律责任及后果相关联,起到顺承作用。如第 1172 条规定:“二人以上分别实施侵权行为造成同一损害,能够确定责任大小的,各自承担相应的责任;难以确定责任大小的,平均承担责任。”该条款通过“实施侵权行为”这一结构,明确了各行为人的侵权行为,并将其与承担责任大小挂钩,突出责任认定的标准,从而形成递进关系。

26.2 译文对比

表 26.1 《民法典》中“实施……行为”结构的翻译对比

序号	出处(条)	原文	北大法宝译文(法宝版译文)	国家法规总库译文(总库版译文)
1	18	成年人为完全民事行为能力人,可以独立实施民事法律行为。	An adult has full capacity for civil conduct, and may perform juridical acts independently.	An adult has full capacity for performing civil juristic acts and may independently perform civil juristic acts.

续表

序号	出处（条）	原文	北大法宝译文（法宝版译文）	国家法规总库译文（总库版译文）
2	34	监护人的职责是代理被监护人实施民事法律行为，保护被监护人的人身权利、财产权利以及其他合法权益等。	The duties of a guardian include but are not limited to representing the ward in performing juridical acts and protecting the personal rights, property rights, and other lawful rights and interests of the ward.	The duties of a guardian are to represent the ward to perform civil juristic acts and to protect the personal, proprietary, and other lawful rights and interests of the ward.
3	161	民事主体可以通过代理人实施民事法律行为。	The parties to civil legal relations may conduct juridical acts through agents.	A person of the civil law may perform a civil juristic act through his agent.
4	1016	民事主体变更姓名、名称的，变更前实施的民事法律行为对其具有法律约束力。	Where a party to civil legal relations changes his name, the civil legal acts conducted before the change shall be legally binding upon him or it.	For a person of the civil law who changes the name or entity name, the civil juristic acts performed by the person before the name change is legally binding on the person.
5	1060	夫妻一方因家庭日常生活需要而实施的民事法律行为，对夫妻双方发生效力，但是夫妻一方与相对人另有约定的除外。	A juridical act performed by one of the spouses to meet the needs of the family's daily life shall be binding on both of them, except as otherwise agreed between one spouse and an opposite party.	A civil juristic act performed by one of the spouses to meet the daily needs of the family is binding on both spouses unless otherwise agreed between the third person and the spouse performing the act.

续表

序号	出处（条）	原文	北大法宝译文（法宝版译文）	国家法规总库译文（总库版译文）
6	1168	二人以上共同实施侵权行为，造成他人损害的，应当承担连带责任。	Where two or more persons jointly commit a tort, causing harm to another person, they shall be liable jointly and severally.	Where two or more persons jointly commit a tortious act causing damage to another person, they shall bear joint and several liability.
7	1172	二人以上分别实施侵权行为造成同一损害，能够确定责任大小的，各自承担相应的责任；难以确定责任大小的，平均承担责任。	Where two or more persons commit torts respectively, causing the same harm, if the seriousness of liability of each tortfeasor can be determined, the tortfeasors shall assume corresponding liability respectively; or if the seriousness of liability of each tortfeasor is hard to be determined, the tortfeasors shall evenly assume the liability.	Where the tortious acts separately committed by two or more persons cause the same damage to another person, each of them shall bear the liability in proportion to their respective share of fault if it can be determined, or in equal share if it cannot be determined.
8	1195	网络用户利用网络服务实施侵权行为的，权利人有权通知网络服务提供者采取删除、屏蔽、断开链接等必要措施。	Where a network user commits a tort through the network services, the right holder shall be entitled to notify the network service provider to take such necessary measures as deletion, block or disconnection.	Where a network user commits a tortious act through using the network service, the right holder is entitled to notify the network service provider to take such necessary measures as deletion, block, or disconnection.

26.3 译文分析

我们针对《民法典》中“实施……行为”结构的两种运用情况，分别对比分析两个版本的对应译文，同时探讨更为可取的翻译方法。

26.3.1 “实施民事法律行为”结构的翻译

例句1—5属于该结构。法宝版译文有“perform...act”和“conduct...act”两种译法；总库版译文则统一翻译为“perform...act”。

通过查阅《韦氏法律词典》，perform的定义为to adhere to the terms of (eg. a contract); to execute a duty or task；conduct的定义为to direct or take part in the operation or management of。可见，在法律语境中，“perform”一般强调完成或履行某种具体的职责或任务，通常与合同法和责任相关。例如，“perform a contract”(履行合同)、“perform duties”(执行职责)或“perform a legal procedure”(执行法律程序)等。而“conduct”则侧重对过程、活动或事务的管理和引导，适用于描述负责组织、协调或执行某项活动，常用于行政法、商业法等领域。例如“conduct a hearing”(主持听证会)或“conduct business”(进行商业活动)，强调对过程的管理和组织。在《民法典》中，“实施……行为”主要用于描述行为人主动完成、履行、采取或执行《民法典》规定的各种民事法律行为、权利义务、救济措施和法律程序等。因此，perform一词更适用于表达“实施……行为”。

关于“民事法律行为”的翻译，法宝版译为juridical acts，总库版译为civil juristic acts。juridical的词根是拉丁语“juridicus”(司法的)，更贴近“jurisdiction”(司法权)和“judicial”(司法的)，在《柯林斯英语词典》中的定义为“of or relating to law, to the administration of justice, or to the office or function of a judge; legal”。可见juridical强调制度性、程序性，侧重法律的实际运行和司法体系的操作。“juridical act”通常指国家机构或司法部门在法律框架内行使权力的行为，如法院判决、立法机关通过法律、行政机关颁布规章等,多用于公法领域;尽管也有时用于私法领域(如 in the civil law of Louisiana),其意为"an expression of will that is intended to have legal consequences",更侧重于法律行为的正式性和法律后果。juristic 的词根是"jurist"(法学家、法律学者),与"jurisprudence"(法理学)直接相关。《柯林斯英语词典》对其的定义为"1. of or relating to jurists; 2. of, relating to, or characteristic of the study of law or the legal profession"。因此 juristic 天然带有理论性、学术性色彩,侧重法律背后的原则、逻辑和学者的解释。"juristic act"意思为 an action intended and capable of having a legal effect; any conduct by a private individual designed to originate, terminate, or alter a right (West's Encyclopedia of American Law, 2008),其核心概念为个人或实体通过意思表示设立、变更或终止法律关系的行为,如签订合同、立遗嘱等。《民法典》第 133 条规定:"民事法律行为是民事主体通过意思表示设立、变更、终止民事法律关系的行为。"可见,用"juristic act"翻译"民事法律行为"更能准确反映民事法律行为的主体意图和法律效果。

26.3.2 "实施侵权行为"结构的翻译

在例句 6—8 中,北大法宝将该结构译为"commit a tort",而总库版的译文是"commit a tortious act"。commit 意为做非法的事、犯……罪。侵权行为属于犯罪行为,因此,"实施"应译为"commit"。

"侵权行为"是指违反法律义务或社会责任,给他人造成损害的行为。根据《布莱克法律词典》,"tort"指可在民事法庭而非刑事法庭处理的不法行为。该词本身已包含了"行为"这一含义,如将其译为"tortious act"则较为冗余。此外,在四大数据库中检索两词的使用频次(见表 26.2)和情境,其结果也验证了我们的结论。"tort"在各类法规术语库的出现频次都远高于"tortious act"。因此"commit a tort"更适合用作汉语语境中"实施侵权行为"一词的普适性翻译。

表 26.2 “侵权行为”的英文表达方式及检索频次

表达方式	国内	国外		
	香港法例库	英国立法库	美国联邦法规库	美国法典库
tort	2	＞200	705	252
tortious act	0	37	11	20

小　结

在《民法典》中,“实施……行为”结构通常用于描述完成的某种法律行为,以及行为主体的主动作为。完成的某种法律行为,体现了行为的结果性质,其典型句式为“实施民事法律行为”,可译为“perform juristic acts”;行为主体的主动作为,强调行为的主观能动性,该结构的典型句式为“实施侵权行为”,可译为“commit a tort”。

27 “适用……规定”结构的翻译

27.1 结构特点及其在《民法典》中的运用

27.1.1 结构特点

“适用……规定”结构在法律条文中，主要指在特定情境下对某一法律规则、条款或规定的引用或适用。“适用”一词前通常是某个具体的条件或情境，“适用”一词后常是具体法律条文、编章，但在某些情况下，为了保持法律条文的简洁性和灵活性，“适用”一词后可能采用概括性表述，如“适用有关法律、行政法规以及章程的规定”。该结构体现了《民法典》内部各编章、条文之间的逻辑关联和体系性，也凸显了法律体系之间的协调性和互补性。

27.1.2 在《民法典》中的运用

《民法典》中“适用……规定”共出现了 86 次，其中“参照适用……规定”共出现 28 次。当某一法律条文或规定直接适用于某一具体情形或案件时，应使用“适用……规定”这一普遍结构，该结构体现了法律的直接性和明确性，如第 474 条规定：“要约生效的时间**适用**本法第一百三十七条的**规定**。”而“参照适用……规定”结构则更具灵活性，表示某一法律条款或规定在处理某一具体情形或案件时，需要参照其他法律条款或规定的内容来适用。如第414条规定:“其他可以登记的担保物权,清偿顺序参照适用前款规定。”

(1)“适用……规定”结构

该结构通常指向的法律规范较为明确、具体。在法律语境中,该结构前往往伴随特定的条件限制,保证法律适用的逻辑严密性;其后通常直接引用具体条款或规定,减少法律适用过程中的歧义和不确定性。如第21条规定:“八周岁以上的未成年人不能辨认自己行为的,适用前款规定。”其中,“……的”为条件限制部分,“适用前款规定”指的是前一条款中关于无民事行为能力或限制民事行为能力的未成年人的相关规定,确保了法律条文之间的连贯性和一致性。

(2)“参照适用……规定”结构

该结构指向的法律规范更为模糊,是指在特定情况下,可以参照另一法律条文的规定来处理相关问题,但这需要根据具体情况的相似性和适用范围予以判断。通过参照适用,可以避免对类似事项作出重复规定,也能够进一步完善法律体系。该结构在《民法典》中的句式通常为“法律关系或法律事实,(由于……原因,)参照适用……的规定”。如第966条规定:“本章没有规定的,参照适用委托合同的有关规定。”该句式采用“前提条件+参照适用”的逻辑结构,表明在本章没有规定的前提基础上,可以借鉴或参考委托合同章节中的相关规定来处理问题。该结构通过明确参照适用的对象和范围,让法律体系更具完整性。

27.2 译文对比

表 27.1 《民法典》中"适用……规定"结构的翻译对比

序号	出处(条)	原文	北大法宝译文(法宝版译文)	国家法规总库译文(总库版译文)
1	21	八周岁以上的未成年人不能辨认自己行为的,适用前款规定。	The provision of the preceding paragraph shall also apply to a minor attaining the age of eight without the power of discernment of his or her conduct.	The preceding paragraph is applicable to a minor aged eight or above who is unable to comprehend his own conduct.
2	474	要约生效的时间适用本法第一百三十七条的规定。	The effective time of an offer shall be governed by the provisions of Article 137 of this Code.	The time when an offer becomes effective is governed by the provisions of Article 137 of this Code.
3	198	法律对仲裁时效有规定的,依照其规定;没有规定的,适用诉讼时效的规定。	Where any law prescribes arbitration, such a law shall apply; otherwise, the provisions on extinctive prescription for actions shall apply.	Any provisions of law regulating the limitation period for arbitration shall be followed; in the absence of such provisions, the provisions on limitation period for litigation provided herein shall be applied *mutatis mutandis*.
4	556	合同的权利和义务一并转让的,适用债权转让、债务转移的有关规定。	Where contractual rights and obligations are transferred together, the provisions on the assignment of claims and delegation of obligations shall apply.	Where the rights and obligations under a contract are assigned and delegated concomitantly, the provisions on assignment of claims and delegation of obligations shall be applied.

续表

序号	出处（条）	原文	北大法宝译文（法宝版译文）	国家法规总库译文（总库版译文）
5	842	货物的毁损、灭失发生于多式联运的某一运输区段的，多式联运经营人的赔偿责任和责任限额，适用调整该区段运输方式的有关法律规定。	Where damage to or loss of the cargo occurred within a particular segment of the course of a multimodal carriage, the multimodal carriage operator's liability for damages and any limitation thereon are governed by the applicable transportation law of the jurisdiction which such segment is under.	Where destruction, damage, or loss of goods occurs in one section of the multi-modal transport, the provisions of the relevant laws regulating the transport modes of the section shall apply to the liability for compensation to be assumed by the operator of multi-modal transport and the limit of the liability.
6	269	营利法人以外的法人，对其不动产和动产的权利，适用有关法律、行政法规以及章程的规定。	The rights enjoyed by a legal person other than for-profit legal persons over its immovables and movables shall be governed by the provisions of relevant laws and administrative regulations as well as its bylaws.	The provisions of the relevant laws, administrative regulations, and articles of association shall apply to the rights of a legal person other than a for-profit legal person with respect to its immovable and movable property.
7	464	婚姻、收养、监护等有关身份关系的协议，适用有关该身份关系的法律规定。	Agreements concerning personal relations such as marriage, adoption, and guardianship shall be governed by the provisions of laws on the relevant personal relations.	An agreement on establishing a marriage, adoption, guardianship, or the like personal relationships shall be governed by the provisions of laws providing for such personal relationships.

续表

序号	出处(条)	原文	北大法宝译文(法宝版译文)	国家法规总库译文(总库版译文)
8	310	两个以上组织、个人共同享有用益物权、担保物权的,**参照适用**本章的有关**规定**。	The provisions of this Chapter **shall apply, mutatis mutandis**, **to** usufruct or security interest enjoyed by two or more organizations or individuals.	The relevant provisions of this Chapter **shall be applied *mutatis mutandis* to** the situation where two or more organizations or individuals are jointly entitled to a right to usufruct or a security interest.
9	414	其他可以登记的担保物权,清偿顺序**参照适用**前款**规定**。	The provisions of the preceding paragraph **shall apply, mutatis mutandis, to** the order of payment with respect to any other security interest that may be registered.	The preceding paragraph **shall be applied *mutatis mutandis*** with regard to the priority order of payment for other security interests that are registrable.
10	966	本章没有规定的,**参照适用**委托合同的有关**规定**。	Where this Chapter is silent, the provisions on contracts of mandate **shall apply mutatis mutandis**.	For matters not provided in this Chapter, the relevant provisions on entrustment contracts **shall be applied *mutatis mutandis***.

27.3 译文分析

以下对比分析两个版本中"适用……规定"的相应译文,探讨各种情况下较为可取的翻译方法。

27.3.1 “适用……规定”结构的翻译

例句1—7同属该句式。法宝版和总库版的译文给出了“shall apply to”“shall apply”“shall be applied”“(shall) be governed by”“be applicable to”几种表达方式。根据两个版本的译文,可从是否使用shall和该结构的词汇翻译两方面进行分析。

根据《布莱克法律词典》的释义,shall在现代法律文本中只有“has a duty to; more broadly, is required to”一种标准用法,表示“命令”“义务”的意义。但是受英语立法文本中shall过度使用现象(Garner, 1995; Wydick, 1998)的影响,我国立法文本的译者误认为使用shall能够体现出译文的法律英语特征,维护法律权威,更符合目的语读者的期待,结果造成shall在译文中的使用具有垄断性和排他性(陈忠诚,1992;陈小全、刘劲松,2011;李晋、董晓波,2021),“为读者埋下许多陷阱”,可能导致法庭对shall进行任意解读(Wydick, 1998: 66-67)。随着法律英语简明化运动的开展,英国、澳大利亚、加拿大、美国都开始减少甚至清除shall“病毒”(陈小全、刘劲松,2011;李晋、董晓波,2021),立法文本中与shall搭配的主语多为有灵主语(各种义务承担者)和少数无灵主语(各种义务,如decision、conviction、evidence等)。从例句1—7的语境分析可知,“适用”强调了相关规定与其约束对象之间的恰当性,明确了法律使用的范围,并非强调该规定的“责任”或“义务”,因此该结构不应使用shall。

对于该结构词汇的翻译,可结合词汇内涵和中文句式结构进行分析。

(1)词汇内涵

①apply:通过查询《柯林斯英语词典》可知,apply的定义为:If something such as a rule or a remark applies to a person or in a situation, it is relevant to the person or the situation。该词作为动词单独使用时,其一般含义为“应用”“适用”,但由于没有明确指出应用的对象和范围,通常需要根据上下文来确定所指范围。

②apply to:通过查询《剑桥词典》可知,apply to的定义为:If

something such as a rule or law applies to you, it involves you or is important to you。该短语译为"适用于",通过介词 to 明确指出了某个规则、法律或原则将应用于某个特定的情况、对象或范围。该短语常与具体的法律条款、规定、原则或情境搭配使用,明确指出其适用范围和对象,相比 apply 一词更强调适用性和针对性。

③be governed by:通过查询《柯林斯英语词典》可知,govern 的定义为:If a situation or activity is governed by a particular factor, rule, or force, it is controlled by that factor, rule, or force。该短语意为"受……管辖"或"由……控制",强调的是一种管理或控制关系,即某个行为、规则或实体受到某法律、规则或实体的约束或指导。该短语常与法律、法规、合同等规范性文件搭配使用,更强调法律的管辖和控制作用。

④be applicable to:通过查询《柯林斯英语词典》可知,applicable 的定义为:being appropriate or relevant; able to be applied; fitting。该短语可译为"可应用于",表达的是某项规定或原则在特定情况下具有潜在的适用性,但不一定要求必须应用,更多的是在描述一种可能性或适用范围。

综上,"apply"和 "apply to"均意为"适用","be governed by"意为"受……管辖","be applicable to"意为"可应用于"。在法律英语中,"apply"一词若单独使用需要根据上下文来确定所指范围,"apply to"用于表达法律条款的明确适用性和强制性,"be governed by"侧重于表达法律、法规或合同对特定行为或实体的约束关系,"be applicable to"则用于描述潜在的适用性范围。

(2)中文句式结构

基于上文对不同词汇含义的分析,以下将结合例句给出适当翻译,并总结归纳一般情况下不同句式的翻译规律。

例句 1、例句 2 均强调某一具体的条款对某种特定情况的适应性。其中,例句 1 是"前款规定"这个明确的、已存在的规定对"八周岁以上的未成年人不能辨认自己行为的"这一情况的规定,例句 2 是"本法第一百三十七条"对要约生效时间的具体规定,因此该两句中的结构都应翻译成 apply to。例句3—5同样强调法律的适用性，但并不特指某个具体条款对某个具体对象的直接适用性，而是描述了一个更广泛、更原则性的法律适用情境。如例句3中"诉讼时效的规定"主要集中于《民法典》第一百八十八条至第一百九十九条等条款中，例句4和例句5也是泛泛指出了应当适用的法律规定范围，因此应翻译成apply。例句6、例句7强调的是这些规定对某一情况或行为的强制性和管理性。例句6表达的是特定法人（营利法人以外的法人）的行为（对其不动产和动产的权利）受到某些规定（法律、行政法规以及章程）的约束和管理，例句7强调"婚姻、收养、监护等有关身份关系的协议"受到"有关该身份关系的法律规定"的约束，因此应译为be governed by。

根据上述案例分析，结合中文句式结构特点，我们将"适用……规定"结构细分为三类，给出普适性翻译的参考：

①"适用（某）规定"和"适用……（第几条）的规定"：例句1、例句2同属该结构。这两个短语中，"适用"作为动词，直接指向其后的名词"（某）规定"或"（第几条）的规定"，所指的内容为具体、明确的法律条款，均译为apply to。

②"适用……（某类）的规定"和"适用……的有关规定"：例句3—5同属该结构。其中，"（某类）的规定"描述的是一个更为广泛的法律使用情境；"……的有关规定"明确指向与某一对象或情况直接相关的法律范围，这里的"有关"强调了规定与对象或情况之间的直接联系，意味着这些规定是专门为该对象或情况制定的，或者至少在该对象或情况的适用范围内，均译为apply。

③"适用有关……的规定"：例句6、例句7同属该结构。该句式结构更加宽泛，涉及某对象或某情况相关的多方面规定。这里的"有关"不仅强调了规定与对象或情况之间的联系，还暗示了这种联系可能是多方面的、复杂的。这种结构通常用于描述一个对象或情况受到多个不同但相互关联的法律规定的共同管辖，因此应译为be governed by。

27.3.2 "参照适用……规定"结构的翻译

例句 8—10 同属该句式。法宝版的译文为"shall apply，mutatis mutandis，(to)"，总库版的译文为"shall be applied *mutatis mutandis* (to)"。

法律适用和参照适用有着显著区别，前者强调的是法律规范直接应用于具体案件，具有较高的确定性和广泛的适用范围；后者是指法律明文规定将某种事项的规定适用于最相类似的其他事项，它需要裁判者进行相似性判断，可能存在一定的自由裁量空间。"mutatis mutandis"是一个源自拉丁语的术语，表示在进行比较或应用某项规定时，需要进行必要的调整或修改，用于翻译"参照"非常合适。但是无论是"适用"还是"参照适用"，虽然都是立法者设置的强制性义务，义务的主体都不是相关规定"provisions"。具体而言，在参照适用条款中，裁判者才是义务主体，"参照适用"是裁判者的强制性义务（李伟平，2023），例句 8—10 都使用"provisions"作句子主语，其后不应使用 shall。

关于 apply 应当使用主动态还是被动态的问题。"apply"的主动语态，即作不及物动词时，表示条款自身具有适用性，暗示适用是条款的固有属性；"be applied"作为被动语态，强调条款的适用依赖外部行为，隐含责任主体（裁判者）需主动采取行动。而"参照适用……规定"在立法文本中并不强调主体适用规定的主动过程和行为，因为"参照适用"条款是立法者为了简化法律条文、避免重复规定而采用的立法技术。立法者通过明确的条款表述，授权裁判者在特定情形下适用相关规范，这种适用是基于立法者的预先安排，具有一定的自动性；在立法者已经明确设定"参照适用"条款的情况下，裁判者应当首先考虑适用这些条款，而不是自行类推或适用习惯法（李伟平，2023）。可见"参照适用……规定"更强调条款的自动适用性，因此，apply 的主动语态更适合该句式结构的翻译。

小 结

在《民法典》中,“适用……规定”结构主要体现了法律适用的原则和规则,该结构可分为“适用……规定”的一般结构和“参照适用……规定”结构。

“适用……规定”可细分为三类,从词汇内涵和句式结构对案例进行分析,可提出如下参考性翻译建议:①“适用(某)规定”和“适用……(第几条)的规定”可译为 apply to;②“适用……(某类)的规定”和“适用……的有关规定”可译为 apply;③“适用有关……的规定”可译 be governed by。译者仍需结合语境进行具体分析。

“参照适用……规定”可译为 “apply mutatis mutandis (to)”。

28 “享有……权利”结构的翻译

28.1 结构特点及其在《民法典》中的运用

28.1.1 结构特点

“享有……权利”结构在法律条文中,指明确赋予特定主体(如自然人、法人或其他组织)以特定权利的法律表述方式。“享有”一词前通常为权利主体,如“法人”“所有权人”等;“享有”一词后常是对权利内容的具体描述,包括但不限于财产权、人身权、知识产权等。该结构与“承担……责任”相对应,保证权利义务的一致性。

28.1.2 在《民法典》中的运用

《民法典》中“享有……权利”结构一共出现了 99 次,用于宣告法律赋予的权利,保障民事主体的合法权益,为权利的保护、行使及救济提供了明确的法律依据。该结构有“享有……(的)权利”“由……享有……权利”和“……的,享有……权利”三种句式。

(1)“享有……(的)权利”

该句式结构简洁,“享有”一词直接连接所列举的具体权利或权利类别。如果权利前需要加定语以进一步说明,可添加“的”字短语。如第 240 条规定:“所有权人对自己的不动产或者动产,依法享有占有、使用、收益和处分的权利。”句中直接阐明“所有权人”为权利的享有者，以避免权利归属的模糊性；“占有、使用、收益和处分”四项权利共同构成了所有权的核心内容。此类句式简洁明了，确保了法律条文的清晰度，减少歧义。

(2)“由……享有……权利”

该句式结构通过“由”字，明确指出权利的主体，强调了权利的动态变化或特定归属。在涉及多方主体时，该结构能够清晰界定享有特定权利的一方。如第67条规定：“法人合并的，其权利和义务由合并后的法人享有和承担。”其中“由……享有和承担”是一个并列的动词短语结构，清晰地表明了权利与义务的主体变化。

(3)“……的，享有……权利”

该结构在“享有”前加入描述性短语或条件性短语，用以说明主体享有权利的前提、条件或范围，使得权利的行使更加规范。如第859条规定：“研究开发人转让专利申请权的，委托人享有以同等条件优先受让的权利。”其中，“……的”为条件状语从句，“委托人享有……权利”为结果，指出了在特定条件下，委托人享有的具体的权利。

28.2 译文对比

表28.1 《民法典》中“享有……权利”结构的翻译对比

序号	出处(条)	原文	北大法宝译文(法宝版译文)	国家法规总库译文(总库版译文)
1	124	自然人依法享有继承权。	Natural persons enjoy the right of succession in accordance with the law.	A natural person has the right to succession in accordance with law.

续表

序号	出处(条)	原文	北大法宝译文(法宝版译文)	国家法规总库译文(总库版译文)
2	836	托运人或者收货人不支付运费、保管费或者其他费用的，承运人对相应的运输货物**享有**留置**权**，但是当事人另有约定的除外。	Where the consignor or consignee fails to pay the freight, storage fees or other expenses, the carrier **is entitled to** lien on the relevant carried cargoes, except as otherwise agreed upon by the parties.	If a consignor or consignee fails to pay freight, storage fee, or other expenses, the carrier **has the right to** retain the goods under a lien, unless otherwise agreed by the parties.
3	240	所有权人对自己的不动产或者动产，依法**享有**占有、使用、收益和处分**的权利**。	The owner of an immovable or movable **has the right to** possess, use, enjoy, and dispose of such an immovable or movable in accordance with the law.	An owner **is entitled to** possess, use, benefit from, and dispose of his own immovable or movable property in accordance with law.
4	263	城镇集体所有的不动产和动产，依照法律、行政法规的规定由本集体**享有**占有、使用、收益和处分**的权利**。	An urban collective **has the right to** possess, use, enjoy, and dispose of any immovable or movable owned by it in accordance with the provisions of laws and administrative regulations.	With respect to the immovable and movable property owned by an urban-town collective, the collective **is entitled to** possess, use, benefit from, and dispose of such property in accordance with laws and administrative regulations.

续表

序号	出处(条)	原文	北大法宝译文(法宝版译文)	国家法规总库译文(总库版译文)
5	519	实际承担债务超过自己份额的连带债务人,有权就超出部分在其他连带债务人未履行的份额范围内向其追偿,并相应地**享有**债权人**的权利**,但是不得损害债权人的利益。	A joint and several debtor who actually pays the obligation in excess of its share shall have the right to recover the excess from the other joint and several debtors to the extent of the shares not performed and be subrogated to **the right of** the creditor accordingly without prejudice to the interest of the creditor.	A debtor subjected to joint and several liabilities who has assumed obligation in excess of his own share has the right to contribution against the other debtors subjected to joint and several liabilities to the extent of the share not performed by the other debtors, and accordingly **shall be entitled to** the rights of a creditor, provided that the other creditors' interests may not be harmed.
6	739	出租人根据承租人对出卖人、租赁物的选择订立的买卖合同,出卖人应当按照约定向承租人交付标的物,承租人**享有**与受领标的物有关的买受人**的权利**。	Under the sales contract concluded by the lessor according to the lessee's selection of the seller and the leased property, the seller shall deliver the subject matter to the lessee in accordance with the contract, and the lessee **enjoys the rights of** the buyer in respect of taking delivery of the subject matter.	Where a lessor concludes a sales contract based on a lessee's selection of the seller and the leased object, the seller shall deliver the subject matter to the lessee as agreed by the parties, and the lessee **shall enjoy the rights of** a buyer with regard to the subject matter received.

续表

序号	出处(条)	原文	北大法宝译文(法宝版译文)	国家法规总库译文(总库版译文)
7	1058	夫妻双方平等享有对未成年子女抚养、教育和保护的权利,共同承担对未成年子女抚养、教育和保护的义务。	Both husband and wife equally enjoy the rights to support, educate and protect their minor children, and shall jointly assume the duties to support, educate, and protect their minor children.	Both spouses have equal rights and joint duties to raise, educate, and protect their minor children.
8	67	法人合并的,其权利和义务由合并后的法人享有和承担。	In case of combination of a legal person, the surviving legal person shall enjoy the rights and assume the obligations of the legal person.	In case of a merger between or among legal persons, the rights and obligations of such legal persons shall be enjoyed and assumed by the surviving legal person.
9	268	国家、集体和私人所有的不动产或者动产投到企业的,由出资人按照约定或者出资比例享有资产收益、重大决策以及选择经营管理者等权利并履行义务。	If the immovable or movable owned by the state, the collective or an individual is invested in an enterprise, the investor shall enjoy such rights as obtaining asset returns, making major decisions and selecting business managers, and shall perform duties as agreed upon or in proportion to the amount of investment.	Where the immovable or movable property of the State, collectives, and private individuals are invested in an enterprise, the investors are, in accordance with their agreement or in proportion to their investment, entitled to receive returns on the assets, make major decisions, and select business managers, and obligated to perform their duties.

续表

序号	出处(条)	原文	北大法宝译文(法宝版译文)	国家法规总库译文(总库版译文)
10	859	研究开发人转让专利申请权的,委托人享有以同等条件优先受让的权利。	Where the developer is to assign the right to apply for patent on the Invention or innovation resulting from the commissioned development, the commissioning party shall have the right to priority in acquiring such right under the same conditions.	Where a researcher-developer is to transfer his patent application right, the client has a priority right to acquire the right on equivalent conditions.
11	382	需役地以及需役地上的土地承包经营权、建设用地使用权等部分转让时,转让部分涉及地役权的,受让人同时享有地役权。	When the dominant land and the conventional usufruct on rural land for agricultural operations or the right to use land for construction thereon, among others, is partially transferred, if servitude is involved in the transferred part, the transferee shall enjoy the servitude at the same time.	Where a right to easement is involved when the dominant land and a right to contractual management of land, a right to use a lot of land for construction purposes, and the like rights thereon are partially transferred, the transferee is simultaneously entitled to the easement.

28.3 译文分析

对比两个版本中“享有……权利”结构的相应译文,可以发现,差别主要出现在“享有……权利”的词汇翻译和是否应使用 shall 两个方面。以下将就此进行分析讨论。

28.3.1 “享有……权利”的翻译

例句1—11中,对于该结构的翻译,法宝版和总库版的译文都给出了“enjoy the right”“have/has the rights to”“be entitled to”三种表述。

(1)“享有”的翻译

在中文里,“享有”表达某人或某实体在法律上或某种规定下所拥有的权利、特权、利益或地位,并有权行使或享受这些权利、特权、利益所带来的好处。

在《布莱克法律词典》中,enjoyment作为enjoy的名词形式,其释义为the exercise of a right; the possession and fruition of a right, privilege, or incorporeal hereditament。由此可知,“enjoy”不仅仅指单纯地拥有或持有某项权利,更强调权利的积极使用或体验,传递出愉悦和积极的体验情感,适用于强调权利所带来的利益。而have的基本含义为“拥有”,当与“权利”相结合时,强调了对权利的拥有状态,即表达权利的存在和归属,而并未突出权利行使或享受的过程。

在《民法典》中,“享有”一词传达的重点在于法律权利的赋予和确认。

例句1中“自然人依法享有继承权”,直接表达了自然人对继承权的合法拥有和行使的资格,更多地侧重了权利的归属,并未突出权利的实际运用或享受,因此译为have更为恰当。例句3和例句4中,虽然“享有”包含了所有权人对财产的全面控制和利用,包括占有、使用、收益和处分,但使用“have”在法律语境中更显中立,避免了情感色彩,使得表述更加严谨,符合法律文件的正式风格。再如例句8,“法人合并的,其**权利**和义务由合并后的法人**享有**和承担”。此处“享有权利”与“承担义务”虽然相提并论,但并未强调对权利的“享受”,仍然表达的是权利的归属。

可见,《民法典》中“享受……权利”结构表达的是对权利的确认和权责的描述,译文使用“have”更适合表达对权利的拥有和控制,尤其与“enjoy”相比,后者通常带有积极等情感的色彩,而立法文本通常更注重严谨性和客观性。

(2)“权利”的翻译

“权利”指公民依法应享有的权力和利益，或者法律关系主体在法律规定的范围内，为满足其特定的利益而自主享有的权能和利益。

李克兴(2012)对“权利”一词进行了分析，并指出，be entitled to 实际上指的是由于权利主体做出了某种贡献、符合某一标准或获得某种资格而可以享有或被某权力机构赋予的权利，并非同一语境中人人可以享有的、平等的权利。而 right 所涉及的“有权”不涉及明显的“职权”“代理权”或“特权”，即权利主体本身就有权利做某事，无须任何其他方面授权或许可。

例如，例句 5 中，连带债务人可以享有债权人的权利，但必须符合“实际承担债务超过自己份额”“就超出部分在其他连带债务人未履行的份额范围内”“不得损害债权人的利益”多个条件。在这一语境下，并非所有连带债务人都可以享有该权利，所以这是一个“特权”，使用“be entitled to”会更加贴切。例句 9 亦然，出资人权利的获得并非法律自然赋予的，而是因为出资或约定而获得的。

而在例句 8 中，权利和义务是由合并后的法人承担，这里权利主体无须任何其他方面授权或特殊限制，且该内容只是强调权利的存在，因此应当将“权利”译为“right”。

28.3.2 是否使用 shall

根据《布莱克法律词典》，shall 的定义为：As used in statutes and similar instruments, this word is generally imperative or mandatory; but it may be construed as merely permissive or directory, (as equivalent to “may,”) to carry out the legislative intention and in cases where no right or benefit to any one depends on its being taken in the imperative sense, and where no public or private right is impaired by its interpretation in the other sense。这也就意味着，在法律语境中，shall 有强制性及指令性的意味，但该词也可以解释为“可以”。shall 语义的多样性与法律起草必须遵循“表达一致”的原则(Dickerson，1986)相悖，势必造成读者理解困难，导致目

的语的法律功能与源语的法律功能产生错位。因此，避免滥用 shall 已经是立法界和法律翻译界的共识。陈小全和刘劲松(2011)指出，随着简明英语运动不断发展，许多欧美国家的法律文本中 shall 的使用呈逐渐减少趋势，且 shall 已经失去了其情态动词的价值，而法律文本中 shall 的意义在律师行业中也很难达成一致，故认为应除去 shall 的使用。是否应彻底除去 shall，我们不敢断言，但慎重使用 shall 确为必然。

《布莱克法律词典》第十版中明确注明，在现代法律文本中 shall 只有“has a duty to; more broadly, is required to”一种标准用法，表示“命令”“义务”的意义。本章中的“享有……权利”结构，权利人和享有权利之间没有“义务”或“责任”的关系，不符合 shall 的程式语搭配要求，因此使用 shall 实为冗余。

小 结

本章从词汇和情态动词 shall 的使用两方面分析总结了“享有……权利”结构的翻译。

针对“享有……权利”的词汇翻译，译者需要根据语境进行判断。“right”是同一语境下，人人都享有的权利，“have the right”强调权利存在和归属。而“be entitled to”需要权利主体做出某种贡献、符合某一标准或资格，从而被某权力机构赋予一定权利。

此外，在“享有……权利”结构中，权利人和享有权利之间没有“义务”或“责任”的关系，不符合 shall 的程式语搭配要求，翻译中不应使用 shall。

29 “遵循……原则”结构的翻译

29.1 结构特点及其在《民法典》中的运用

29.1.1 结构特点

“遵循……原则”“按照……原则”和“根据……原则”在法律条文中结构相似，用于明确表达某种行为或决策所依据的原则及标准，以确保法律条文的明确性、规范性和可操作性。“遵循”“按照”“根据”前常跟描述某一民事活动或法律关系的背景或情境，其后会具体阐述该原则的内容或要求。“原则”一词后为产生的法律效果。在法律语境中，“遵循”常作为动词使用；“按照”在多数情况下作介词，少数情况下为动词，表示主体要依照某原则行事；“根据”常作介词使用，表示行为或决策的来源。

29.1.2 在《民法典》中的运用

在《民法典》中，“遵循/按照/根据……原则”共出现了 19 次。其中，“遵循……原则”结构出现 8 次，“按照……原则”结构出现 8 次，“根据……原则”结构出现 3 次。

(1)“遵循……原则”结构

该结构在《民法典》中用于规范民事主体从事民事活动的场景。其中“遵循”一词在句中常作动词，表示行为主体要主动遵守特定的原则或准则，强调对某一原则或准则的严格执行，与后面“……原则”构成动宾关系，因此，该结构在句式中作谓语成分。如第 5 条规定：“民事主体从事民事活动，应当**遵循**自愿**原则**，按照自己的意思设立、变更、终止民事法律关系。”其中，“民事主体”是主语，“从事民事活动”是状语，用来描述主体的行为场景。“应当遵循自愿原则”作为谓语部分，其中“遵循”与“自愿原则”构成动宾关系，明确了民事主体在民事活动中的行为方式。“按照自己的意思设立、变更、终止民事法律关系”是对“遵循自愿原则”这一行为的进一步说明，强调民事主体在遵循自愿原则的基础上，按照自己的意思来操作民事法律关系的设立、变更和终止。

(2)“按照……原则”结构

在该结构中，“按照”常作介词，用于引出行为所依据的准则、标准或方式，强调按照既定的程序或原则来行动或进行决策。该结构在句中主要充当状语，修饰谓语动词，表明动作的原则依据。如第 288 条规定：“不动产的相邻权利人应当**按照**有利生产、方便生活、团结互助、公平合理的**原则**，正确处理相邻关系。”“不动产的相邻权利人”是句子主语，“按照有利生产、方便生活、团结互助、公平合理的原则”是介词短语作状语，用于修饰谓语动词“处理”。此处“按照”将原则与行动紧密相连，体现了法律对于相邻关系处理方式的规范性要求，有助于避免纠纷，维护社会稳定。

(3)“根据……原则”结构

在该结构中，“根据”一词前通常为法律规则适用的前提条件，或是对具体事件和行为场景的描述。“根据”常作介词，与“……原则”连用，形成状语成分修饰谓语，表示基于某种原则或理由来作出判断或决策。如第 533 条规定：“人民法院或者仲裁机构应当结合案件的实际情况，**根据**公平**原则**变更或者解除合同。”该条中，“根据”一词前为法律规则适用的前提条件描述，意味着在考虑变更或解除合同时，需要先对具体案件的各种实际状况进行综合考量。“根据公平原则”为介词短语，在句中充当状语成分，修饰“变更或者解除”这一谓语动词。该句式结构在条款中的运用有利于引导当事人在订立、履行合同过程中自觉遵循公平原则。

29.2 译文对比

表 29.1 《民法典》中"遵循……原则"结构的翻译对比

序号	出处(条)	原文	北大法宝译文(法宝版译文)	国家法规总库译文(总库版译文)
1	5	民事主体从事民事活动,应当遵循自愿原则,按照自己的意思设立、变更、终止民事法律关系。	The parties to civil legal relations shall conduct civil activities under the principle of free will, and create, modify, or terminate civil legal relations according to their own wills.	When conducting a civil activity, a person of the civil law shall, in compliance with the principle of voluntariness, create, alter, or terminate a civil juristic relationship according to his own will.
2	509	当事人应当遵循诚信原则,根据合同的性质、目的和交易习惯履行通知、协助、保密等义务。	The parties shall abide by the principle of good faith, and perform obligations of notification, assistance, confidentiality, etc. in accordance with the nature and purpose of the contract and the usage of trade.	The parties shall comply with the principle of good faith, and perform such obligations as sending notification, rendering assistance, and keeping confidentiality in accordance with the nature and purpose of the contract and the course of dealing.
3	558	债权债务终止后,当事人应当遵循诚信等原则,根据交易习惯履行通知、协助、保密、旧物回收等义务。	After the termination of an obligation, the parties shall observe the principles such as good faith and perform obligations such as notification, assistance, confidentiality, and recycling of used things in accordance with the relevant usage of trade.	After the parties' claims and obligations are terminated, the parties shall, in compliance with the principle of good faith and the like, perform such obligations as sending notification, rendering assistance, keeping confidentiality, and recycling the used articles according to the course of dealing.

续表

序号	出处（条）	原文	北大法宝译文（法宝版译文）	国家法规总库译文（总库版译文）
4	1035	处理个人信息的，应当**遵循**合法、正当、必要**原则**，不得过度处理，并符合下列条件：	The personal information of a natural person shall be processed **under the principles of** lawfulness, justification and necessity, shall not be excessively processed, and shall meet the following conditions:	The processing of personal information shall be **in compliance with the principles of** lawfulness, justification, and within a necessary limit, and may not be excessively processed; meanwhile, the following conditions shall be satisfied;
5	1044	收养应当**遵循**最有利于被收养人的**原则**，保障被收养人和收养人的合法权益。	Adoption shall **follow the principle of** serving the best interest of the adopted person, and protect the lawful rights and interests of the adopter and the adopted person.	Adoption shall be **in compliance with the principle of** acting in the best interest of the adoptee, and the lawful rights and interests of both the adoptee and the adopter shall be protected.
6	288	不动产的相邻权利人应当**按照**有利生产、方便生活、团结互助、公平合理的**原则**，正确处理相邻关系。	The right holders of neighboring immovables shall properly handle their neighboring relations **under the principles of** being conducive to production, convenience for daily life, unity and mutual assistance, and fairness and rationality.	The persons entitled to adjacent rights in immovable property shall properly deal with adjacent relationships **in accordance with the principles of** facilitation to production, convenience for daily lives, solidarity and mutual assistance, and fairness and reasonableness.

续表

序号	出处（条）	原文	北大法宝译文（法宝版译文）	国家法规总库译文（总库版译文）
7	322	法律没有规定的，**按照**充分发挥物的效用以及保护无过错当事人的**原则**确定。	If it is not provided for by laws, the ownership shall be determined **under the principles of** maximum use of the property and protection of innocent parties.	..., in the absence of any provisions in law, be determined **in compliance with the principles of** making full use of the thing and protecting the party without fault.
8	1087	离婚时，夫妻的共同财产由双方协议处理；协议不成的，由人民法院根据财产的具体情况，**按照**照顾子女、女方和无过错方权益的**原则**判决。	In the case of divorce, the community property shall be disposed of by the two parties upon agreement. If they fail to reach an agreement, the people's court shall make a judgment in light of the actual circumstance of the property and **under the principle of** caring for the rights and interests of the child or children, the wife, and the no-fault party.	Upon divorce, the community property of the spouses shall be partitioned by them through agreement, or, where no such an agreement is reached, adjudicated by the people's court in light of the actual state of the property and **in compliance with the principle of** favoring the rights and interests of their children, the wife, and the no-fault party.
9	533	人民法院或者仲裁机构应当结合案件的实际情况，**根据**公平**原则**变更或者解除合同。	The people's court or arbitration institution shall change or rescind the contract based on the actual circumstances of the case, **in accordance with the principle of** fairness.	The people's court or an arbitration institution shall, taking account of the actual circumstances of the case, rectify or rescind the contract **in compliance with the principle of** fairness.

续表

序号	出处(条)	原文	北大法宝译文(法宝版译文)	国家法规总库译文(总库版译文)
10	1054	同居期间所得的财产，由当事人协议处理；协议不成的，由人民法院**根据**照顾无过错方的**原则**判决。	The property acquired by them during their cohabitation shall be disposed of by both parties upon agreement; if they fail to reach an agreement, the people's court shall make a judgment **under the principle of** favoring the no-fault party.	Property acquired during the cohabitation period shall be disposed of by mutual agreement. Where the parties fail to reach such an agreement, the people's court shall adjudicate the case **in compliance with the principle of** favoring the no-fault party.

29.3 译文分析

以下对比分析两个版本中"遵循……原则"及类似结构的相应译文，探讨各种情况下较为可取的翻译方法。

29.3.1 "遵循……原则"结构的翻译

例句1—5同属该句式。法宝版译文为"under the principle of""abide by the principle""observe the principle of""follow the principle of"；总库版译文为"in compliance with the principle of""comply with the principle of"。

从词汇角度分析，under本身具有"受……支配"的含义，因此"under the principle of"更侧重于表明行动是在某个原则框架内进行的，突出了法律原则对法律适用或法律决策的指导和限定作用，但不具体强调"遵循"这一行为。因此，当介绍某法律制度或法律体系基本架构时，通常使用该短语来明确一些基础性原则。

通过查阅《柯林斯英语词典》可知，abide by 的定义为：to act in accord with; to submit to; agree to; to remain steadfast or faithful to。第三条释义明确了 abide by 的核心特点，即侧重于主体内心对原则的认可和自觉遵守。该短语强调内在的道德或原则的约束，暗含主体不会轻易违背原则的意味。“abide by the principle of”与具有道德和伦理色彩的词汇搭配较多，如 good faith（诚信）、fairness（公平）等，强调主体的自我约束和内在道德。

observe 的定义为：If you observe a person or thing, you watch them carefully, especially in order to learn something about them; If you observe something such as a law or custom, you obey it or follow it。observe 本身有观察、注意、遵守的意思，因此短语“observe the principle of”更强调行为主体带有留意、自我监督的态度来遵守规则。这意味着主体在遵守原则的过程中，可能会有意识地审视自己的行为是否符合原则要求。该短语常与司法审判和证据规则等词汇搭配，体现行动主体在具体操作过程中对原则的遵从和自我监督，侧重表达的是对原则实施的状态。

follow 的定义为：to keep to the course or track of; If you follow advice, an instruction, or a recipe, you act or do something in the way that it indicates。在短语“follow the principle of”中，principle 更像是一种行为路线，强调行为主体将原则作为指南，在行动过程中参照原则进行活动。因此，该短语通常与一些具有行为导向性的法律原则搭配使用，例如 follow the principle of traffic safety（遵循交通安全原则），以引导行为主体按照特定原则规范其行为，但是缺乏法律强制性。

comply 的定义为：If someone or something complies with an order or set of rules, they are in accordance with what is required or expected。在释义中，“be required or expected”表示行为主体必须按照既定的法律要求或期望来行动，体现了法律的强制性、权威性和规范性。因此 comply 的相关短语常与具有明确法律规定和强制要求的词汇搭配，以表明法律主体必须遵守特定法律原则，否则将面临相应的责任。

在《民法典》中，中文句式“遵循……原则”通常会先给出适用的条件背景，再依据该背景提出具体的法律原则和规范，以及违反法律所面临的后果。因此译文中使用 comply 更显客观，表达了主体在行为上必须按照原则行事的规范性要求，并带有一定的强制性。如例句 1 中"遵循"表达了民事主体在从事民事活动时，需要按照"自愿原则"来实施后续行为，否则行为可能会被认定为无效或可撤销。例句 2 中"遵循诚信原则"是对当事人的一种强制要求，是在履行合同相关义务时必须依照的准则，以保障合同履行过程符合法律和道德规范。同样，例句 3—5 分别规范了行为主体在债权、处理个人信息和收养方面的法律行为，以此明确和保护各方权益，体现了法律的客观性和强制约束力。因此，从词汇角度分析，comply 的相关短语更适合作为该结构的普适性翻译。

从句式结构角度分析，"遵循……原则"短语在句中作谓语成分，构成了"主语＋应当＋遵循……原则＋(其他行为描述)"的句式，强调主体需依照特定原则去实施后续行为。在翻译成英文时，通常要准确体现出动作"遵循"及其对应的"原则"，以使译文符合英文的表达习惯，从而确保句子结构合理、逻辑清晰。"comply with"本身是一个动词短语，能够直接充当谓语，较好地契合原句式结构。而"in compliance with the principle"是介词短语，在句中作状语，主要修饰动词、形容词或其他副词，用来表示行为与原则相符的状态或方式，无法直接表达行为主体遵循原则的具体动作。

从句式风格角度分析，法律文本要求语言风格严谨、正式，具有很强的专业性。"comply with the principle of" 采用动宾结构，句式简洁，符合法律语言简明严谨的风格。相比之下，"abide by the principle of"在风格上稍显柔和，更侧重于道德或个人意志层面的遵守；"observe the principle of"则更强调细致的监督，在风格上可能会使句子显得略为烦琐；"follow the principle of" 在法律专业性和严谨性方面相对薄弱；"under the principle of" 则主要用于描述宏观框架，不适用于具体的行为原则。因此，在法律文本中，选择"comply with the principle of"能够更有效地传达合规的强制性和必要性。

29.3.2 “按照……原则”结构的翻译

例句6—8同属该句式。法宝版译文为“under the principles of”,总库版译文为“in accordance with the principle of”“in compliance with the principle of”。

从词汇角度分析,根据上文分析可知,under the principles of 侧重于表明主体的行为处于原则的框架之下,强调个人行为在法律原则构建的体系中,但并未阐明行为如何依据具体原则进行。compliance 来源于动词 comply,意为“遵从,服从”,暗示原则是一种既定的、具有权威性的规范,行为主体必须按照原则调整自己的行为,体现了主体对原则的服从性,以及原则本身的规范性和权威性。在“按照……约定”一节中,分析了 in accordance with 的意义与用法,该短语更强调行为和原则之间的内在逻辑一致性,即行为的各个方面都要与原则相符合。在中文语境中,“按照”有依照的意思,“按照……原则”的核心语义是将某原则确立为行为的参照标准,强调行为与原则之间的一致性和平行关系,而非强调行为主体对原则的服从行为。因此,从词汇语义角度来看,in accordance with the principle of 更符合“按照……原则”的最佳译文。

从句式结构角度分析,“按照……原则”结构通常在句中作状语,用于说明动作行为的依据。其句子结构一般为“主体+按照+原则+(谓语动词+宾语)”,重点在于表明主体要按照给定的原则进行具体的行动。如例句6中“不动产的相邻权利人”是行为主体,“正确处理相邻关系”作为谓语,表明该行为应按照“有利生产、方便生活、团结互助、公平合理”的原则进行。例句8的句子结构呈现出前提条件(离婚时、协议不成的情况),接着引出行为主体(人民法院),然后说明行为主体依据特定原则(按照……原则)实施具体行为(判决),形成逻辑链条。这使得夫妻财产分配问题能够做到有法可依,有原则可依。

在翻译该短语时,译者应选用能充当状语且体现行为与原则之间依据关系的短语。“under the principles of”“in accordance with the principle of" 和"in compliance with the principle of"在英文句子中均可作状语,但"under the principles of"往往将句子的重点放在原则所构建的大环境或整体架构上,"in compliance with the principle of"侧重于表达行为主体对原则的服从性,而"in accordance with the principle of"则更直接体现行为与原则之间的紧密对应关系。此外,"in accordance with the principle of"的位置灵活,放在句首可以强调原则,放在句中能使句子结构更加紧凑,将行为和原则紧密结合,放在句尾则可对行为与原则的关系做进一步补充说明。无论该短语位于句子的哪个位置,都能有效突出行为和原则之间的对应关系,从而清晰地传达信息,避免歧义。

29.3.3 "根据……原则" 结构的翻译

例句 9—10 同属该结构。法宝版译文为"in accordance with the principle of" "under the principle of",总库版译文为"in compliance with the principle of"。

"按照……约定"一节中分析了"根据"一词,"根据"作介词时,意为以某种事务作为结论的前提或语言行动的基础,该词在法律语境中更侧重于引出某个结论或判断的前提,这个前提可能是一个法律条文、原则、广泛的事实或数据等,强调以这些前提为基础来做决策或判断。值得注意的是,"根据"一词并不强调行动和原则的紧密一致性,而是为行动提供了基础性的规范框架与准则指引,保障了法律行为在宏观原则上的合法性。然而在具体的法律实践过程中,只要处于该广泛原则所界定的范畴之内,无论是行动主体的具体行为举措,或是法律量裁的判定过程,均存在着一定程度的弹性操作区间。如"根据公平公正原则做出裁决",表明裁决这一行为是以公平公正原则为前提基础的,但不同的人可能对"公平"有不同的理解,这种差异就为在具体案件中如何依据公平原则进行裁决提供了一定的可操作空间。

在上文的分析中可知,"in accordance with the principle of"更强调行为与原则的紧密一致性,"under the principle of"侧重于描述在原则所营造的大环境下的状态，对于行为如何以原则为基础进行（特别是作为结论或判断的前提依据）的表达不够直接和明确，“in compliance with the principle of”则侧重于表达行为主体对原则的服从性。三者皆不是该短语的最佳译文。相比之下，短语“based on”有“基于，以……为基础；建立在……之上”的含义。《柯林斯英语词典》对 base on 的定义为：If you base one thing on another thing, the first thing develops from the second thing。这意味着“based on”强调的是一种依存关系，即某个事物的产生、存在或某种行为的实施是以另一个事物作为根基或前提条件。在表达“根据……原则”时，该短语能够更好地体现出行为是以某个原则为基础开展的这一核心语义。

此外，从句式角度分析，“根据……原则”和“按照……原则”较为相似，均采用“主体＋根据＋原则＋（谓语动词＋宾语）”的句式结构。在该结构中，“根据＋原则”作为状语修饰谓语动词，限定了行为的依据范围。在英文语句中，“based on the principle of”主要充当状语，用于修饰动词，其语法功能与“根据……原则”在中文句子中的作用完全一致。同时，该短语可以放在句首、句中或句尾，位置的灵活性使得它在翻译“根据……原则”时能够很好地适应中文句子结构的变化，从而准确把握句子重点。

小　结

“遵循……原则”的类似结构还包括“按照……原则”和“根据……原则”这两种形式。针对该类结构的翻译，从词汇和句式等角度进行了分析总结，可提出如下一般性翻译建议：

“遵循……原则”结构可译为“comply with the principle of”。

“按照……原则”结构可译为“in accordance with the principle of”。

“根据……原则”结构可译为“based on the principle of”。

译者在实际翻译中仍需根据具体情况进行灵活调整。

30 “行使……权”结构的翻译

30.1 结构特点及其在《民法典》中的运用

30.1.1 结构特点

“行使……权”结构在法律文本中通常由“行使”加上某种具体的“权利”组成，用于描述权利主体主动、依法行使自身权利的情况。该结构通常明确了权利行使的具体方式和程序，如“依法行使”；同时也为权利受到侵害时的救济提供了法律依据，如“行使撤销权”“行使请求权”等。

30.1.2 在《民法典》中的运用

《民法典》中该结构一共出现了 69 次。多数情况下，该结构的主语为拥有国家权力的官方机构和个体民事主体。如第 80 条规定：“**权力机构**行使修改法人章程，选举或者更换执行机构、监督机构成员，以及法人章程规定的其他职权。”第 163 条规定：“**委托代理人**按照被代理人的委托行使代理权。”其中，“权力机构”属于拥有国家权力的官方机构，“委托代理人”属于个体民事主体。少数情况下，该结构的主语为集体组织，如第 262 条规定：“分别属于村内两个以上农民集体所有的，由村内各该**集体经济组织或者村民小组**依法代表集体行使所有权。”其中，集体经济组织介于个人和官方机构之间，是由农民集体自愿结合而成的经济实体，代表着集体成员的共同利益，享有相应的民事权利并承担民事义务。

根据“行使……权”在《民法典》中的使用频率，该结构可主要分为两种情况：

(1)主体为拥有国家权力的官方机构

本结构在《民法典》中出现了 5 次。这种情况下，该结构强调国家公权力的性质、边界、程序正义和公共利益取向，突出权力机构的管理权、监督权，以及国家代表行使国有财产所有权等不同类型的公权力。如第 246 条规定：“国有财产由国务院代表国家行使所有权。”该权利表明国家通过国务院对国有财产行使所有权和决策权，是国家宏观调控和权力配置的一个重要体现。

(2)主体为个体民事主体

本结构在《民法典》中共出现了 61 次。《民法典》对个体民事主体的各类重要权利作出了明确规定和保护，旨在维护个体民事主体的人格尊严、财产安全、身份地位以及经济自主权等。如第 130 条规定：“民事主体按照自己的意愿依法行使民事权利，不受干涉。”该结构突出民事主体的自主决定权，明确了权利行使的具体程序为“依法行使”，以及权利的使用范围，包括物权、债权、人身权等各类民事权利。

30.2 译文对比

表 30.1 《民法典》中“行使……权”结构的翻译对比

序号	出处(条)	原文	北大法宝译文(法宝版译文)	国家法规总库译文(总库版译文)
1	80	权力机构行使修改法人章程，选举或者更换执行机构、监督机构成员，以及法人章程规定的其他职权。	The supreme organ exercises the powers of amending the bylaws of the legal person and electing or replacing members of the executive organ and supervisory organ and other powers stated in the bylaws of the legal person.	The governing body has the authority to revise the articles of association of the legal person, elect or replace members of the executive or supervisory body, and perform other responsibilities stipulated in the articles of association.

续表

序号	出处（条）	原文	北大法宝译文（法宝版译文）	国家法规总库译文（总库版译文）
2	82	营利法人设监事会或者监事等监督机构的，监督机构依法**行使**检查法人财务，监督执行机构成员、高级管理人员执行法人职务的行为，以及法人章程规定的其他职**权**。	Where a for-profit legal person has a supervisory organ such as the board of supervisors or a supervisor, the supervisory organ shall, in accordance with the law, **exercise the powers of** inspecting the legal person's financial affairs and overseeing the performance of duties by the members of the executive organ and the senior executives of the legal person and the powers stated in the bylaws of the legal person.	Where a for-profit legal person establishes a supervisory body such as a board of supervisors or a supervisor, the supervisory body **has**, in accordance with law, **the authority to** inspect the financial matters of the legal person, supervise the performance of duty by the members of the executive body and the senior management officers of the legal person, and perform other responsibilities stipulated in the articles of association.
3	246	国有财产由国务院代表国家**行使**所有**权**。法律另有规定的，依照其规定。	The State Council **exercises** the ownership of state-owned property on behalf of the state, except as otherwise provided for by any law.	The ownership rights over the State-owned property **shall be exercised by** the State Council on behalf of the State, unless otherwise provided by law.
4	248	无居民海岛属于国家所有，国务院代表国家**行使**无居民海岛所有**权**。	Uninhabited sea islands belong to the state, and the State Council **exercises** the ownership of uninhabited sea islands on behalf of the state.	Uninhabited islands are owned by the State, and the State Council **exercises** the ownership rights over the uninhabited islands on behalf of the State.

续表

序号	出处（条）	原文	北大法宝译文（法宝版译文）	国家法规总库译文（总库版译文）
5	130	民事主体按照自己的意愿依法行使民事权利，不受干涉。	The parties to civil legal relations shall, based on their free will, exercise civil rights in accordance with the law without any interference.	The persons of the civil law enjoy their civil-law rights according to their own will and in accordance with law free from any interference.
6	163	委托代理人按照被代理人的委托行使代理权。	An agent under a mandate shall exercise the power conferred by the principal.	An agent under agreement shall act in accordance with the principal's authorization.
7	306	其他共有人应当在合理期限内行使优先购买权。	Other co-owners shall exercise the preemptive right within a reasonable period.	The other co-owners shall exercise their right of pre-emption within a reasonable period of time.
8	419	抵押权人应当在主债权诉讼时效期间行使抵押权；未行使的，人民法院不予保护。	The mortgagee shall exercise mortgage within the prescriptive period of the principal claim, failing which the mortgagee will not be protected by the people's court.	A mortgagee shall exercise his right to mortgage within the limitation period for claiming against the principal obligation; otherwise no protection may be provided by the people's court.
9	743	承租人行使索赔权利时，未及时提供必要协助。	Failing to provide necessary assistance in a timely manner when the lessee exercises the right to claims.	when the lessee exercises the right to claim, the lessor fails to provide necessary assistance in a timely manner.
10	262	分别属于村内两个以上农民集体所有的，由村内各该集体经济组织或者村民小组依法代表集体行使所有权；	If it is owned by two or more farmers' collectives of a village, the ownership shall be exercised by all the collective economic organizations or the villagers' groups of the village on behalf of the collective in accordance with the law.	where they are owned by two or more farmer collectives within a village, the ownership shall be exercised by the respective collective economic organizations or the villagers' groups on behalf of the collectives in accordance with law.

30.3 译文分析

我们针对《民法典》中“行使……权”结构的两种运用情况，分别对比分析两个版本的对应译文，同时探讨更为可取的翻译方法。

30.3.1 主体为拥有国家权力的官方机构时，“行使……权”结构的翻译

例句 1—4 同属该句式。法宝版译文为“exercise the powers of”“exercise”。总库版译文为“have the authority to”“exercise”。

基于对于“行使……权”结构在《民法典》中运用情况的分析，当主语为拥有国家权力的官方机构时，该结构强调官方机构有权力、权限或授权来进行特定行为或决策。通过查阅《布莱克法律词典》和相关文本可知，exercise the powers of 的定义为：to exercise a right or power is to do something which it enables the holder to do。(U. S. v. Souders，27 Fed. Cas. 1267；Cleaverv.Comm.，34)

have the authority 的定义为：In the English law relating to public administration，an authority is a body having jurisdiction in certain matters of a public nature. In governmental law. Legal power；a right to command or to act；the right and power of public officers to require obedience to their orders lawfully issued in the scope of their public duties。[Com. Dig.“Attorney，” 7 Term，207；1 Holt，141；Blood v. Goodrich，9 Wend. (N. Y.) 68，75，24 Am. Dec. 121；Banorgee v. Hovey，5 Mass. 11，4 Am. Dec. 17；Cooper v. Rankin，5 Bin. (Pa.) 613.]

exercise 的定义为：①行使合法权利。例如，“exercise the right to vote” 意味着行使投票权。②履行职责和义务。例如，“exercise due diligence” 意味着履行尽职调查的责任。③进行活动或行为。例如，“exercise caution” 意味着

谨慎行事。④实施或执行法律规定。例如,"exercise a judgment" 意味着执行判决。⑤在合同或法规中,用于描述当事人行使合同中规定的某些权利。例如,"the right to exercise an option" 意味着行使选择权。

通过上述释义和例子可以得出,exercise 和 exercise the powers of 均强调某人使用或实施所拥有的特权或权利,而 have the authority 强调官方有权力或授权,从而进行公共事务的管辖。因此,当"行使……权"结构的主体为拥有国家权力的官方机构时,have the authority 更适合作为普适性翻译。

30.3.2 主体为个体民事主体时,"行使……权"结构的翻译

例句 5—9 同属该句式。法宝版译文为 "exercise the power""exercise the right"。总库版译文为"exercise the right""shall act""enjoy right"。

基于对"行使……权"结构在《民法典》中的运用情况分析,当主语为个体民事主体时,该结构强调权利行使的自主性、依法性,保护个体的自由、利益和安全。

(1)"exercise the power" 和 "exercise the right"

徐蕊(2017)对权利和权力进行对比,表示在法律背景中,权利是指由特定的法律制度所规定的赋予个人的某些特定或专有的利益,而权力基本指国家权力机关或者指政府行使的职权、权限。通过查阅《元照英美法词典》和《布莱克法律词典》可以得出,"right"通常指的是个人或实体依法享有的利益、特权或自由;"power"一词既可以指个人或组织依法享有的支配力或影响力,也可以指法律赋予的某种特权或授权。李克兴(2012)在对"权利"和"权力"的翻译中也阐明,right 所指的"权利""利益"成分往往大于"权力"成分,而 power 主要指在法律上具有的通过作出或不作出一定行为而改变一定法律关系的能力或资格,即纯粹的"实权"。

(2)"exercise the right", "shall act" 和 "enjoy right"

通过上文的分析可以得出,"exercise the right" 适用于描述个体民事主体依法行使其自由权,包括选择作为或不作为的自主权,并维护其对特

定利益或财产的所有权或主张。"shall act" 在法律条文中表示个人或实体必须按照法律规定或合同条款来采取行动,倾向于强调行为的必要性与合法性,而非主体所拥有的权利或权力本身。换言之,其暗示了"遵循"但没有强调"行使"这个动作。"enjoy right" ,根据"享有……权利"一节中对 enjoy 的分析,更强调主体可以享受某种利益,传递出愉悦和积极的体验情感,不适用正式、严谨、客观的立法文本。

结合上述分析,在例句 5—10 中,例句 5 的"民事权利"指的是个人在法律框架内所享有的权益,强调的是权益的享有而非权力的行使;例句 6 的"代理权"涉及代理人代替委托人行使的权力,"权"更像是权力或授权的体现;例句 7"优先购买权"是基于法律或合同的特定权益,表明共有人在购买权上享有的一种优先权;例句 8"抵押权"通常指的是抵押权人(如银行)依托贷款合同对抵押财产所享有的权益;例句 9"索赔权利"是指承租人或权益人基于损失而享有的权益,强调权利的性质;例句 10"所有权"表示的是一项法定的权益,包括对财产的全面控制和使用权。可见,除例句 6 的"权"强调的是行为的能力和执行的授权,应当译为 power 外,其余各句的"权"强调的是个体的合法权益和法律保护,应当译为 right。

小　结

在《民法典》中,"行使……权"结构通常用于描述个体或组织依法享有并实际运用某种权利的行为。当行为的主体为拥有国家权力的官方机构时,该结构可译为 "have the authority"。当主体为个体民事主体时,需要区分所涉"权"的性质,如果该"权"为个体因法律而拥有的合法权益和法律保护的利益,该结构可译为"exercise the right";如果该"权"涉及法律赋予的执行特定行为的能力和权限,则该结构可译为"exercise the power"。

参考文献

一、中文论著

陈小全，刘劲松. 法律文本中 shall 的问题及解决途径. 中国翻译，2011 (3).

陈忠诚. 驱除法律英译中的“shall”病毒. 上海科技翻译，1992 (3).

董秀芳. “的”字短语做后置关系小句的用法——兼评法律文献中“的”字短语的用法. 语言文字应用，2003 (4).

高雅蓉，钟玲俐. 表原因词组在法律英语中的用法——基于“中国法律法规汉英平行语料库”的统计与分析. 湖南工业大学学报(社会科学版)，2022 (2).

胡道华，蒋长刚. “自指”与“转指”视角下立法条文“的”字结构的翻译. 语言与翻译，2016 (3).

李奉栖. 基于平行语料库的汉语立法语篇禁止性规范词英译研究——以“不得”的英译为例. 语言与翻译，2017 (1).

李晋，董晓波.我国立法文本翻译中“shall”的失范分析及改进策略研究.外语教学理论与实践，2021(3).

李克兴. 英语法律文本中主要情态动词的作用及其翻译. 中国翻译，2007 (6).

李克兴. 英汉法律翻译案例讲评. 北京：外文出版社，2011.

李克兴. 论法律文本中“权利”和“权力”的表述和翻译. 中国翻译，2012 (4).

李克兴. 英文立法文本写作解密之一——“where-句”与“if-句”的对比研究. 中国翻译，2013 (2).

李伟平. 认真对待《民法典》中的参照适用条款. 中国社会科学报，2023-7-13.

林克难，籍明文. 法律文书中“的”字结构翻译探讨. 上海科技翻译，2002 (3).

刘月华，潘文娱，赵淑华. 实用现代汉语语法：第 3 版. 北京：商务印书馆，2019.

陶博. 法律英语：中英双语法律文书制作. 上海：复旦大学出版社，2004.

汪全胜，张鹏. 法律文本中“定义条款”的设置论析. 东方法学，2013(2).

王芳，汤文华.《中华人民共和国民法典》英译本问题及分析——基于高频程式语搭配. 外国语文(双月刊)，2023 (2).

王洁. 法律语言研究. 广州：广东教育出版社，1999.

王子颖. 法律语篇中 shall 和 may 的翻译对比研究. 上海翻译，2013 (4).

中国社会科学院语言研究所词典编辑室编. 现代汉语词典：第 7 版. 商务印书馆，2016.

邢伟星.《民法典》“另有规定”条款的法理分析. 青海民族大学学报(社会科学版)，2022 (1).

徐蕊. “权利”与“权力”辨析. 中国科技术语，2017 (2).

姚海萍. 论现代汉语“为＋O＋V/VP”的构式义. 学术交流，2013 (11).

张海燕. “推定”和 “视为”之语词解读？——以我国现行民事法律规范为样. 法制与社会发展(双月刊)，2012 (3).

张文. 现代法律文本中的文言成分及其应用. 北华大学学报(社会科学版)，2020 (5).

朱景松. 现代汉语虚词词典. 北京：语文出版社，2007.

邹玉华. 论立法文本中“有下列情形(行为)之一”的句式的规范. 语言文字应用，2008 (4).

二、外文论著

Cambridge Dictionary. Retrieved from cambridge. org on August 27, 2024.

Collins Online Dictionary. Retrieved from collinsdictionary. com on November 21, 2024.

Dickerson, R. (1986). *The Fundamentals of Legal Drafting* (2nd Edition). Boston: Little Brown.

Garner, B. A. (1995). *A Dictionary of Modern Legal Usage* (2nd ed.). New York: Oxford University Press.

Garner, B. A. (2014). *Black's Law Dictionary*. Minnesota: Thomson Reuters West.

Garner, B. A. (2016). *Garner's Modern English Usage* (4th ed.). New York: Oxford University Press.

Halliday M. A. K. (1994 /2000). *An Introduction to Functional Grammar*. 北京：外语教学与研究出版社.

Juristic Act. (n.d.) *West's Encyclopedia of American Law, edition 2*. (2008). Retrieved from https://legal-dictionary.thefreedictionary.com/Juristic+Act on February 3, 2025.

Oxford Learner's Dictionary. Retrieved from liability noun- Definition, pictures, pronunciation and usage notes | Oxford Advanced Learner's Dictionary at oxfordlearnersdictionaries.com on August 6, 2024.

"Prohibited degree of kinship." (2014) Retrieved from https://encyclopedia. thefreedictionary. com/Prohibited+degree+of+kinship on August 23, 2024.

Wydick, R. C. (1998). *Plain English for Lawyers*. New York: Carolina Academic Press.